红衣少女

THE GIRL IN RED

A Study Guide for the Film

Vivian Ling

ISBN 0-89264-116-9

Printed in the United States of America

5 4 3 2 1

紅衣少女

一. 電影對白及生詞表

Part I: Script and Vocabulary Annotations

CONTENTS OF PART I

SCRIPT AND VOCABULARY ANNOTATIONS

FOREWORD

The set of materials presented here - the videotaped film 《紅衣少女》 *The Girl in Red*, the filmscript and vocabulary annotations, and the grammatical notes and exercises - is designed to respond to the need for teaching materials for developing aural comprehension and speech skills at the intermediate level. In the West, the teaching of Chinese language beyond the beginning level has traditionally emphasized reading to the neglect of the other three skills: aural comprehension, speech, and writing. The concept of using films to teach comprehension and speech is not new, but it is only in the last few years that the popularization of videotape technology and the availability of films appropriate for our pedagogical purpose have made it feasible to carry this concept into practice. The film *The Girl in Red* is ideal for our purpose in that it fulfills the following criteria: 1) Its language - in terms of pronunciation, vocabulary, and discourse patterns - conforms with the standard spoken in contemporary China. The vocabulary is rich, containing some common colloquialisms not normally found in traditional language texts. Moreover, it contains many "irregular" discourse structures which are excluded from dictionaries and textbooks, but which occur with high frequency in authentic Chinese. 2) Its subject matter consists of significant and common societal phenomena in the early 1980's, and thereby provides a glimpse of contemporary Chinese society while serving as a vehicle for language development. 3) It has an engaging plot that is neither too simplistic nor too complicated to follow. 4) It embodies considerable cinematic artistry and human interest, and therefore promises to have long-lasting value. Materials based on films are not intended to replace traditional texts, but to supplement them. Through film-based materials, students will be exposed to language use in simulated real life situations, and will thereby develop their proficiency in comprehension and speech. It is also hoped that film-based materials will add variety and fun along the hard road toward mastery of Chinese.

This set of materials is designed for students who have completed two years of Chinese in a typical American college Chinese program. However, it has some built-in flexibility to accommodate students at varying levels of proficiency. The filmscript is divided into twelve segments, each one corresponding to approximately ten minutes of the film.

The vocabulary annotations are pitched at approximately the 800 character level. However, because students using these materials presumably have studied Chinese from a wide variety of prior textbooks, the choice of vocabulary items to be annotated is based on a "common denominator," that is, on a "generic" background at a level slightly lower than two years of study. Some students may find many annotations unnecessary, others may need to resort to a dictionary occasionally. Students may find the number of annotated vocabulary items overwhelming. Therefore, as an aid in determining which items one should commit to memory, they are categorized into three levels of importance. The top priority vocabulary items - those that occur most commonly in the language and are therefore most useful - are marked with " * ". The vocabulary items of secondary priority are marked with " ˆ ". Those which remain unmarked are of least importance. The vocabulary items of top and secondary priority appear in two lists - in complex and simplified characters - in the back of Part I: Script and Vocabulary Annotations. These lists can be used as an inventory of vocabulary for required learning.

To promote comprehension of the plot and the "substance" of the film, a set of discussion questions (討論問題) is provided at the end of each segment of the script. The instructor may use the discussion questions as a comprehension and discourse exercise after viewing the segment, either before or after having read through the script. Students may also preview these questions before viewing the segment so as to be prepared to look for certain things in the development of the plot. The discussion questions may even be used as prompts for short essays. Thus, this set of questions may be used variously depending on the relative emphasis the instructor wishes to give to the oral and written aspects of the course.

The discourse patterns included in Part II: Grammatical Notes and Exercises are selected with the intermediate student in mind. As in the selection of vocabulary items to be annotated, a "common denominator" is used. Often, a pattern typically introduced at the beginning level is included for review and reinforcement, in order to help the student advance from the "passive knowledge" to the "active usage" level. Many patterns included in this section occur only in colloquial spoken Chinese. Some are in fact not "sentence patterns" per se, but discourse structures. These colloquial sentence patterns and discourse structures are typically excluded from traditional reading texts even though they are an important component of the spoken language. In this part, each pattern is labeled by a pattern heading, followed by the contextual example, an explanation in English, then a couple of further examples, and exercises to be done either orally or in writing. The clarity of the explanations is sometimes limited by the nature of these discourse patterns. Often they convey nuances which cannot be translated or explained easily, and therefore can be "brought to life" only through examples given by a skilled teacher.

In Part II: Grammatical Notes and Exercises, aside from the exercises under each discourse pattern, each segment ends with a set of inclusive translation exercises in which the patterns are represented in random order to foster their active use. In these inclusive exercises as well as those under each pattern, an attempt has been made to reinforce the student's newly-acquired key vocabulary and to place the patterns and vocabulary in a larger linguistic context beyond that of the film.

I wish to express special thanks to my colleague Prof. Kai Li, who has provided valuable comments and suggestions based on his test-use of this set of materials, and to all those patient students who have served as guinea pigs.

ABBREVIATIONS OF GRAMMATICAL TERMS

adv.	adverb
AV	auxiliary verb
colloq.	colloquial
CV	coverb
BF	bound form
M	measure word
MA	movable adverb
N	noun
NP	noun phrase
Nu	number
O	object
PN	pronoun
PW	place word
QW	question word
RE	resultative verb ending
subj.	subject
SV	stative verb (sometimes called "adjective")
V	verb
VP	verb phrase

紅衣少女

峨眉電影制片廠	峨眉电影制片厂
原著：鐵凝，《沒有紐扣的紅襯衫》	原著：铁凝，《沒有纽扣的红衬衫》
十月 1983.2	十月 1983.2
導演：周力	导演：周力

人物　CAST OF CHARACTERS

安然	安然	Ān Rán	teenage protagonist, sometimes affectionately called 然然
安靜	安静	Ān Jìng	An Ran's older sister, a journal editor
爸爸	爸爸		father of Ran and Jing
媽媽	妈妈		mother of Ran and Jing
馬編輯	马编辑	Mǎ Biānjí	Editor Ma, An Jing's senior colleague
韋婉	韦婉	Wéi Wǎn	Ran's teacher, former classmate of Jing's
米曉玲	米晓玲	Mǐ Xiǎolíng	Ran's friend and classmate
祝文娟	祝文娟	Zhū Wénjuān	another classmate of Ran's, class monitor
劉冬虎	刘冬虎	Liú Dōnghǔ	classmate and neighbor of Ran's
王紅衛	王红卫	Wáng Hǒngwèi	classmate of Ran's
王麗萍	王丽萍	Wáng Lìpíng	classmate of Ran's
宋振國	宋振国	Sòng Zhènguó	classmate of Ran's
洪鈞	洪钧	Hóng Jūn	classmate of Ran's
白雲	白云	Bái Yún	classmate of Ran's
高力偉	高力伟	Gāo Lìwěi	classmate of Ran's
王小容	王小容	Wáng Xiǎoróng	classmate of Ran's
張曉英	张晓英	Zhāng Xiǎoyīng	classmate of Ran's
女老師	女老师	Nǔ Lǎoshī	Teacher Wei's colleague, Ran's former teacher

*1. 少女	少女	shàonǚ	young (adolescent or teenage) girl
2. 峨眉	峨眉	Éméi	name of a sacred mountain in Sichuan province; here, name of a film studio
3. 製片廠	制片厂	zhìpiān-chǎng	film production studio (-廠: factory)
^4. 原著	原著	yuánzhù	original work (here, referring to the novelette from which the film is made)
5. 鐵凝	铁凝	Tiě Níng	name of the author of the original work
^6. 紐扣	纽扣	niǔkòu	(same as kòuzi 扣子) button
*7. 襯衫	衬衫	chènshān	shirt, blouse
8. 十月	十月	Shíyuè	October; here, name of a literary magazine
^9. 導演	导演	dǎoyǎn	director (of a film or play)
10. 周力	周力	Zhōu Lì	name of the director
*11. 人物	人物	rénwù	characters (in a film or play), personage
^12. 編輯	编辑	biānjí	editor

SEGMENT I

Scene 1 ─────────────────

A mother, carrying a little girl on her back and baggage in her hands, trudges along in the wilderness. She tries in vain to hitch a ride from a passing truck.

安然：　媽媽，汽車爲什麼跑得那麼快？
媽媽：　然然自己跑，媽媽追你，哦？

The little girl, An Ran, runs ahead while her mother follows behind. We hear the voice of the inquisitive little girl...

安然：　汽車爲什麼跑得那麼快？紅棗爲什麼是紅的？螞蟻爲什麼那麼小？飛機爲什麼會飛？

Arriving in a town, the mother is again carrying the little girl and their baggage.

安然：　媽媽，人爲什麼要吃飯呢？
媽媽：　不吃飯要餓死的！
安然：　那爲什麼會餓死？
媽媽：　爲什麼？你長大就知道了！
安然：　那我什麼時候能長大呀？
媽媽：　嗯……

Scene 2 ─────────────────

The little girl's adolescent sister, An Jing, washes her hair for her.

*1. 追	追	zhuī	to chase
^2. 哦	哦	ó, ò	an interjection expressing surprise, doubt, comprehension (as in "Oh! Now I understand."), or suggestion (as in "How about it? What do you say?")
3. 棗	枣	zǎo	date (a fruit)
^4. 螞蟻	蚂蚁	mǎyǐ	ants

S E G M E N T   I

Scene 1 ────────────────

A mother, carrying a little girl on her back and baggage in her hands, trudges along in the wilderness. She tries in vain to hitch a ride from a passing truck.

安然： 妈妈，汽车为什么跑得那么快？

妈妈： 然然自己跑，妈妈追你，哦？

The little girl, An Ran, runs ahead while her mother follows behind. We hear the voice of the inquisitive little girl...

安然： 汽车为什么跑得那么快？红枣为什么是红的？蚂蚁为什么那么小？飞机为什么会飞？

Arriving in a town, the mother is again carrying the little girl and their baggage.

安然： 妈妈，人为什么要吃饭呢？

妈妈： 不吃饭要饿死的！

安然： 那为什么会饿死？

妈妈： 为什么？你长大就知道了！

安然： 那我什么时候能长大呀？

妈妈： 嗯……

Scene 2 ────────────────

The little girl's adolescent sister, An Jing, washes her hair for her.

*5. 饿死	饿死	èsǐ	to die from hunger
^6. 呀	呀	ya	a form of the sentence particle 啊, but used after words ending in "a, e, i, o, ü" due to sandhi (cf. Note 16 below)
7. 嗯	嗯	m	hmm, uh, um-hum

安然：　你是個好姐姐！

安靜：　你是個小<u>黃毛</u>！

安然：　我是小<u>白毛女</u>！

Jing carries the basin of water out of the room. Ran sings as she combs her hair.

安然：　"北<u>風</u>那個<u>吹</u>，<u>雪花</u>那個<u>飄</u>。"

Returning to the room, Jing hands Ran some walnuts.

安靜：　<u>喏</u>！

安然：　你為什麼老給我<u>核桃</u>吃<u>啊</u>？

安靜：　吃了核桃，<u>頭髮會變黑</u>呀！

In time, Ran becomes a teenager.

Scene 3 ──────────────

The two sisters stroll on a street crowded with vendors and shoppers.

<u>小販甲</u>：唉，賣<u>膨香酥嘞</u>，賣膨香酥啊。

安然：　<u>欸</u>！姐，你看！

─────────────────────────────

8. 黃毛	黃毛	huáng máo	"yellow fuzz" (the brownish hair of small children)
9. 白毛女	白毛女	bái máo nǚ	"White-Haired Girl," heroine of a model opera during the Cultural Revolution
*10. 風	风	fēng	wind
*11. 吹	吹	chuī	to blow
^12. 雪花	雪花	xuěhuā	snow flake
^13. 飄	飘	piāo	to float, flutter
14. 喏	喏	nuò	"There!" "Look!" "Here you are!"
15. 核桃	核桃	hétao	walnut
^16. 啊	啊	a	a particle used in the following ways (each carrying a different intonation): a) used alone or at the beginning of an utterance as an expletive or to convey surprise; b) tagged on after a sentence,

安然：　　你是个好姐姐！
安静：　　你是个小<u>黄毛</u>！
安然：　　我是小<u>白毛女</u>！

Jing carries the basin of water out of the room. Ran sings as she combs her hair.

安然：　　"北<u>风</u>那个<u>吹</u>，<u>雪花</u>那个<u>飘</u>。"

Returning to the room, Jing hands Ran some walnuts.

安静：　　<u>喏</u>！
安然：　　你为什么老给我<u>核桃</u>吃<u>啊</u>？
安静：　　吃了核桃，<u>头发会变</u>黑<u>呀</u>！

In time, Ran becomes a teenager.

Scene 3 ————————————————

The two sisters stroll on a street crowded with vendors and shoppers.

小<u>贩甲</u>：<u>唉</u>，卖<u>膨香酥勒</u>，卖膨香酥啊。
安然：　　<u>欸</u>！姐，你看！

---

				meaning "OK?" c) sentence final particle used optionally to round off the tone of the sentence
*17.	頭髮	头发	tóufa	hair (on the head)
*18.	變	变	biàn	to change, become
19.	-販	-贩	-fàn	(BF) vendor, pedlar
^20.	甲	甲	jiǎ	the first in a series (equivalent to "A" in English)
21.	唉	唉	āi, ài	a particle to call attention; a sigh
22.	膨香酥	膨香酥	péngxiāngsū	a puffed confection made of corn flour and sugar
23.	勒	勒	lei	a sentence final particle conveying alacrity or "lightness"
^24.	欸	欸	ē, é, ě, è	Hey! Eh! Eh? (a particle conveying different meanings depending on the tone and intonation used)

小販：　　膨香酥。

安然：　　八十年代新農民。

安靜：　　嘻嘻嘻。

安然：　　我買一根兒哦？

安靜：　　你多大了？

Ran holds out her hand for some money from her sister.

小販乙：五香瓜子兒！五香大瓜子。

Jing puts some money in Ran's hand.

安然：　　(to the vendor) 買一根兒。　(Holding her purchase, Ran rejoins Jing.)

安靜：　　還笑，好意思。

安然：　　(commenting on people on the street)　欸，姐，你看！多精彩的木刻。欸，
　　　　　嘻嘻！哈哈！熊貓歡歡。嘿嘿！

安靜：　　怎麼能指人家呢？　(takes the stick out of Ran's hand and throws it away.)
　　　　　扔了！

安然：　　(stopping in front of a store with two mannequins in the window) 欸，姐，
　　　　　你來！哈哈哈！怪可憐的！哈哈哈！這麼熱的天，連衣服也不給換！這位女士和先生，
　　　　　好像都有黃疸性肝炎！

安靜：　　防冷塗的蠟。小點兒聲，……

安然：　　(Spotting a classmate, she calls after her.)　噯，祝文娟！

*25. 農民	农民	nóngmín	peasant, farmer
26. 嘻	嘻	xī	laughter (onomatopoeia)
^27. 乙	乙	yǐ	second in a series (equivalent to "B" in English)
28. 五香	五香	wǔxiāng	a mixture of five spices
29. 瓜子	瓜子	guāzǐ	melon seeds
^30. 好意思	好意思	hǎoyìsi	(sarcastic) to have the nerve (to do something disgraceful or embarrassing)
^31. 精彩	精彩	jīngcǎi	splendid, brilliant, wonderful
^32. 木刻	木刻	mùkè	wood sculpture
33. 哈	哈	ha	laughter (onomatopoeia)
^34. 熊貓	熊猫	xióngmāo	panda bear
35. 嘿	嘿	hēi	laughter (onomatopoeia); Hey!
^36. 指	指	zhǐ	to point at

小贩：　膨香酥。

安然：　八十年代新农民。

安静：　嘻嘻嘻。

安然：　我买一根儿哦？

安静：　你多大了？

Ran holds out her hand for some money from her sister.

小贩乙：五香瓜子儿! 五香大瓜子。

Jing puts some money in Ran's hand.

安然：　(to the vendor) 买一根儿。　(Holding her purchase, Ran rejoins Jing.)

安静：　还笑，好意思。

安然：　(commenting on people on the street)　欸，姐，你看! 多精彩的木刻。欸，嘻嘻! 哈哈! 熊猫欢欢。嘿嘿!

安静：　怎么能指人家呢？ (takes the stick out of Ran's hand and throws it away.) 扔了!

安然：　(stopping in front of a store with two mannequins in the window) 欸，姐，你来! 哈哈哈! 怪可怜的! 哈哈哈! 这么热的天，连衣服也不给换! 这位女士和先生，好象都有黄疸性肝炎!

安静：　防冷涂的蜡。小点儿声，……

安然：　(Spotting a classmate, she calls after her.)　嗳，祝文娟!

*37.	人家	人家	rénjia	other people; that person (in particular)
*38.	扔	扔	rēng	to throw away, toss
ˆ39.	怪	怪	guài	quite, rather; strange, odd; to blame
*40.	可憐	可怜	kělián	pitiful
*41.	换	换	huàn	to change (clothes, etc.)
ˆ42.	女士	女士	nǔshì	lady, professional woman
43.	黄膽性肝炎	黄胆性肝炎	huángdǎnxìng gānyán	hepatogenous jaundice
ˆ44.	防	防	fáng	to prevent
ˆ45.	塗	涂	tú	to spread on, apply
46.	蠟	蜡	là	wax
47.	嗳	嗳	ài	Ah! Oh!

祝文娟：安然。

安然：　祝文娟，這是我姐姐，安靜！

祝文娟：安姐姐，你好！

安靜：　你好！<u>怎麼</u>，星期天喜歡出來走走？

祝文娟：不，我是有事兒，到我媽的朋友家裡去。

安靜：　嗯！

祝文娟：再見！

安靜：　好，再見！　(Zhu Wenjuan leaves.)

安然：　她是去找人<u>輔導</u>英語。她不願意跟別人説。她媽對她學習<u>抓</u>得可<u>緊</u>呢！

安靜：　她<u>挺</u>懂<u>禮貌</u>的！

安然：　那我還有禮貌呢。不過，她學習是好，特別是<u>古文</u>和<u>歷史</u>，講起<u>三國演義</u>來一<u>套</u>一套的！

Scene 4 ——————————————

Strolling through a furniture store, Jing stops to inspect a bed.

安然：　姐，你要<u>結婚</u>？

安靜：　<u>誰</u>説的？這不是<u>單人</u>床嗎？

安然：　那就為你自己？<u>嘎</u>？不明白！

安靜：　結了婚就不要單人床<u>啦</u>？<u>比方</u>説，兩個人<u>吵了嘴</u>，就得到單人床去睡呀！

安然：　結婚就<u>意味</u>着吵嘴嗎？

安靜：　話不能這麼説。可天下沒有不吵嘴的<u>夫妻</u>。

安然：　比如，劉冬虎的爸爸媽媽，還有<u>咱們</u>家二老？

^48. 怎麼	怎么	zěnme	an interjection
*49. 輔導	辅导	fǔdǎo	to tutor
^50. 抓	抓	zhuā	to grasp, stress, pay special attention to
*51. 緊	紧	jǐn	tight
^52. 挺	挺	tǐng	rather, quite
*53. 禮貌	礼貌	lǐmào	etiquette, courtesy; courteous, polite
^54. 古文	古文	gǔwén	ancient literature
*55. 歷史	历史	lìshǐ	history
56. 三國演義	三国演义	Sānguó Yǎnyì	Romance of the Three Kingdoms, a classic historical novel
^57. 套	套	tào	(M) set, suit

祝文娟：安然。

安然：　祝文娟，这是我姐姐，安静！

祝文娟：安姐姐，你好！

安静：　你好！<u>怎么</u>，星期天喜欢出来走走？

祝文娟：不，我是有事儿，到我妈的朋友家里去。

安静：　嗯！

祝文娟：再见！

安静：　好，再见！　(Zhu Wenjuan leaves.)

安然：　她是去找人<u>辅导</u>英语。她不愿意跟别人说。她妈对她学习<u>抓</u>得可<u>紧</u>呢！

安静：　她挺<u>懂</u><u>礼貌</u>的！

安然：　那我还有礼貌呢。不过，她学习是好，特别是<u>古文</u>和<u>历史</u>，讲起<u>三国演义</u>来<u>一套</u>
一套的！

Scene 4 ——————————

Strolling through a furniture store, Jing stops to inspect a bed.

安然：　姐，你要<u>结婚</u>？

安静：　谁说的？这不是<u>单人</u>床吗？

安然：　那就为你自己？<u>嘎</u>？不明白！

安静：　结了婚就不要单人床<u>啦</u>？<u>比方</u>说，两个人<u>吵了嘴</u>，就得到单人床去睡呀！

安然：　结婚就<u>意味</u>着吵嘴吗？

安静：　话不能这么说。可天下沒有不吵嘴的<u>夫妻</u>。

安然：　比如，刘冬虎的爸爸妈妈，还有<u>咱们</u>家二<u>老</u>？

*58.	結婚	结婚	jiéhūn	to get married
59.	單人-	单人-	dānrén-	(BF) single, for one person
60.	嘎	嘎	á	an interjection conveying surprise or dismay
61.	啦	啦	la	a sentence final particle, sometimes serving as a contraction of 了 and 啊 (cf. Note I.16.)
*62.	比方	比方	bǐfang	for example
^63.	吵嘴	吵嘴	chǎozuǐ	to bicker, quarrel
^64.	意味	意味	yìwèi	to imply, signify
*65.	夫妻	夫妻	fūqī	husband and wife
*66.	咱們	咱们	zánmen	(Northern Mandarin, sometimes just zán 咱) inclusive "we" (including the person being spoken to)
^67.	老	老	lǎo	(as a noun) the old folks

Scene 5 ─────────────────────

The two sisters walk along a major modern road.

安然：　姐，你説在咱們家二老身上，怎麼看不見人們常説的那個愛情？

安靜：　沒愛情，怎麼會有你和我？

安然：　不懂，實在不懂！

安靜：　唔，……

安然：　欸，姐，我去買幾根冰棍兒！

Ran runs off and buys a bunch of popsicles from a vendor.

安然：　給！

安靜：　買這麼多幹嘛？

安然：　你忘啦？我的最高記錄是十二枝！

冰棍販：對！這個玩意兒吃多了沒事兒，到肚子裡就化了，啊？

安靜、安然：呵呵呵！

安然：　欸，姐，你説，媽怎麼會愛上爸的？媽那麼漂亮，爸那麼不漂亮……

安靜：　這我可沒想過。什麼叫漂亮？

安然：　佐羅就漂亮，特別是他的下巴！我頂喜歡佐羅的下巴！

安靜：　哈哈哈！哈哈哈！

Now, they are strolling on a tree-lined avenue.

安然：　怎麼，姐，你還在想那張床？

安靜：　哪兒啊！我在想，今天是個星期天。

安然：　是個沉悶的星期天，是個快樂的星期天……咳！是個害怕的星期天！

^68. 身上	身上	shēnshang	(lit. "on one's body") in one's person
*69. 愛情	爱情	àiqíng	love (usually in the romantic or sexual sense)
*70. 實在	实在	shízài	truly
71. 冰棍兒	冰棍儿	bīnggùnr	popsicle
^72. 幹嘛	干嘛	gànmá	(colloquial) 爲什麼？做什麼？
*73. 記錄	记录	jìlù	record; to record
74. 枝	枝	zhī	M for stick-like things such as popsicles
^75. 玩意兒	玩意儿	wányìr	plaything; (colloquial) 東西

Scene 5 ——————————————

The two sisters walk along a major modern road.

安然：　姐，你说在咱们家二老身上，怎么看不见人们常说的那个爱情？

安静：　沒爱情，怎么会有你和我？

安然：　不懂，实在不懂！

安静：　咡，……

安然：　欸，姐，我去买几根冰棍儿！

Ran runs off and buys a bunch of popsicles from a vendor.

安然：　给！

安静：　买这么多干嘛？

安然：　你忘啦？我的最高记录是十二枝！

冰棍贩：对！这个玩意儿吃多了沒事儿，到肚子里就化了，啊？

安静、安然：呵呵呵！

安然：　欸，姐，你说，妈怎么会爱上爸的？妈那么漂亮，爸那么不漂亮……

安静：　这我可沒想过。什么叫漂亮？

安然：　佐罗就漂亮，特别是他的下巴！我顶喜欢佐罗的下巴！

安静：　哈哈哈！哈哈哈！

Now, they are strolling on a tree-lined avenue.

安然：　怎么，姐，你还在想那张床？

安静：　哪儿啊！我在想，今天是个星期天。

安然：　是个沉闷的星期天，是个快乐的星期天…… 咳！是个害怕的星期天！

*76. 沒事兒	沒事儿	méi shìr	no problem, it's nothing
^77. 肚子	肚子	dùzi	tummy, stomach
78. 化	化	huà	to melt
79. 呵	呵	hē	laughter (onomatopoeia)
80. 佐羅	佐罗	Zuǒluó	Zorro (hero in a widely known Western film)
81. 下巴	下巴	xiàba	chin
^82. 沉悶	沉闷	chénmèn	subdued, depressing
83. 咳	咳	hai	a sigh
*84. 害怕	害怕	hàipà	to fear; scared; scary

安靜：   你怎麼了？

安然：   明天進行總複習，再過幾天就要期末考試了！

安靜：   然然！你可不是個害怕考試的人！你是怕……

安然：   欸！姐，你看！(pointing to knots on a tree trunk) 這麼多眼睛！這是思考的
         眼睛，這是憤怒的眼睛，這是呆滯的眼睛，這是流淚的眼睛，這是憂慮的眼睛。

安靜：   然然，你不願意聽，我也要説！你是怕考試完以後的評"三好生"，是吧？

安然：   我不稀罕！

安靜：   可我希望你評上。欸，韋老師對你印象怎麼樣？

安然：   我不知道！她不是你小學同學嗎？你應該比我了解她！

安靜：   Eh……

安然：   韋老師的心，實在摸不透！

^85. 怎麼了	怎么了	zěnmele	What's up? What's wrong?
*86. 進行	进行	jìnxíng	to proceed with
*87. 總	总	zǒng	general, overall, total
*88. 複習	复习	fùxí	to review; review
^89. 期末	期末	qīmò	end of the term or semester
*90. 眼睛	眼睛	yǎnjing	eye
^91. 思考	思考	sīkǎo	to contemplate; contemplative
^92. 憤怒	愤怒	fènnù	indignant, angry
93. 呆滯	呆滞	dāizhì	dull
^94. 流淚	流泪	liú lèi	to shed tears
^95. 憂慮	忧虑	yōulù	worried, anxious

討論問題：

1)   安然小時候愛問媽媽那麼多問題。從這一點，你能不能想到她從小是一個什麼樣的女孩？

2)   安靜替安然洗頭髮能不能表現出 (biǎoxiàn-chū: to manifest) 她們姐妹的關係是怎麼樣的？

3)   十幾歲的安然又是個什麼樣的女孩？跟她小時候一樣嗎？

4)   在街上，姐妹倆看見了誰？這個同學有什麼特點？跟安然有什麼不同？

5)   安然看見了樹上的不同的"眼睛"。從這一點你能不能看出她的心情 (xīnqíng: mood) 怎麼樣？

6)   你猜 (cāi: to guess) 安然為什麼會怕評"三好生"？

安静：	你怎么了？
安然：	明天进行总复习，再过几天就要期末考试了！
安静：	然然！你可不是个害怕考试的人！你是怕……
安然：	欸！姐，你看！(pointing to knots on a tree trunk) 这么多眼睛！这是思考的眼睛，这是愤怒的眼睛，这是呆滞的眼睛，这是流泪的眼睛，这是忧虑的眼睛。
安静：	然然，你不愿意听，我也要说！你是怕考试完以后的评"三好生"，是吧？
安然：	我不稀罕！
安静：	可我希望你评上。欸，韦老师对你印象怎么样？
安然：	我不知道！她不是你小学同学吗？你应该比我了解她！
安静：	Eh……
安然：	韦老师的心，实在摸不透！

^96. 評	评	píng	to evaluate
97. 三好生	三好生	sān hǎo shēng	"three-goods student," an honor bestowed on high school students deemed superior in the three aspects of moral character, wisdom, and physical fitness
^98. 稀罕	稀罕	xīhan	rare, scarce; to value as a rarity, cherish
*99. 印象	印象	yìnxiàng	impression
*100.了解	了解	liǎojiě	to understand, comprehend
101.摸不透	摸不透	mōbutòu	(V不RE) unable to get a feel for

讨论问题：

1) 安然小时候爱问妈妈那么多问题。从这一点，你能不能想到她从小是一个什么样的女孩？

2) 安静替安然洗头发能不能表现出 (biǎoxiàn-chū: to manifest) 她们姐妹的关系是怎么样的？

3) 十几岁的安然又是个什么样的女孩？跟她小时候一样吗？

4) 在街上，姐妹俩看见了谁？这个同学有什么特点？跟安然有什么不同？

5) 安然看见了树上的不同的"眼睛"。从这一点你能不能看出她的心情 (xīnqíng: mood)怎么样？

6) 你猜 (cāi: to guess) 安然为什么会怕评"三好生"？

Scene 6 ──────────────

In Ran's classroom, the entire class reads a classical Chinese passage in unison while Teacher Wei strolls between rows of desks.

韋老師：下面一句："<u>故曰</u>：良劍期乎斷，不期乎鏌鋣；良馬期乎千里，不期乎驥驁。"
　　　　鏌鋣，是古代的一把名<u>劍</u>。
安然：　(to her deskmate) 欸，老師<u>讀錯</u>了！
男生甲：是嗎？
祝文娟：是<u>讀錯</u>了！(checks in a dictionary, then puts it on her desk.)
韋老師：好，下面我來講講這句…(Ran raises her hand.)　安然，你要說什麼？
安然：　韋老師，應該讀鏌<u>yé</u>，不讀 <u>xié</u>，您讀錯了！

Shocked at Ran's audacity, all heads turn in her direction.

韋老師：你說的，也不一定對。先<u>按</u>我的讀，下課，<u>查</u>查字典再說！
安然：　這兒有字典。
韋老師：那好吧。誰有字典……就拿出來吧。
安然：　(tapping Wenjuan's shoulder)　欸，祝文娟，你不是有字典嗎？
祝文娟：沒有，我沒有字典。
安然：　不，你有。我剛才看見你拿着在<u>翻</u>。
祝文娟：那你可能看錯了，這是<u>英漢小辭典</u>。

Commotion breaks out.　The teacher taps the board to hush the class.

---

1. 故	故	gù	(literary) therefore
2. 曰	曰	yuē	(literary) 説; it is said
3. 良劍期乎 斷，不期 乎鏌鋣； 良馬期乎 千里，不 期乎驥驁	良剑期乎 断，不期 乎镆铘； 良马期乎 千里，不 期乎骥骜	liángjiàn qīhū duàn, bù qīhū Mòxié [sic]; liángmǎ qīhū qiānlǐ, bù qīhū Jì Áo	(a passage from the classical text 呂氏春秋 <u>Lǔ-shì Chūn-qiū</u>) "a good sword may expect to break and cannot aspire to be like the super sword Mòyé; a good horse may expect to cover 10,000 <u>lǐ</u>, but cannot aspire to be like the super steeds Jì and Áo"

SEGMENT II

Scene 6 ————————————

In Ran's classroom, the entire class reads a classical Chinese passage in unison while Teacher Wei strolls between rows of desks.

韦老师：下面一句：" <u>故曰</u>：良剑期乎断，不期乎镆铘；良马期乎千里，不期乎骥骜。"
　　　　镆铘，是古代的一把名<u>剑</u>。

安然：　（to her deskmate）欸，老师<u>读</u>错了!

男生甲：是吗？

祝文娟：是读错了!　（checks in a dictionary, then puts it on her desk.）

韦老师：好，下面我来讲讲这句…（Ran raises her hand.）　安然，你要说什么？

安然：　韦老师，应该读镆 y℩，不读 xi℩，您读错了!

Shocked at Ran's audacity, all heads turn in her direction.

韦老师：你说的，也不一定对。先<u>按</u>我的读，下课，<u>查查</u>字典再说!

安然：　这儿有字典。

韦老师：那好吧。谁有字典……就拿出来吧。

安然：　（tapping Wenjuan's shoulder）　欸，祝文娟，你不是有字典吗？

祝文娟：没有，我没有字典。

安然：　不，你有。我刚才看见你拿着在<u>翻</u>。

祝文娟：那你可能看错了，这是<u>英汉小辞典</u>。

Commotion breaks out. The teacher taps the board to hush the class.

---

4. 劍	剑	jiàn	sword
*5. 讀	读	dú	to read aloud, study
*6. 按	按	àn	according to
^7. 查	查	chá	to look up in a dictionary; to examine, investigate
^8. 翻	翻	fān	to turn (here, to turn the pages)

韋老師：安然，你先坐下。

As Ran sits down slowly, a boy makes a sneering remark at her.

男生乙：這是咱<u>班</u>的<u>大能人</u>吧。
韋老師：我<u>順便</u>地說幾句。我們<u>進入高一</u>下學期<u>之後</u>，學習<u>難度</u>加大了，所以，大家在學習上，要<u>更加</u>踏實。上課，要認真地聽老師<u>講解</u>。大家要想學習好，<u>必須</u>要<u>端正</u>學習<u>態度</u>，做到<u>謙虛</u>謹慎，<u>戒驕戒躁</u>。

Knowing that these remarks are directed at Ran, many eyes turn toward her. Tears well up in her eyes.

Scene 7 ————————————

Ran and Jing stroll along a quiet street.

安靜：　　她不是說要來<u>家訪</u>嗎？怎麼總沒見她來呢？
安然：　　那誰知道！

Scene 8 ————————————

A couple in the Ans' apartment building is having a fight. As the neighbors (and we) hear the crying and yelling, their son, wiping his eyes, runs out of the apartment and down the stairs.

^9. 班	班	bān	class
^10. 大能人	大能人	dà néngrén	a greatly capable person
^11. 順便	顺便	shùnbiàn	conveniently, in passing, to do something along the way
*12. 進入	进入	jìnrù	to enter
^13. 高一	高一	gāo yī	高中一年級
*14. 之	之	zhī	literary equivalent of the particle 的 in vernacular; here 之後 is equivalent to 以後 in vernacular
^15. 難度	难度	nándù	(-度: degree of) degree of difficulty
^16. 更加	更加	gèngjiā	even more

韦老师：安然，你先坐下。

As Ran sits down slowly, a boy makes a sneering remark at her.

男生乙：这是咱<u>班</u>的<u>大能人</u>吧。

韦老师：我<u>顺便</u>地说几句。我们<u>进入</u><u>高一</u>下学期<u>之后</u>，学习<u>难度</u>加大了，所以，大家在学习上，
          要<u>更加</u><u>踏实</u>。上课，要<u>认真</u>地听老师<u>讲解</u>。大家要想学习好，<u>必须</u>要<u>端正</u>学习<u>态度</u>，
          做到<u>谦虚</u><u>谨慎</u>，<u>戒骄戒躁</u>。

Knowing that these remarks are directed at Ran, many eyes turn toward her. Tears
well up in her eyes.

Scene 7 ————————————

Ran and Jing stroll along a quiet street.

安静：   她不是说要来<u>家访</u>吗？怎么总沒见她来呢？

安然：   那谁知道！

Scene 8 ————————————

A couple in the Ans' apartment building is having a fight. As the neighbors (and
we) hear the crying and yelling, their son, wiping his eyes, runs out of the
apartment and down the stairs.

---

17. 踏實	踏实	tāshi	steadfast (in work)
*18. 認真	认真	rènzhēn	earnest
^19. 講解	讲解	jiǎngjiě	to explain
*20. 必須	必须	bìxū	must
^21. 端正	端正	duānzhèng	to set straight, rectify
*22. 態度	态度	tàidu	attitude
^23. 謙虛	谦虚	qiānxū	modest, self-effacing
^24. 謹慎	谨慎	jǐnshèn	prudent, cautious, circumspect
25. 戒驕戒躁	戒骄戒躁	jiè jiāo jiè zào	to guard against conceit and impetuosity
^26. 家訪	家访	jiāfǎng	home visit (by a teacher)

冬虎爸：你哭什麼你哭。

冬虎媽：打人，你<u>欺負</u>我，你。

冬虎爸：你讓人聽着好聽是怎麼着？…

冬虎媽：…你欺負人，…   冬虎爸：我怎麼欺負你了？

冬虎媽：…小心想想，…   冬虎爸：你好好想想吧你！…

冬虎媽：…我不是容易…   冬虎爸：你不容易啊。

冬虎媽：你到外面<u>幹</u>的好事兒。

⋯⋯⋯⋯⋯

冬虎爸：我幹什麼我？

Her curiosity piqued, Ran is about to go upstairs to see what the commotion is all about when Jing pulls her back into their apartment.

安靜：   (to Ran) 你<u>精力</u>太<u>過剩</u>了。幹自己的事兒去。

Scene 9 ──────────

In the Ans' apartment, a tape of "The Sound of Music" is playing loudly in the sisters' room. Ran sings along.

媽媽：   然然，你幹什麼呢？怎麼還不抓緊時間複習功課？要考試了。

安然：   (shutting off the tape recorder) 媽，您不是病了嗎？別<u>管</u>這麼多了。老<u>嚷嚷</u>。

媽媽：   誰說我病了？

安然：   爸爸。

媽媽：   我什麼時候病了？

爸爸：   <u>哼</u>，你不是說你<u>不舒服</u>嗎？

媽媽：   我哪兒不舒服過？<u>丟掉專業</u>的<u>滋味</u>，你們知道。就會畫那些<u>不被賞識</u>的畫兒。

^27. 欺負	欺负	qīfu	to bully, take advantage of
^28. 幹	干	gàn	(colloquial) 做
*29. 精力	精力	jīnglì	energy, vim, vigor
^30. 過剩	过剩	guòshèng	excessively abundant
*31. 管	管	guǎn	to be concerned with, to mind; to be in charge of, manage
32. 嚷	嚷	rǎng	to yell, make an uproar or a fuss
33. 哼	哼	hng!	humph!
*34. 不舒服	不舒服	bùshūfu	to not feel well, be sick

冬虎爸：你哭什么你哭。

冬虎妈：打人，你<u>欺负</u>我，你。

冬虎爸：你让人听着好听是怎么着？…

冬虎妈：…你欺负人，…	冬虎爸：我怎么欺负你了？
冬虎妈：…小心想想，…	冬虎爸：你好好想想吧你！…
冬虎妈：…我不是容易…	冬虎爸：你不容易啊。

冬虎妈：你到外面<u>干</u>的好事儿。

‥‥‥‥‥‥

冬虎爸：我干什么我？

Her curiosity piqued, Ran is about to go upstairs to see what the commotion is all about when Jing pulls her back into their apartment.

安靜：　(to Ran) 你<u>精力</u>太<u>过剩</u>了。干自己的事儿去。

Scene 9 ─────────────

In the Ans' apartment, a tape of "The Sound of Music" is playing loudly in the sisters' room.　Ran sings along.

妈妈：　然然，你干什么呢？怎么还不抓紧时间复习功课？要考试了。

安然：　(shutting off the tape recorder) 妈，您不是病了吗？别<u>管</u>这么多了。老<u>嚷嚷</u>。

妈妈：　谁说我病了？

安然：　爸爸。

妈妈：　我什么时候病了？

爸爸：　<u>哼</u>，你不是说你<u>不舒服</u>吗？

妈妈：　我<u>哪儿</u>不舒服过？<u>丢掉</u><u>专业</u>的<u>滋味</u>，你们知道。就会画那<u>些</u>不<u>被</u><u>赏识</u>的画儿。

---

^35.　哪兒	哪儿	năr	(used rhetorically to indicate denial) "Where...?" "How...?"
*36.　丢掉	丢掉	diūdiào	to discard, cast away, lose
*37.　專業	专业	zhuānyè	professional specialty
^38.　滋味	滋味	zīwèi	flavor, taste
*39.　被	被	bèi	(a coverb indicating the agent in a passive sentence) by (the object of 被 may be understood and omitted, as in this context)
^40.　賞識	赏识	shăngshí	to recognize the worth of, appreciate

安静： 媽，洗衣機停了。

媽媽： <u>倒霉</u>。

安静： 爸。(puts a glass on a stand for him, then to Ran.) 然然，<u>洗頭</u>。

安然： 哦。 (to her dad) 爸，你又<u>抽煙</u>。第幾枝啦？(He gestures "two.") 幾枝？我得<u>檢查</u>檢查。

爸爸： 欸，去去。你姐姐叫你呢。跟姐姐好好學習學習。

安然： 才不呢，她<u>儘偷着</u>給你買煙。

Jing is now washing Ran's hair.

安静： 小黄毛的頭髮現在又黑又<u>密</u>了。

安然： 你給我吃核桃吃的。

安静： 嗐，這麼大了，還要我<u>伺候</u>你。

安然： 姐，你可不能結婚，你結婚了，誰給我洗頭啊。

安静： 那當然。

Scene 10 ————————————

In another corner of the Ans' apartment...

媽媽： 我聽説，從高一到高三，<u>連任</u>三好生，考大學有<u>照顧</u>。

爸爸： 嗯，嗯？照顧誰？

媽媽： 我説的是然然。現在是高一，很<u>關鍵</u>。

爸爸： 考試<u>嘛</u>，還照顧。怪事，我就沒讓誰照顧過。

媽媽： 你這個人哪，就一條<u>優點</u>，<u>倔</u>。然然就像你。

^41.	倒霉	倒霉	dǎoméi	in bad luck, "Darn!" "What lousy luck!"
^42.	洗頭	洗头	xǐtóu	to wash hair
^43.	抽煙	抽烟	chōuyān	to smoke
*44.	檢查	检查	jiǎnchá	to inspect, check up, examine
*45.	儘	尽	jǐn	(dialectal) to keep on (doing something)
^46.	偷着	偷着	tōuzhe	on the sly
47.	密	密	mì	dense, thick
^48.	伺候	伺候	cìhou	to wait upon, serve
49.	連任	连任	liánrèn	to be reappointed or reelected consecutively
*50.	照顧	照顾	zhàogu	to give special consideration to, look after

安静：   妈，洗衣机停了。

妈妈：   <u>倒霉</u>。

安静：   爸。(puts a glass on a stand for him, then to Ran.) 然然，<u>洗头</u>。

安然：   哦。 (to her dad) 爸，你又<u>抽烟</u>。第几枝<u>啦</u>？(He gestures "two.") 几枝？我得
         <u>检查</u>检查。

爸爸：   欸，去去。你姐姐叫你呢。跟姐姐好好学习学习。

安然：   才不呢，她<u>尽</u>偷着给你买烟。

Jing is now washing Ran's hair.

安静：   小黄毛的头发现在又黑又<u>密</u>了。

安然：   你给我吃核桃吃的。

安静：   嗯，这么大了，还要我<u>伺候</u>你。

安然：   姐，你可不能结婚，你结婚了，谁给我洗头啊。

安静：   那当然。

Scene 10 ————————————————

In another corner of the Ans' apartment...

妈妈：   我听说，从高一到高三，<u>连任</u>三好生，考大学有<u>照顾</u>。

爸爸：   嗯，嗯？照顾谁？

妈妈：   我说的是然然。现在是高一，很<u>关键</u>。

爸爸：   考试<u>嘛</u>，还照顾。怪事，我就没让谁照顾过。

妈妈：   你这个人哪，就一条<u>优点</u>，<u>倔</u>。然然就象你。

^51	關鍵	关键	guānjiàn	hinge, crux, key
^52.	嘛	嘛	ma	1) a sentence-final particle reinforcing or "rubbing in" the sense of the statement; 2) (as in this context) a particle setting the subject or topic of a sentence apart to give it emphasis, thus reinforcing the comma that serves the same function (cf. Grammatical Note I.14.)
*53.	優點	优点	yōudiǎn	strong point, virtue, advantage
54.	倔	倔	jué	stubborn

安然：　我又怎麼了？

媽媽：　我說，你一定要<u>爭取</u>個<u>三好生</u>。

Scene 11 —————————————

In the girls' room, Ran picks up a letter addressed to Jing.

安然：　唉，<u>郵票</u>？是<u>紀念</u><u>羅伯特·柯赫</u><u>發現</u><u>結核菌</u>一百<u>週年</u>的。這套就一張。
　　　　(reading the return address) <u>秦皇島</u>三二三二信箱。這是誰給你寫的信呀？

安靜：　我是編輯，給我寫信的人可多了。

Scene 12 —————————————

Mi Xiaolin calls from the yard outside the Ans' apartment.

米曉玲：安然。

安然：　(goes to the window) 欸。

米曉玲：嘿，(makes a gesture signifying a notebook) <u>哎呀</u>，<u>物理作業本兒</u>。

Ran wraps up some papers for her friend.

米曉玲：安然，快點兒啊。

安然：　(tosses a bundle of papers out the window) 給。

Xiaoling opens the bundle and finds these words on top: <u>只許參考</u>，<u>不準照抄</u>。

^55.	爭取	争取	zhēngqǔ	to strive for
^56.	郵票	邮票	yóupiào	postage stamp
*57.	紀念	纪念	jìniàn	to commemorate
58.	羅伯特·柯赫	罗伯特·柯赫	Luóbótè Kēhè	Robert Coch
*59.	發現	发现	fāxiàn	to discover
60.	結核菌	结核菌	jiéhéjùn	tuberculosis bacillus
^61.	週年	周年	zhōunián	anniversary
62.	秦皇島	秦皇岛	Qínhuáng Dǎo	"Emperor Qin Island," name of a seaport in Hobei Province

安然：　我又怎么了？

妈妈：　我说，你一定要争取个三好生。

Scene 11 ——————————————

In the girls' room, Ran picks up a letter addressed to Jing.

安然：　唉，邮票？是纪念罗伯特·柯赫发现结核菌一百周年的。这套就一张。

　　　　（reading the return address）秦皇岛三二三二信箱。这是谁给你写的信呀？

安静：　我是编辑，给我写信的人可多了。

Scene 12 ——————————————

Mi Xiaolin calls from the yard outside the Ans' apartment.

米晓玲：安然。

安然：　（goes to the window）欸。

米晓玲：嘿，（makes a gesture signifying a notebook）哎呀，物理作业本儿。

Ran wraps up some papers for her friend.

米晓玲：安然，快点儿啊。

安然：　（tosses a bundle of papers out the window）给。

Xiaoling opens the bundle and finds these words on top: 只许参考，不准照抄。

^63. 哎呀	哎呀	āiyā	an expletive
*64. 物理	物理	wùlǐ	physics
*65. 作業	作业	zuòyè	homework
^66. 本兒	本儿	běnr	notebook
*67. 許	许	xǔ	to permit
^68. 參考	参考	cānkǎo	to use as reference
*69. 準	准	zhǔn	to permit (synonymous with 許)
70. 照抄	照抄	zhàochāo	to copy word for word

米曉玲：放心吧，再見。

安靜：　誰呀？

安然：　米曉玲。

Scene 13 ——————————

In Wei Wan's apartment.

安靜：　　韋婉，小學畢業以後，你好像念的是十三中吧？

韋老師：哦，是，我知道你念的是二中。

安靜：　　那幾年中學就這麼回事。

韋老師：可不是啊。

安靜：　　欸，你後來也下鄉了吧？

韋老師：呵呵呵，去了幾天，後來啊，又到了部隊，上過幾天學，這不，又到了教育部門兒，
　　　　　呵……噯，你坐呀。

安靜：　　哦，好。

韋老師：別客氣哦，呵呵。

*71. 畢業	毕业	bìyè	to graduate
72. 十三中	十三中	shísān zhōng	Middle School Number 13
^73. 這麼回事	这么回事	zhème huí shì	that's the way it is; that's all there is to it
*74. 下鄉	下乡	xiàxiāng	"to go down to the countryside," (here) the rustication of youths during the Cultural Revolution

討論問題：

1)　在安然的一堂 (táng: M for classes) 古文課中發生 (fāshēng: to occur) 了什麼事情？

2)　從這件事，你能看出安然、韋老師、和祝文娟的一些什麼？

3)　劉冬虎父母的關係怎麼樣？別人知道他們的情況 (qíngkuàng: situation) 嗎？

4)　爸爸和媽媽對於"三好生"的看法一樣嗎？

5)　安然怎麼幫助米曉玲？你認為 (rènwéi: to construe, consider) 她這樣做對嗎？

6)　安靜和韋老師小學的時候是同學，現在她們是好朋友嗎？你猜安靜為什麼去找韋老師？

米晓玲：放心吧，再见。

安静：　谁呀？

安然：　米晓玲。

Scene 13 —————————————

In Wei Wan's apartment.

安静：　韦婉，小学<u>毕业</u>以后，你好象念的是<u>十三中</u>吧？

韦老师：哦，是，我知道你念的是二中。

安静：　那几年中学就<u>这么回事</u>。

韦老师：可不是啊。

安静：　欸，你后来也<u>下乡</u>了吧？

韦老师：呵呵呵，去了几天，后来啊，又到了<u>部队</u>，上过几天学，<u>这不</u>，又到了<u>教育部门</u>儿，
　　　　呵……嗳，你坐呀。

安静：　哦，好。

韦老师：别客气哦，呵呵。

^75. 部隊	部队	bùduì	the armed forces, particularly the army
76. 這不	这不	zhèbu	(colloquial, mid-statement interjection) "Now, can't you see? ..." (i.e., "As you can see, ...)
*77. 教育	教育	jiàoyù	education; educational
^78. 部門	部门	bùmén	sector, department, branch

讨论问题：

1)　在安然的一堂 (táng: M for classes) 古文课中发生 (fāshēng: to occur) 了什么事情？

2)　从这件事，你能看出安然、韦老师、和祝文娟的一些什么？

3)　刘冬虎父母的关系怎么样？别人知道他们的情况 (qíngkuàng: situation) 吗？

4)　爸爸和妈妈对于"三好生"的看法一样吗？

5)　安然怎么帮助米晓玲？你认为 (rènwéi: to construe, consider) 她这样做对吗？

6)　安静和韦老师小学的时候是同学，现在她们是好朋友吗？你猜安静为什么去找韦老师？

SEGMENT III

Continued from the last scene in Segment II.

韋老師：欸，我看過你寫的小説。

安靜：　那只能算習作。安然，在班裡怎麼樣？

韋老師：怎麼跟你説呢？其實啊，我是準備專門到你們家去和你談談的。你妹妹呀，很聰明，也很用功。

安靜：　哦。

韋老師：就是……用形容成人的話來説，呵，就是有點兒羣眾關係不大好。

安靜：　她怎麼了？

韋老師：怎麼跟你説呢？……反正，咱們可是老同學了，有啥説啥。

安靜：　哦。

韋老師：不知為什麼，安然總喜歡和一個叫米曉玲的女同學在一起，這個同學學習成績又不好……嗯……安然和……和她唱過一首什麼歌，這首歌的歌詞，我就不便重複了。嗯，還有，她最近老愛和一個叫劉冬虎的男同學在一起接觸。

安靜：　哦，這個男孩兒我好像認識，（韋老師：嗯？）他就住在我們一個樓裡。

韋老師：噢。還有……欸，你坐呀。

安靜：　噢，好好好。呵呵。

韋老師：今天你可是稀客。

安靜：　欸，你接着説吧。

韋老師：其實啊，也沒什麼。

安靜：　不不不，沒關係，你説吧。

韋老師：嗯，她過去挺朴素的。現在，也愛打扮起來了。嘻嘻。上個星期，還穿了件大紅襯衫兒。對了，前面沒有扣子，後面還帶了條拉鍊兒。

---

1. 習作	习作	xízuò	an exercise in composition, drawing, etc.
*2. 其實	其实	qíshí	actually
^3. 專門	专门	zhuānmén	especially; special
*4. 聰明	聪明	cōngming	intelligent
^5. 形容	形容	xíngróng	to describe
*6. 成人	成人	chéngrén	adult
^7. 羣眾	群众	qúnzhòng	the masses, people
*8. 關係	关系	guānxi	relationship
*9. 反正	反正	fǎnzhèng	(adv.) in any case
10. 啥	啥	shá	(colloquial) 什麼
^11. 成績	成绩	chéngjī	achievements
12. 首	首	shǒu	M for songs and poems

SEGMENT III

Continued from the last scene in Segment II.

韦老师：欸，我看过你写的小说。

安静：　那只能算习作。安然，在班里怎么样？

韦老师：怎么跟你说呢？其实啊，我是准备专门到你们家去和你谈谈的。你妹妹呀，很聪明，
　　　　也很用功。

安静：　哦。

韦老师：就是……用形容成人的话来说，呵，就是有点儿群众关系不大好。

安静：　她怎么了？

韦老师：怎么跟你说呢？……反正，咱们可是老同学了，有啥说啥。

安静：　哦。

韦老师：不知为什么，安然总喜欢和一个叫米晓玲的女同学在一起，这个同学学习成绩又不
　　　　好……唔……安然和……和她唱过一首什么歌，这首歌的歌词，我就不便重复了。唔，
　　　　还有，她最近老爱和一个叫刘冬虎的男同学在一起接触。

安静：　哦，这个男孩儿我好象认识，（韦老师：唔？）他就住在我们一个楼里。

韦老师：噢。还有……欸，你坐呀。

安静：　噢，好好好。呵呵。

韦老师：今天你可是稀客。

安静：　欸，你接着说吧。

韦老师：其实啊，也没什么。

安静：　不不不，没关系，你说吧。

韦老师：唔，她过去挺朴素的。现在，也爱打扮起来了。嘻嘻。上个星期，还穿了件大红
　　　　衬衫儿。对了，前面没有扣子，后面还带了条拉链儿。

13. 歌詞	歌词	gēcí	song lyrics
^14. 不便	不便	búbiàn	"不方便," inappropriate
^15. 重複	重复	chóngfù	to repeat
^16. 還有	还有	háiyǒu	moreover
^17. 接觸	接触	jiēchù	to have contact with
18. 噢	噢	o	Oh!
19. 稀客	稀客	xīkè	a rare visitor
^20. 接着	接着	jiēzhe	to continue (doing something)
^21. 樸素	朴素	pǔsù	simple and plain, free of adornment
^22. 打扮	打扮	dǎbàn	to dress up, put on make-up
^23. 扣子	扣子	kòuzi	button
24. 拉鏈兒	拉链儿	lāliànr	zipper

安靜：　噢，那是新買的。

韋老師：對，問題就在這兒。這是一種跡象，可得引起注意啊。

安靜：　呵呵。

韋老師：呵呵。

韋老師：你作爲安然的姐姐，作爲我的老同學，可要協助我，幫安然把路子走正，呵呵呵。

安靜：　嗯。

韋老師：欸，你也別往心裡去。

安靜：　噢，呵呵呵

韋老師：呵呵呵。孩子嘛，呵呵呵。

韋老師：嗯……你最近收到我一封信了嗎？

安靜：　沒有啊？

韋老師：我寄了篇稿子給你。

安靜：　噢？

韋老師：那是瞎寫的。我是教語文的，想練練筆。呵呵呵。

安靜：　是。

韋老師：還得請你多幫忙啊。呵呵呵。欸，吃這個。

Scene 14 ───────────────

Coming home, Jing enters the apartment. Ran is doing her homework while playing a
tape of vocal music.

安靜：　爸，媽。我回來了。

安然：　姐，你上哪兒啦？

安靜：　噢，去一個業餘作者那兒了。

---

^25. 跡象	迹象	jīxiàng	sign, indication
^26. 引起	引起	yǐnqǐ	to arouse, give rise to
^27. 作爲	作为	zuòwéi	as, in the role or position of...
^28. 協助	协助	xiézhù	to assist
29. 把路子走正	把路子走正	bǎ lùzi zǒuzhèng	to walk a straight path
30. 往心裡去	往心里去	wǎng xīnli qù	to take it to heart, to be overly concerned about something
^31. 篇	篇	piān	M for a literary work (short story, article, etc., but not book)

安静：　噢，那是新买的。

韦老师：对，问题就在这儿。这是一种迹象，可得引起注意啊。

安静：　呵呵。

韦老师：呵呵。

韦老师：你作为安然的姐姐，作为我的老同学，可要协助我，帮安然把路子走正，呵呵呵。

安静：　嗯。

韦老师：欸，你也别往心里去。

安静：　噢，呵呵呵

韦老师：呵呵呵。孩子嘛，呵呵呵。

韦老师：嗯……你最近收到我一封信了吗？

安静：　沒有啊？

韦老师：我寄了篇稿子给你。

安静：　噢？

韦老师：那是瞎写的。我是教语文的，想练练笔。呵呵呵。

安静：　是。

韦老师：还得请你多帮忙啊。呵呵呵。欸，吃这个。

Scene 14 ————————————

Coming home, Jing enters the apartment. Ran is doing her homework while playing a
tape of vocal music.

安静：　爸，妈。我回来了。

安然：　姐，你上哪儿啦？

安静：　噢，去一个业余作者那儿了。

---

^32. 稿子	稿子	gǎozi	manuscript, draft
^33. 瞎	瞎	xiā	blind; (adv., colloquial) blindly, groundlessly, foolishly
*34. 語文	语文	yǔwén	language and literature
35. 練筆	练笔	liànbǐ	to "exercise the pen," write something as an exercise
^36. 上	上	shàng	(colloquial) 去
^37. 業餘	业余	yèyú	sparetime, after hours, amateur
*38. 作者	作者	zuòzhě	author, writer

安靜：　你呀，又聽音樂，又作功課。把錄音機關了！

安然：　(turning up the tape player) 姐，你聽這是誰唱的？

安靜：　呵呵呵，<u>歌壇</u><u>新秀</u>安然唱的。

安然：　哈哈哈。

安靜：　你呀，精力也太過剩啦！(shuts off the tape player.)

安靜：　(about to unzip Ran's red blouse) 那衣服<u>髒</u>啦，該換了。

安然：　哎呀，我再穿一天。

安靜：　不，一會兒我洗衣服，<u>順手</u>給你帶。

安然：　那太好啦。謝謝您<u>同志</u>。我看這件衣服，就是好看。你說呀。

安靜：　唔，我們的小然然，真長成大姑娘了啊？

安然：　本來嘛。我<u>早就</u>看出來了，你老把我當男孩子<u>看待</u>，老讓我穿<u>夾克衫</u>。其實，(takes off her blouse and hands it to Jing) 我是個女的，女的，別忘了。

安靜：　放心，忘不了。你是個<u>地地道道</u>挺不錯的女孩兒。

Scene 15 ─────────────

Mother walks into the room, reading a letter, then collapses dejectedly onto the sofa.

爸爸：　怎麼，又不舒服啦？

媽媽：　(hands the letter to Father) 看嘛！

爸爸：　(reads the letter) 噢，開<u>校友</u>會，去吧。

媽媽：　我去幹什麼？

爸爸：　老同學嘛，<u>聚會</u>聚會。

媽媽：　人家現在是<u>翻譯家</u>，作家，有的還出了國，<u>當了官兒</u>，我呢？是你們畫院的一個<u>辦事員</u>。我去幹什麼？

爸爸：　那幾年我就<u>勸</u>你，別把專業丟掉，你就是不聽。在那兒瞎<u>積極</u>。

39. 歌壇	歌坛	gētán	musical circles (particularly vocal music)
40. 新秀	新秀	xīnxiù	a new star, a new talent
^41. 髒	脏	zāng	dirty
^42. 順手	顺手	shùnshǒu	conveniently, without extra trouble
*43. 同志	同志	tóngzhì	comrade
*44. 早就	早就	zǎojiù	(adv.) long ago, long since
^45. 看待	看待	kàndài	to regard as, treat as
46. 夾克衫	夹克衫	jiákè-shān	"jacket shirt"

安静： 你呀，又听音乐，又作功课。把录音机关了！

安然： (turning up the tape player) 姐，你听这是谁唱的？

安静： 呵呵呵，歌坛新秀安然唱的。

安然： 哈哈哈。

安静： 你呀，精力也太过剩啦！(shuts off the tape player.)

安静： (about to unzip Ran's red blouse) 那衣服脏啦，该换了。

安然： 哎呀，我再穿一天。

安静： 不，一会儿我洗衣服，顺手给你带。

安然： 那太好啦。谢谢您同志。我看这件衣服，就是好看。你说呀。

安静： 嗯，我们的小然然，真长成大姑娘了啊？

安然： 本来嘛。我早就看出来了，你老把我当男孩子看待，老让我穿夹克衫。其实，(takes off her blouse and hands it to Jing) 我是个女的，女的，别忘了。

安静： 放心，忘不了。你是个地地道道挺不错的女孩儿。

Scene 15 ————————————

Mother walks into the room, reading a letter, then collapses dejectedly onto the sofa.

爸爸： 怎么，又不舒服啦？

妈妈： (hands the letter to Father) 看嘛！

爸爸： (reads the letter) 噢，开校友会，去吧。

妈妈： 我去干什么？

爸爸： 老同学嘛，聚会聚会。

妈妈： 人家现在是翻译家，作家，有的还出了国，当了官儿，我呢？是你们画院的一个办事员。我去干什么？

爸爸： 那几年我就劝你，别把专业丢掉，你就是不听。在那儿瞎积极。

^47.	地地道道	地地道道	dìdìdàodào	typical, authentic, genuine
^48.	校友	校友	xiàoyǒu	alumni
^49.	聚會	聚会	jùhuì	get-together, reunion
*50.	翻譯	翻译	fānyì	to translate (翻译家: cf. next gloss)
^51.	-家	-家	-jiā	a professional or expert in...
52.	當官兒	当官儿	dāngguānr	to be an official
^53.	辦事員	办事员	bànshìyuán	office worker
*54.	勸	劝	quàn	to urge, persuade
*55.	積極	积极	jījí	positive, enthusiastic, gungho

媽媽：　我不是為了給孩子們<u>創造</u>點<u>政治</u><u>條件</u>嗎？
爸爸：　政治條件？

Mother sits down with a basin to start preparing a meal. Father pulls up a stool to help.

媽媽：　洗洗手去。
爸爸：　<u>到底</u>什麼是政治？　(goes to wash his hands.)

Scene 16 ——————————————

In the yard, several girls are jumping a rubber band rope.

<u>眾</u>小朋友：<u>大蘋果</u>，<u>香蕉梨</u>，<u>馬藍</u>開花二十一，二八二五六，二八二五七，二八二九三十一。
小朋友：安然姐姐，安然姐姐。
安然：　欸。
小朋友：你再借一本書給我看，好嗎？
安然：　好吧！再借一本<u>安徒生</u>的<u>童話</u>給你看。一會兒來拿吧。
小朋友：那好吧，謝謝啦。

Scene 17 ——————————————

At her office, Jing sorts through the mail and hands a letter to Editor Ma.

安靜：　馬老師。

Jing goes to her own desk and opens a piece of her mail. Ma looks up from reading a manuscript.

^56. 創造	创造	chuàngzào	to create
*57. 政治	政治	zhèngzhì	politics; political
*58. 條件	条件	tiáojiàn	conditions, qualifications
*59. 到底	到底	dàodǐ	(adv.) after all
^60. -眾-	-众-	zhòng-, -zhòng	(BF) many, numerous (of people); a crowd of...

妈妈：　我不是为了给孩子们<u>创造点</u><u>政治条件</u>吗？

爸爸：　政治条件？

Mother sits down with a basin to start preparing a meal. Father pulls up a stool to help.

妈妈：　洗洗手去。

爸爸：　<u>到底</u>什么是政治？（goes to wash his hands.)

Scene 16 ———————————

In the yard, several girls are jumping a rubber band rope.

众小朋友：大<u>苹果</u>，<u>香蕉梨</u>，<u>马蓝</u>开花二十一，二八二五六，二八二五七，二八二九三十一。

小朋友：安然姐姐，安然姐姐。

安然：　欸。

小朋友：你再借一本书给我看，好吗？

安然：　好吧！再借一本<u>安徒生</u>的<u>童话</u>给你看。一会儿来拿吧。

小朋友：那好吧，谢谢啦。

Scene 17 ———————————

At her office, Jing sorts through the mail and hands a letter to Editor Ma.

安静：　马老师。

Jing goes to her own desk and opens a piece of her mail. Ma looks up from reading a manuscript.

---

61. 蘋果	苹果	píngguǒ	apple
62. 香蕉	香蕉	xiāngjiāo	banana
63. 梨	梨	lí	pear
64. 馬藍	马蓝	mǎlán	a kind of flower (acanthaceous indigo)
65. 安徒生	安徒生	Āntúshēng	Anderson (Hans Christian Anderson)
^66. 童話	童话	tónghuà	children's story, fairy tale

馬編輯：完蛋啦，我們完蛋啦。世界是你們的。太陽是你們的。才二十歲，寫出這樣的好詩，
　　　　多麼清新哪！欸，安靜啊。你記得艾青在詩論裡是怎麼闡述"清新"這個詞兒的嗎？
安靜：　他好像是這麼說的：　清新是在感覺完全清醒的場合的對世界的一種明晰的反射。是嗎？
馬編輯：對，完全準確。可以打滿分。

Jing begins to read the manuscript that just came in her mail.

安靜：　　(The voice of Wei Wan, author of the manuscript, sounds in Jing's mind.)
　　　　　"我攀着民族靈魂的火箭，
　　　　　我執着鋒利的赤誠，
　　　　　用自己的紅心，
　　　　　遙望那滿宇宙的紅旗，
　　　　　啊，甩開膀子，大幹快上啊，
　　　　　大幹快上啊！"
　　　　　(in Jing's own mind's voice) 天哪！這也叫詩？！

---

^67. 完蛋	完蛋	wándàn	(colloquial) done for, finished
*68. 世界	世界	shìjiè	world
^69. 太陽	太阳	tàiyáng	sun
^70. 詩	诗	shī	poetry, poem
71. 清新	清新	qīngxīn	pure and fresh
72. 艾青	艾青	Ai Qīng	a well-known twentieth century Chinese poet
73. 詩論	诗论	Shīlùn	Discourse on Poetry
74. 闡述	阐述	chǎnshù	to expound, to elaborate
*75. 感覺	感觉	gǎnjué	feeling, perception
^76. 清醒	清醒	qīngxǐng	clear-headed, fully conscious
^77. 場合	场合	chǎnghé	circumstance, occasion
78. 明晰	明晰	míngxī	distinct, clear
^79. 反射	反射	fǎnshè	reflex, reflection
*80. 準確	准确	zhǔnquè	accurate, correct

马编辑：完蛋啦，我们完蛋啦。世界是你们的。太阳是你们的。才二十岁，写出这样的好诗，
多么清新哪！欸，安静啊。你记得艾青在诗论里是怎么阐述"清新"这个词儿的吗？

安静： 他好象是这么说的： 清新是在感觉完全清醒的场合的对世界的一种明晰的反射。是吗？

马编辑：对，完全准确。可以打满分。

```
Jing begins to read the manuscript that just came in her mail.
```

安静： (The voice of Wei Wan, author of the manuscript, sounds in Jing's mind.)

"我攀着民族灵魂的火箭，

我执着锋利的赤诚，

用自己的红心，

遥望那满宇宙的红旗，

啊，甩开膀子，大干快上啊，

大干快上啊！"

(in Jing's own mind's voice) 天哪！这也叫诗？！

---

81. 打滿分	打满分	dǎ mǎnfēn	to give a perfect score
82. 攀	攀	pān	to climb, clamber
*83. 民族	民族	mínzú	a nation (in the sense of a united people), ethnic group
84. 靈魂	灵魂	línghún	soul, spirit
85. 火箭	火箭	huǒjiàn	rocket
86. 執	执	zhí	to hold, grasp
87. 鋒利	锋利	fēnglì	sharp
88. 赤誠	赤诚	chìchéng	absolute sincerity
89. 遙望	遥望	yáowàng	to gaze from afar
^90. 宇宙	宇宙	yǔzhòu	cosmos, universe
^91. 旗	旗	qí	flag, banner
^92. 甩開	甩开	shuǎikāi	to swing wide
93. 膀子	膀子	bǎngzi	arms

討論問題：

1)　為什麼韋老師說安然"有點兒羣眾關係不大好"？　她舉了些什麼例子 (jǔ...lìzi: to give an example)？

2)　韋老師對安然的那件紅襯衫有什麼看法？

3)　韋老師給安靜寫過一封信。你想她為什麼在這時候提這封信？為什麼最後還說"還得請你多幫忙啊"？

4)　為什麼安靜回家後叫安然別穿那件紅襯衫？安靜對那件紅襯衫有什麼看法？和韋老師的看法一樣嗎？為什麼她要拿去洗？

5)　媽媽為什麼"不舒服"了？"丟掉專業"和"創造政治條件"有什麼關係？

6)　你覺得安靜讀的那首詩稿怎麼樣？為什麼她說"天哪！這也叫詩？！"？　馬編輯和安靜談到詩的"清新"，這在劇 (jù: play, drama, film) 中有什麼作用？

讨论问题：

1) 为什么韦老师说安然"有点儿群众关系不大好"？ 她举了些什么例子 (jǔ...lìzi: to give an example)？

2) 韦老师对安然的那件红衬衫有什么看法？

3) 韦老师给安静写过一封信。你想她为什么在这时候提这封信？为什么最后还说"还得请你多帮忙啊"？

4) 为什么安静回家后叫安然别穿那件红衬衫？安静对那件红衬衫有什么看法？和韦老师的看法一样吗？为什么她要拿去洗？

5) 妈妈为什么"不舒服"了？"丢掉专业"和"创造政治条件"有什么关系？

6) 你觉得安静读的那首诗稿怎么样？为什么她说"天哪！这也叫诗？！"？马编辑和安静谈到诗的"清新"，这在剧 (jù: play, drama, film) 中有什么作用？

SEGMENT IV

Scene 18 ———————————

Ran is excitedly watching a ballgame on TV at home.

安然： 噢，好。…… 太<u>棒</u>了！

媽媽： 喏，洗了衣服也不<u>收</u>。(moves to front of the TV.)

安然： 哎呀，別<u>搗亂</u>了。

媽媽： 別<u>傻</u>了，看個電視那麼認真啊？

安然： 噢，<u>贏</u>了，贏了！

媽媽： 快複習功課去啦！(shuts off the TV.)

安然： 真棒！

Coming home, Father walks into the apartment.

媽媽： 回來啦。

爸爸： 欸。

媽媽： <u>噫</u>，你不是去大學<u>講課</u>了嗎？

爸爸： 啊。

媽媽： 怎麼就穿這條褲子去的？這像個什麼樣子啊？小靜，然然，你們都來看看啊。人家把你爸爸<u>當成</u>什麼美術家呢。

爸爸： 他們來聽我講課呀，不是來看我穿什麼……

媽媽： 人家<u>背後</u>會議論你啊。

爸爸： 議論我褲子怕什麼？

媽媽： 我怕。人家<u>該</u>以為我<u>虐待</u>你了。

---

^1. 棒	棒	bàng	(colloquial) great, excellent
*2. 收	收	shōu	to put away, collect
^3. 搗亂	搗乱	dǎoluàn	to make trouble, create disturbance
^4. 傻	傻	shǎ	silly
*5. 贏	赢	yíng	to win
6. 噫	噫	yí	an expletive conveying surprise
*7. 講課	讲课	jiǎngkè	to teach, lecture

SEGMENT IV

Scene 18 ———————————

Ran is excitedly watching a ballgame on TV at home.

安然： 噢，好。…… 太棒了！

妈妈： 喏，洗了衣服也不收。(moves to front of the TV.)

安然： 哎呀，别捣乱了。

妈妈： 别傻了，看个电视那么认真啊？

安然： 噢，赢了，赢了！

妈妈： 快复习功课去啦！(shuts off the TV.)

安然： 真棒！

Coming home, Father walks into the apartment.

妈妈： 回来啦。

爸爸： 欸。

妈妈： 噢，你不是去大学讲课了吗？

爸爸： 啊。

妈妈： 怎么就穿这条裤子去的？这象个什么样子啊？小静，然然，你们都来看看啊。人家把你爸爸当成什么美术家呢。

爸爸： 他们来听我讲课呀，不是来看我穿什么……

妈妈： 人家背后会议论你啊。

爸爸： 议论我裤子怕什么？

妈妈： 我怕。人家该以为我虐待你了。

---

*8. 褲子	裤子	kùzi	slacks
^9. 當成	当成	dāngchéng	to take as, construe as
^10. 美術家	美术家	měishùjiā	artist
^11. 背後	背后	bèihòu	behind one's back
*12. 議論	议论	yìlùn	to discuss, comment
13. 該	该	gāi	should; (colloq.) would, probably, likely
^14. 虐待	虐待	nüèdài	to maltreat

Ran turns on the TV, which adds to the furor of the family argument.   Ironically, the TV program is something about 美滿家庭.   The argument continues, but we cannot hear it clearly.   Then Mother shuts off the TV.

安然：   媽，我有看法。大事你老看不着，一天到晚爲這些雞毛蒜皮的小事兒嘮叨。這對您身體也不好。

媽媽：   這家大事小事都是我在管。

安然：   我的事兒你就沒管過。

媽媽：   你這沒良心的東西。什麼事我沒管過你？抱你躲武鬥，抱你去幹校，抱你去外婆家，⋯⋯

安然：   那也不能吃老本兒。

安然：   叫你幫我請個你老同學幫我輔導一下外語都不幹。

媽媽：   我不是在給你輔導嗎？

安然：   你？早忘得差不多了。上次我問你，"上帝保佑我們： God bless us" 爲什麼第三人稱單數不加 "s," 都答不上來。

爸爸：   (to Ran)   就你知道。

媽媽：   我怎麼會忘的？還不是因爲這個家！因爲你們。

安然：   老拿人撒氣。

媽媽：   我才那麼積極，我才變得現在這個樣！

安靜：   (handing Father a cup)   爸！

Scene 19 ————————————————

In the parents' room, Father tries to console Mother.

*15. 美滿	美满	měimǎn	perfectly satisfactory
*16. 看法	看法	kànfǎ	view, opinion
*17. 一天到晚	一天到晚	yìtiān dàowǎn	all day long
18. 雞毛蒜皮	鸡毛蒜皮	jīmáo suànpí	"chicken feathers and garlic peelings," i.e., trivial domestic matters
19. 嘮叨	唠叨	láodao	chatter, garrulousness
*20. 良心	良心	liángxīn	conscience
*21. 抱	抱	bào	to carry in the arms, embrace
*22. 躲	躲	duǒ	to hide, evade, flee
23. 武鬥	武斗	wǔdòu	violence, armed struggle

Ran turns on the TV, which adds to the furor of the family argument. Ironically, the TV program is something about 美满家庭. The argument continues, but we cannot hear it clearly. Then Mother shuts off the TV.

安然： 妈，我有看法。大事你老看不着，一天到晚为这些鸡毛蒜皮的小事儿唠叨。这对您
　　　 身体也不好。

妈妈： 这家大事小事都是我在管。

安然： 我的事儿你就没管过。

妈妈： 你这没良心的东西。什么事我没管过你？抱你躲武斗，抱你去干校，抱你去外婆
　　　 家，……

安然： 那也不能吃老本儿。

安然： 叫你帮我请个你老同学帮我辅导一下外语都不干。

妈妈： 我不是在给你辅导吗？

安然： 你？早忘得差不多了。上次我问你，"上帝保佑我们：God bless us"
　　　 为什么第三人称单数不加 "s," 都答不上来。

爸爸： (to Ran) 就你知道。

妈妈： 我怎么会忘的？还不是因为这个家！因为你们。

安然： 老拿人撒气。

妈妈： 我才那么积极，我才变得现在这个样！

安静： (handing Father a cup) 爸！

Scene 19 ———————————

In the parents' room, Father tries to console Mother.

^24. 幹校	干校	gànxiào	school for cadres (labor farm for political reeducation)
25. 外婆	外婆	wàipó	maternal grandmother
26. 吃老本兒	吃老本儿	chī lǎo běnr	"to eat one's old capital," i.e., to rest on one's past credit
*27. 外語	外语	wàiyǔ	foreign language
28. 上帝	上帝	shàngdì	god
29. 保佑	保佑	bǎoyòu	to bless and protect
30. 人稱	人称	rénchēng	person (in terms of grammar, as in "first person singular")
31. 單數	单数	dānshù	singular
32. 撒氣	撒气	sāqì	to vent anger or temper

爸爸：　嘿嘿，嘻嘻，你看然然，像不像你年輕的時候？

媽媽：　你別<u>提</u>我年輕的時候！

Outside the room, Jing catches on to what's going on and calls Ran to join her in peeping in on their parents.

安靜：　(to Ran)　欸，來，來呀。

媽媽：　誰<u>理解</u>我呀？

爸爸：　我理解你呀。好啦，別哭啦。然然還小嘛。

媽媽：　還小啊？都十六歲了。

爸爸：　嘻嘻。

The girls giggle from outside the door.

安靜、安然：嘻嘻嘻嘻。

爸爸：　(to the girls)　去去，回屋去。

The girls close the parents' door and walk away.

安靜、安然：哈哈哈。

安然：　欸，姐，媽今天怎麼像個小孩兒？

安靜：　別瞎說。不過，大人也有像小孩兒的時候。

安然：　我是不是不太了解媽媽？

安靜：　反正大人的<u>煩惱</u>，總比小孩兒要多。

安然：　你老是小孩兒小孩兒的，誰是小孩兒啊！

Scene 20 ——————————————————

Jing pulls out an album and hands Ran a photograph of their mother.

安靜：　你看。

安然：　<u>喲</u>，媽媽真年輕！

*33.	提	提	tí	to raise, bring up the subject of...
*34.	理解	理解	lǐjiě	to understand

爸爸：　嘿嘿，嘻嘻，你看然然，象不象你年轻的时候？

妈妈：　你别<u>提</u>我年轻的时候！

Outside the room, Jing catches on to what's going on and calls Ran to join her in peeping in on their parents.

安静：　(to Ran)　欸，来，来呀。

妈妈：　谁<u>理解</u>我呀？

爸爸：　我理解你呀。好啦，别哭啦。然然还小嘛。

妈妈：　还小啊？都十六岁了。

爸爸：　嘻嘻。

The girls giggle from outside the door.

安静、安然：嘻嘻嘻嘻。

爸爸：　(to the girls)　去去，回屋去。

The girls close the parents' door and walk away.

安静、安然：哈哈哈。

安然：　欸，姐，妈今天怎么象个小孩儿？

安静：　别瞎说。不过，大人也有象小孩儿的时候。

安然：　我是不是不太了解妈妈？

安静：　反正大人的<u>烦恼</u>，总比小孩儿要多。

安然：　你老是小孩儿小孩儿的，谁是小孩儿啊！

Scene 20 ——————————————

Jing pulls out an album and hands Ran a photograph of their mother.

安静：　你看。

安然：　<u>哟</u>，妈妈真年轻！

^35. 烦恼	烦恼	fánnǎo	vexed
36. 哟	哟	yō	an expletive conveying slight surprise

(reading the poem on the back of the photograph)

"藍天，白雲，大海！
我爲什麽這樣熱愛你們？
因爲你們就是祖國，
就是我的母親。

　　　　　靈靈，於五五年夏"

是媽媽寫的啊。媽媽還會寫詩？我怎麼不知道？

安靜：　你不知道的事情還多着呢。你看，我喜歡寫點東西，說不定還是媽媽的遺傳基因在
　　　起作用呢。

安然：　你說我像爸爸還是像媽媽？

安靜：　你有的地方像爸爸，有的地方又像媽媽，像……

安然：　我誰也不像，我就像我。

Scene 21 ——————————————

In the yard outside their apartment, Ran is helping Liu Donghu with English. From
a window, Jing watches them while she combs her hair.

劉冬虎：你看這個怎麽念？

安然：　　coffee.

劉冬虎：coffee, coffee.　那這個呢？

安然：　　跟我讀，cough.

劉冬虎：cou-

安然：　　看我嘴，cough.

劉冬虎：cou-.

安然：　　cough.

劉冬虎：cou-f.

安然：　　哈哈哈、哈哈哈。是 "cough," 是咳嗽，不是母牛。母牛才念 "cow," 咳嗽是
　　　　"cough."

*37.	藍	蓝	lán	blue
^38.	雲	云	yún	cloud
^39.	熱愛	热爱	rèài	to love fervently
^40.	祖國	祖国	zǔguó	motherland
41.	靈	灵	líng	quick, clever, sharp; spirit; (here) name of the mother
^42.	於	于	yú	(literary) 在
*43.	說不定	说不定	shuōbudìng	(V不RE) cannot say for sure, perhaps

(reading the poem on the back of the photograph)

"<u>蓝天</u>，白<u>云</u>，大海！

我为什么这样<u>热爱</u>你们？

因为你们就是<u>祖国</u>，

就是我的母亲。

<u>灵灵</u>，<u>于五五年夏</u>"

是妈妈写的啊。妈妈还会写诗？我怎么不知道？

安静： 你不知道的事情还多着呢。你看，我喜欢写点东西，<u>说不定</u>还是妈妈的<u>遗传基因</u>在
<u>起作用</u>呢。

安然： 你说我象爸爸还是象妈妈？

安静： 你有的地方象爸爸，有的地方又象妈妈，象……

安然： 我谁也不象，我就象我。

Scene 21 —————————

In the yard outside their apartment, Ran is helping Liu Donghu with English. From
a window, Jing watches them while she combs her hair.

刘冬虎：你看这个怎么念？

安然： coffee.

刘冬虎：coffee, coffee. 那这个呢？

安然： 跟我读，cough.

刘冬虎：cou-

安然： 看我<u>嘴</u>，cough.

刘冬虎：cou-.

安然： cough.

刘冬虎：cou-f.

安然： 哈哈哈、哈哈哈。是 "cough," 是<u>咳嗽</u>，不是母<u>牛</u>。母牛才念 "cow," 咳嗽是

"cough."

---

^44. 遺傳	遗传	yíchuán	hereditary
^45. 基因	基因	jīyīn	genes
^46. 起作用	起作用	qǐ zuòyòng	to affect, give rise to a certain effect
*47. 嘴	嘴	zuǐ	mouth
^48. 咳嗽	咳嗽	késòu	to cough
^49. 牛	牛	niú	ox, cow

劉冬虎：cow.

安然：　欸，你這<u>舌頭</u>可真<u>別扭</u>，你再好好兒練練吧。

Just as Liu Donghu is being thoroughly humiliated, An Jing walks up to them.

安靜：　嘿，這不是劉冬虎嗎？你忘啦，上次你還幫我拿過東西。

劉冬虎：沒忘。

安靜：　嘿嘿嘿。

劉冬虎：那我走啦，再見。(walks off.)

安靜：　欸，他怎麼走了？你該<u>叫住</u>他呀。

安然：　叫他幹嘛？你聽他那<u>發音</u>沒有？簡直<u>沒治</u>了。

安靜：　人家<u>向</u>你<u>請教</u>，你總該<u>耐心</u>點兒。

安然：　誰叫我耐心我都耐心啊？你沒聽見吧？硬把"咳嗽"念成"母牛"。還 "cow" 呢。

安靜：　哈哈哈哈。我覺得他挺<u>虛心</u>的。走，回家吃飯。

The An sisters walk homeward.

安然：　一個男生，<u>光</u>虛心也沒用，看他那樣兒，那兩道<u>眉毛</u>像<u>雜草叢生</u>。

安靜：　呵呵呵。

安然：　不過，他也怪可憐的。他爸和他媽老<u>打架</u>，誰也不太<u>理</u>他。

安靜：　是。

安然：　姐，我覺得和男生在一塊兒複習功課好，<u>廢話</u>少。我覺得這沒什麼。

安靜：　<u>可不</u>？這沒什麼。

^50. 舌頭	舌头	shétou	tongue
^51. 別扭	別扭	bièniu	awkward
^52. 叫住	叫住	jiàozhù	to stop (someone) by calling to him
*53. 發音	发音	fāyīn	to pronounce; pronunciation
54. 沒治	沒治	méizhì	hopeless, there is no cure
^55. 向	向	xiàng	a coverb indicating the direction of the action
*56. 請教	请教	qǐngjiào	to "request instruction," ask for advice, consult
^57. 耐心	耐心	nàixīn	patient; patience

刘冬虎：cow.

安然：　欸，你这<u>舌头</u>可真<u>别扭</u>，你再好好儿练练吧。

Just as Liu Donghu is being thoroughly humiliated, An Jing walks up to them.

安静：　嘿，这不是刘冬虎吗？你忘啦，上次你还帮我拿过东西。

刘冬虎：沒忘。

安静：　嘿嘿嘿。

刘冬虎：那我走啦，再见。（walks off.）

安静：　欸，他怎么走了？你该<u>叫住</u>他呀。

安然：　叫他干嘛？你听他那发音沒有？简直<u>沒治</u>了。

安静：　<u>人家</u>向你<u>请教</u>，你总<u>该</u><u>耐心</u>点儿。

安然：　谁叫我耐心我都耐心啊？你没听见吧？<u>硬</u>把"咳嗽"念成"母牛"。还 "cow" 呢。

安静：　哈哈哈哈。我觉得他挺<u>虚心</u>的。走，回家吃饭。

The An sisters walk homeward.

安然：　一个男生，<u>光</u>虚心也沒用，看他那样儿，那两道<u>眉毛</u>象<u>杂草丛生</u>。

安静：　呵呵呵。

安然：　不过，他也怪可怜的。他爸和他妈老<u>打架</u>，谁也不太<u>理</u>他。

安静：　是。

安然：　姐，我觉得和男生在一块儿复习功课好，<u>废话</u>少。我觉得这沒什么。

安静：　<u>可不</u>？这沒什么。

---

^58. 硬	硬	yìng	hard, firm; obstinately
^59. 虚心	虚心	xūxīn	open-minded, modest
^60. 光	光	guāng	just, only
61. 眉毛	眉毛	méimao	eyebrows
62. 雜草	杂草	zácǎo	weeds
63. 叢生	丛生	cóngshēng	to grow thickly
^64. 打架	打架	dǎjià	to fight
^65. 理	理	lǐ	to pay attention to, attend to
^66. 廢話	废话	fèihuà	useless brattle, nonsense, rubbish
*67. 可不	可不	kěbu	"Ain't that the truth!" That's right!

討論問題：

1) 媽媽為什麼對安然和爸爸不高興？她關心不關心丈夫 (zhàngfu: husband) 和孩子？爸爸和安然對她的 "關心" 有什麼反應 (fǎnyìng: reaction)？

2) 你覺得安家一家了解不了解媽媽？爸爸和媽媽的關係怎麼樣？

3) 安靜為什麼讓安然看一首媽媽年輕時寫的詩作？媽媽和她年輕時一樣嗎？她真的變了嗎？

4) 從安然說的 "我就像我" 那句話，你能看出些什麼？

5) 你從安然對待 (duìdài: to treat) 劉冬虎的樣子能看出她的一些什麼特點和看法？

6) 在這一幕 (mù: scene) 中，安靜對安然有什麼意見？

讨论问题：

1) 妈妈为什么对安然和爸爸不高兴？她关心不关心丈夫 (zhàngfu: husband) 和孩子？爸爸和安然对她的"关心"有什么反应 (fǎnyìng: reaction)？

2) 你觉得安家一家了解不了解妈妈？爸爸和妈妈的关系怎么样？

3) 安静为什么让安然看一首妈妈年轻时写的诗作？妈妈和她年轻时一样吗？她真的变了吗？

4) 从安然说的"我就象我"那句话，你能看出些什么？

5) 你从安然对待 (duìdài: to treat) 刘冬虎的样子能看出她的一些什么特点和看法？

6) 在这一幕 (mù: scene) 中，安静对安然有什么意见？

SEGMENT V

Scene 22 ─────────────

In the Ans' apartment, Father is working at an easel in the living room, Mother and Jing are preparing a meal in the kitchen.

媽媽：　我在畫院聽一些人説，在你爸爸的畫裡，看不到時代脈膊的跳動。你看，又在畫一些樹林子，還有那麼多的落葉，讓他畫幾檯拖拉機幾根高壓線，他都不幹。能被選上嗎？

Jing walks into the living room carrying bowls of food.

安靜：　爸，你就不能畫點説明性強的東西嗎？
爸爸：　什麼？

While Father puts away his brushes, Jing and Ran are already eating.

安靜：　你是專業畫家，總得……
爸爸：　總得什麼？
安靜：　我的意思是説，你……
爸爸：　你喜歡吃糖嗎？
安然：　她比我能吃糖。　(Mother walks in with more food and sits down at the table.)　媽説，她小時候還拔過一顆蛀牙呢。
爸爸：　喜歡吃糖，還要聲明糖是苦的，嗯？
安靜：　爸，我還不是爲您好。我當然喜歡您的畫。可是……

---

*1. 時代	时代	shídài	era, times
2. 脈膊	脉膊	mòbó	pulse
^3. 跳動	跳动	tiàodòng	to pulsate, beat
^4. 樹林	树林	shùlín	woods
5. 落葉	落叶	luòyè	falling or fallen leaves
6. 檯	台	tái	M for large machinery
7. 拖拉機	拖拉机	tuōlājī	tractor
8. 高壓線	高压线	gāoyā-xiàn	high-tension wire
*9. 選	选	xuǎn	to select, choose; to elect
^10. 説明性	说明性	shuōmíngxìng	elucidativeness
*11. 強	强	qiáng	strong, firm

SEGMENT V

Scene 22 ────────────

In the Ans' apartment, Father is working at an easel in the living room, Mother and Jing are preparing a meal in the kitchen.

妈妈：　我在画院听一些人说，在你爸爸的画里，看不到时代脉搏的跳动。你看，又在画一些树林子，还有那么多的落叶，让他画几台拖拉机几根高压线，他都不干。能被选上吗？

Jing walks into the living room carrying bowls of food.

安静：　爸，你就不能画点说明性强的东西吗？
爸爸：　什么？

While Father puts away his brushes, Jing and Ran are already eating.

安静：　你是专业画家，总得……
爸爸：　总得什么？
安静：　我的意思是说，你……
爸爸：　你喜欢吃糖吗？
安然：　她比我能吃糖。　(Mother walks in with more food and sits down at the table.)
　　　　妈说，她小时候还拔过一颗蛀牙呢。
爸爸：　喜欢吃糖，还要声明糖是苦的，嗯？
安静：　爸，我还不是为您好。我当然喜欢您的画。可是……

───

^12. 糖	糖	táng	candy
^13. 拔	拔	bá	to pull out, uproot
14. 颗	颗	kē	M for kernel-shaped objects such as teeth
15. 蛀牙	蛀牙	zhùyá	decayed tooth
^16. 聲明	声明	shēngmíng	to state, declare
*17. 苦	苦	kǔ	bitter
^18. 嗯	嗯	ń, ň, ǹ	an interjection conveying the following meanings depending on the tone:　n "what?" (questioning);　n "what!" (surprise and objection);　n "h'm" (agreement or acquiescence)

爸爸：　小靜啊，一個人老 "可是可是" 地過日子，那日子沒法兒過，更不要說去<u>追求</u>什麼了。

Ran now stands by the easel, gesturing with a brush as she talks.

安然：　我，作為一個畫家，<u>一輩子</u>要用自己的眼睛，自己的。<u>契訶夫</u>說過，有大<u>狗</u>，有小狗，
　　　　但小狗無須因大狗的<u>存在</u>而<u>惶惑</u>，所有的狗都叫，但都按上帝<u>給予</u>他們的聲音去叫，
　　　　對嗎？
眾人：　呵呵呵。
媽媽：　就會跟你爸爸<u>學舌</u>，快上學去吧。
爸爸：　<u>羅丹</u>有一句<u>名言</u>：<u>拙劣</u>的藝術家，永遠<u>戴</u>別人的<u>眼鏡兒</u>。
安然：　欸，這句話好，我得記到我本兒上去。
媽媽：　別老把你那一套<u>灌輸</u>給孩子們。你<u>自個兒</u>吃<u>虧</u>還沒吃夠？

Bringing a notebook and pen, Ran sits down with the rest of the family.

安然：　爸，你再說一<u>遍</u>。
爸爸：　姆，姆，這都記些什麼？來來來來來，我看一看。
安然：　這可不能給您看。這裡有<u>秘密</u>。
安靜：　這本子是然然的<u>寶貝</u>，每天都要<u>鎖</u>在她的<u>抽屜</u>裡。

Scene 23 ——————————————

At her office, Jing, obviously troubled, is pondering and hesitating over a
manuscript. She finally marks "recommend for publication" on top. The camera
shifts to Editor Ma, who remarks over another manuscript...

^19. 追求	追求	zhuīqiú	to seek, go after
^20. 一輩子	一辈子	yíbèizi	one's whole life
21. 契訶夫	契诃夫	Qìhēfū	Chekov
^22. 狗	狗	gǒu	dog
*23. 存在	存在	cúnzài	existence; to exist
24. 惶惑	惶惑	huánghuò	apprehensive and uneasy
^25. 給予	给予	jǐyǔ	(literary) to give, bestow
26. 學舌	学舌	xuéshé	to parrot
27. 羅丹	罗丹	Luódān	Rodin (a sculptor)
^28. 名言	名言	míngyán	famous saying
29. 拙劣	拙劣	zhuōliè	inferior, clumsy

爸爸：　　小静啊，一个人老"可是可是"地过日子，那日子没法儿过，更不要说去<u>追求</u>什么了。

Ran now stands by the easel, gesturing with a brush as she talks.

安然：　　我，作为一个画家，<u>一辈子</u>要用自己的眼睛，自己的。<u>契诃夫</u>说过，有大<u>狗</u>，有小狗，
　　　　　但小狗无须因大狗的<u>存在</u>而惶惑，所有的狗都叫，但都按上帝<u>给予</u>他们的声音去叫，
　　　　　对吗？

众人：　　呵呵呵。

妈妈：　　就会跟你爸爸<u>学舌</u>，快上学去吧。

爸爸：　　<u>罗丹</u>有一句<u>名言</u>：<u>拙劣</u>的艺术家，永远<u>戴</u>别人的<u>眼镜儿</u>。

安然：　　欸，这句话好，我得记到我本儿上去。

妈妈：　　别老把你那一套<u>灌输</u>给孩子们。你<u>自个儿</u><u>吃亏</u>还没吃够？

Bringing a notebook and pen, Ran sits down with the rest of the family.

安然：　　爸，你再说一<u>遍</u>。

爸爸：　　姆，姆，这都记些什么？来来来来来，我看一看。

安然：　　这可不能给您看。这里有<u>秘密</u>。

安静：　　这本子是然然的<u>宝贝</u>，每天都要<u>锁</u>在她的<u>抽屉</u>里。

Scene 23 ──────────────

At her office, Jing, obviously troubled, is pondering and hesitating over a
manuscript. She finally marks "recommend for publication" on top. The camera
shifts to Editor Ma, who remarks over another manuscript...

---

*30. 戴	戴	dài	to wear (accessories such as glasses and gloves)
^31. 眼鏡	眼镜	yǎnjìng	eye glasses
^32. 灌輸	灌输	guànshū	to instill, inculcate
^33. 自個兒	自个儿	zìgěr	(colloquial) 自己
^34. 吃虧	吃亏	chīkuī	"to eat a loss," i.e., to come to grief
^35. 遍	遍	biàn	(colloquial) 次
^36. 秘密	秘密	mìmì	secret
^37. 寶貝	宝贝	bǎobèi	treasure; precious
^38. 鎖	锁	suǒ	to lock; a lock
39. 抽屜	抽屉	chōutì	drawer

馬編輯：嘿嘿。在沒有<u>激情</u>的時候，還要寫詩？總是喜歡<u>賣弄辭藻</u>。正像人在說<u>謊</u>的時候，<u>偏</u>
　　　　<u>要</u>加大嗓門兒一個樣。是吧，安靜？

安靜：　是…是這樣。

Scene 24 ─────────────

Ran and her classmate Mi Xiaoling are at a crowded swimming pool.

米曉玲：安然，安然，安然，快過來呀。 (Ran swims over.) 欸，快點兒。欸，安然，你還記
　　　　得咱們上個星期看的電影兒嗎？

安然：　啊。

米曉玲：<u>演</u>女<u>主角</u>那個女演員她把自己<u>丈夫殺</u>了。

安然：　咳，你儘瞎說。

米曉玲：這是真的。信不信<u>由</u>你。欸，你快注意，那個男<u>生</u>又在看我。 (The camera shifts
　　　　momentarily to a boy standing by the side of the pool.)　頂不<u>正派</u>了。

安然：　我可沒看出來呀。

米曉玲：欸，你快看。

The camera shifts momentarily to the boy, now about to dive.

安然：　人家<u>跳水</u>呢。

米曉玲：你在這方面太<u>遲鈍</u>。咱們學校好幾個這樣的人。哼，我才不愛理他們呢。哎，哎呀。
　　　　我的<u>腿抽筋</u>了。

安然：　嘿，要不要我給你<u>針灸</u>？

米曉玲：行了，你那點兒<u>技術</u>我<u>領教</u>過。

───

^40.	激情	激情	jīqíng	fervor, passion
41.	賣弄	卖弄	màinòng	to show off
42.	辭藻	辞藻	cízǎo	flowery language, ornate diction
^43.	謊	谎	huǎng	lie, falsehood
^44.	偏要	偏要	piānyào	to insist on (in the sense of being willful or obstinate)
45.	嗓門兒	嗓门儿	sǎngménr	voice
^46.	演	演	yǎn	to perform, play the role of...
^47.	主角	主角	zhǔjiǎo	protagonist in a story or movie
*48.	丈夫	丈夫	zhàngfu	husband
^49.	殺	杀	shā	to kill, murder
^50.	由	由	yóu	to leave it to (someone to do); from, by

马编辑：嘿嘿。在没有<u>激情</u>的时候，还要写诗？总是喜欢<u>卖弄辞藻</u>。正象人在说<u>谎</u>的时候，<u>偏要加大嗓门儿</u>一个样。是吧，安静？

安静：　是…是这样。

Scene 24 ————————

Ran and her classmate Mi Xiaoling are at a crowded swimming pool.

米晓玲：安然，安然，安然，快过来呀。 (Ran swims over.) 欸，快点儿。欸，安然，你还记得咱们上个星期看的电影儿吗？

安然：　啊。

米晓玲：<u>演女主角</u>那个女演员她把自己<u>丈夫</u>杀了。

安然：　咳，你尽瞎说。

米晓玲：这是真的。信不信<u>由</u>你。欸，你快注意，那个男<u>生</u>又在看我。 (The camera shifts momentarily to a boy standing by the side of the pool.) 顶不<u>正派</u>了。

安然：　我可没看出来呀。

米晓玲：欸，你快看。

The camera shifts momentarily to the boy, now about to dive.

安然：　<u>人家跳水</u>呢。

米晓玲：你在这方面太<u>迟钝</u>。咱们学校好几个这样的人。哼，我才不爱理他们呢。哎，哎呀。我的<u>腿抽筋</u>了。

安然：　嘿，要不要我给你<u>针灸</u>？

米晓玲：行了，你那点儿<u>技术</u>我<u>领教</u>过。

^51. -生	-生	-shēng	(preceded by 男 or 女）學生
^52. 正派	正派	zhèngpài	upright, decent
^53. 跳水	跳水	tiàoshuǐ	to dive (into water)
54. 遲鈍	迟钝	chídùn	slow (in thought or action)
^55. 腿	腿	tuǐ	leg
56. 抽筋	抽筋	chōujīn	to have a cramp
57. 針灸	针灸	zhēnjiǔ	acupuncture
*58. 技術	技术	jìshù	skill, technique
^59. 領教	领教	lǐngjiào	(sarcastic) to have learned a lesson (from bad experience in the past); much obliged (for someone's instruction)

安然：   呵呵呵。

Mi Xiaoling gets out of the pool to take care of her leg. An Ran follows her over.

米曉玲：欸，剛剛我跟你說的那個事兒，可是千真萬確。那個傢伙老看着我。頂不要臉了。
安然：   哈哈，(sings)"不要太多情，不要假正經，我看你一眼是因為你太滑稽呀，太滑稽。"
米曉玲：哼！
安然：   啊，哈哈哈，嘻嘻嘻，呵呵呵，咳！ (jumps into the pool.)

Scene 25 ————————————————

Evening, in the An sisters' room. Ran is getting ready for bed while Jing is still working at the desk.

安靜：   欸，怎麼最近米曉玲不來玩兒啦？
安然：   我沒叫她，她最近老跟我說些亂七八糟的事兒。
安靜：   你們韋老師喜歡她嗎？
安然：   韋老師？連看都不看她一眼。
安靜：   少和她在一塊兒也好，省得受她影響。
安然：   她又不是流氓。再說，她幹嘛非影響我不可？我就不能影響影響她？
安靜：   影響她的辦法，就是給她唱那種歌詞的歌？
安然：   欸，你怎麼知道的？
安靜：   我？什麼我不知道？ (walks over and turns out the light by Ran's bed.) 欸，
        你到底喜歡她什麼？
安然：   她辦事說到能做到，關鍵時刻講真話，還愛打抱不平。確實夠姐們兒。

---

^60. 千真萬確	千真万确	qiānzhēn wànquè	absolutely true
^61. 傢伙	家伙	jiāhuo	(colloquial) guy, chap
^62. 不要臉	不要脸	búyàoliǎn	shameless
^63. 多情	多情	duōqíng	full of emotions (for someone of the opposite sex)
*64. 假	假	jiǎ	fake
^65. 正經	正经	zhèngjing	proper, serious, upright
^66. 看一眼	看一眼	kàn yì yǎn	to take a look
^67. 滑稽	滑稽	huáji	comical
^68. 亂七八糟	乱七八糟	luànqī bāzāo	at sixes and sevens, a mess, a muddle
^69. 省得	省得	shěngde	to spare (someone from having to do something)

安然：　呵呵呵。

Mi Xiaoling gets out of the pool to take care of her leg. An Ran follows her over.

米晓玲：欸，刚刚我跟你说的那个事儿，可是千真万确。那个家伙老看着我。顶不要脸了。
安然：　哈哈，(sings)"不要太多情，不要假正经，我看你一眼是因为你太滑稽呀，太滑稽。"
米晓玲：哼！
安然：　啊，哈哈哈，嘻嘻嘻，呵呵呵，咳！ (jumps into the pool.)

Scene 25 ──────────

Evening, in the An sisters' room. Ran is getting ready for bed while Jing is still working at the desk.

安静：　欸，怎么最近米晓玲不来玩儿啦？
安然：　我沒叫她，她最近老跟我说些乱七八糟的事儿。
安静：　你们韦老师喜欢她吗？
安然：　韦老师？连看都不看她一眼。
安静：　少和她在一块儿也好，省得受她影响。
安然：　她又不是流氓。再说，她干嘛非影响我不可？我就不能影响影响她？
安静：　影响她的办法，就是给她唱那种歌词的歌？
安然：　欸，你怎么知道的？
安静：　我？什么我不知道？ (walks over and turns out the light by Ran's bed.) 欸，
　　　　你到底喜欢她什么？
安然：　她办事说到能做到，关键时刻讲真话，还爱打抱不平。确实够姐们儿。

──────────────────────────────

*70. 受	受	shòu	to receive, endure, suffer
*71. 影響	影响	yǐngxiǎng	influence
^72. 流氓	流氓	liúmáng	hoodlum, rogue
73. 說到能做到	说到能做到	shuōdào néng zuòdào	able to follow through on one's promises
^74. 時刻	时刻	shíkè	time, moment
^75. 打抱不平	打抱不平	dǎ bàobùpíng	to defend someone against an injustice
^76. 確實	确实	quèshí	truly
77. 夠姐們兒	够姐们儿	gòu jiěmenr	(colloquial) deserve to be called a true "sister," a true and loyal friend (woman-to-woman)

安靜：　你呀，現在不跟人家好啦，關鍵時候，少了一個羣眾，這"三好"，又少了一票。

Jing looks over at Ran, who seems to have already fallen asleep.
Mother opens their door, walks in, and sees Jing at work.

媽媽：　寫什麼呢？
安靜：　我在改一個短篇。媽，可別跟我説話。
媽媽：　餓了，櫃子裡有點心。

Mother walks over to Ran, who is already asleep. She sees a saying over Ran's bed
and reads it.

媽媽：　科學賜予人類的最大禮物是什麼呢？是使人們相信真理的力量--康普頓。

Mother returns to the living room, searches at the desk for something.

爸爸：　你找什麼？
媽媽：　(finds the dictionary she was looking for) 辭海。
爸爸：　幹嘛啊？
媽媽：　康普頓是誰啊？
爸爸：　好像…… 是美國的一個科學家吧。你查查。

Scene 26 ————————————

In Ran's class, the students are working quietly on essays while the teacher paces
in the aisles between rows of desks. One student whispers to another one behind
him; the teacher taps his desk to make him stop. On the board is written:

---

^78.	跟…好	跟…好	gēn...hǎo	to be chummy with..., in a romantic relationship with...
*79.	票	票	piào	vote, ticket
^80.	短篇	短篇	duǎnpiān	a short piece (of fiction)
81.	櫃子	柜子	guìzi	cupboard
*82.	科學	科学	kēxué	science
83.	賜予	赐予	cìyǔ	to bestow upon
^84.	人類	人类	rénlèi	humankind

安静：　你呀，现在不跟人家好啦，关键时候，少了一个群众，这"三好"，又少了一票。

Jing looks over at Ran, who seems to have already fallen asleep.
Mother opens their door, walks in, and sees Jing at work.

妈妈：　写什么呢？
安静：　我在改一个短篇。妈，可别跟我说话。
妈妈：　饿了，柜子里有点心。

Mother walks over to Ran, who is already asleep. She sees a saying over Ran's bed
and reads it.

妈妈：　科学赐予人类的最大礼物是什么呢？是使人们相信真理的力量--康普顿。

Mother returns to the living room, searches at the desk for something.

爸爸：　你找什么？
妈妈：　(finds the dictionary she was looking for) 辞海。
爸爸：　干嘛啊？
妈妈：　康普顿是谁啊？
爸爸：　好象…… 是美国的一个科学家吧。你查查。

Scene 26 ───────────

In Ran's class, the students are working quietly on essays while the teacher paces
in the aisles between rows of desks. One student whispers to another one behind
him; the teacher taps his desk to make him stop. On the board is written:

---

^85. 禮物	礼物	lǐwù	gift
^86. 真理	真理	zhēnlǐ	truth
*87. 力量	力量	lìliang	strength
88. 康普頓	康普顿	Kāngpǔdùn	Compton (Arthur Holly Compton 1892-1962, American Nobel-prize physicist)
^89. 辭海	辞海	Cíhǎi	name of a widely used authoritative dictionary

作文題目--記我熟悉的一位同學。

安然：　(thinks to herself.)　我們應該怎樣評價一個人呢？用"他很好"，或"他很壞"，
就能完整精確地概括一個人嗎？這顯然太簡單了。就拿我們的班長祝文娟同學講，有
人說她團結同學，從不和人吵架；有人說她尊敬老師，僅此就能概括一個同學嗎？
(Scene 27: The camera shifts to a scene of boys fighting in the rain, to
indicate that this scene is a flashback in Ran's mind.)　我看未必。

In the fight scene (Scene 27), An Ran and Zhu Wenjuan spot a gang of boys beating up
Liu Donghu in a lane. An Ran goes over to break up the fight. After the gang
leaves, An Ran helps Liu Donghu to his feet and hands him his book bag.

Scene 28 ————————————

Another flashback in Ran's mind: In the teachers' office, Teacher Wei is asking
Liu Donghu, Wang Hongwei, An Ran, and Zhu Wenjuan about the incident.

韋老師：你們説説，到底怎麼回事兒。
王紅衛：我沒打。
劉冬虎：撒謊。
安然：　我和祝文娟一起看見的。王紅衛打劉冬虎，還有幾個外校男生。
韋老師：祝文娟，你看見了嗎？
祝文娟：那天，我和安然一塊兒去買文具，可買完以後我就走了。 (Wang looks at Zhu with
a smug expression on his face.) 以後的事兒我就不知道了。
安然：　(thinks to herself while looking askance at Zhu Wenjuan) 這是怎麼回事兒呢？

*90. 作文	作文	zuòwén	essay; to write an essay
^91. 熟悉	熟悉	shúxī	familiar
*92. 評價	评价	píngjià	to evaluate
*93. 完整	完整	wánzhěng	comprehensive, complete
^94. 精確	精确	jīngquè	accurate, precise
^95. 概括	概括	gàikuò	to summarize, epitomize
^96. 顯然	显然	xiǎnrán	obviously, apparently
^97. 班長	班长	bānzhǎng	class monitor

作文题目--记我熟悉的一位同学。

安然： (thinks to herself.) 我们应该怎样评价一个人呢？用"他很好"，或"他很坏"，
就能完整精确地概括一个人吗？这显然太简单了。就拿我们的班长祝文娟同学讲，有
人说她团结同学，从不和人吵架；有人说她尊敬老师，仅此就能概括一个同学吗？
(Scene 27: The camera shifts to a scene of boys fighting in the rain, to
indicate that this scene is a flashback in Ran's mind.) 我看未必。

In the fight scene (Scene 27), An Ran and Zhu Wenjuan spot a gang of boys beating up
Liu Donghu in a lane. An Ran goes over to break up the fight. After the gang
leaves, An Ran helps Liu Donghu to his feet and hands him his book bag.

Scene 28 ─────────────────────

Another flashback in Ran's mind: In the teachers' office, Teacher Wei is asking
Liu Donghu, Wang Hongwei, An Ran, and Zhu Wenjuan about the incident.

韦老师：你们说说，到底怎么回事儿。

王红卫：我没打。

刘冬虎：撒谎。

安然： 我和祝文娟一起看见的。王红卫打刘冬虎，还有几个外校男生。

韦老师：祝文娟，你看见了吗？

祝文娟：那天，我和安然一块儿去买文具，可买完以后我就走了。 (Wang looks at Zhu with
a smug expression on his face.) 以后的事儿我就不知道了。

安然： (thinks to herself while looking askance at Zhu Wenjuan) 这是怎么回事儿呢？

*98. 團結	团结	tuánjié	to unite, rally
^99. 尊敬	尊敬	zūnjìng	to respect
100. 僅此	仅此	jǐn cǐ	(literary) this alone
*101. 未必	未必	wèibì	not necessarily
102. 撒謊	撒谎	sāhuǎng	to lie (to tell a lie)
103. 外校	外校	wàixiào	another school
^104. 文具	文具	wénjù	writing material, stationery

The four leave the school separately. Wang runs off while the other three walk with heavy steps. The scene shifts to the present, back to the classroom where An Ran and others are still writing their essays (Scene 26).

安然：　　(thinks to herself)　我認為，青年人最重要的品質，是正義感和誠實。在我很小的時侯，爸爸就告訴我，對人要誠實……

| *105.認為 | 认为 | rènwéi | to deem, consider |
| 106.品質 | 品质 | pǐnzhì | character, quality |

討論問題：

1) 媽媽為什麼覺得爸爸的畫兒不太好？

2) 爸爸為什麼説"喜歡吃糖，還要聲明糖是苦的，嗯？"？

3) 契柯夫關於狗説的話，有什麼意義 (yìyì: significance)？契柯夫説的跟羅丹説的意義一樣嗎？

4) 安然認為米曉玲有些什麼長處 (chángchù: strong points)？什麼短處 (duǎnchù: shortcomings)？她為什麼最近跟米曉玲不那麼好了？安靜對這個有什麼看法？

5) 媽媽要查康普頓是誰，這表現 (biǎoxiàn: to reveal) 出些什麼？

6) 安然認為應該怎樣評價一個人？

7) 最後那一幕 (mù: scene) 讓我們看出祝文娟的哪一面？

The four leave the school separately. Wang runs off while the other three walk with heavy steps. The scene shifts to the present, back to the classroom where An Ran and others are still writing their essays (Scene 26).

安然：　　(thinks to herself)　我<u>认为</u>，青年人最重要的<u>品质</u>，是<u>正义感</u>和<u>诚实</u>。在我很小的时候，爸爸就告诉我，对人要诚实……

107.正義感	正义感	zhèngyìgǎn	sense of righteousness
*108.誠實	诚实	chéngshí	honest; honesty

讨论问题：

1)　妈妈为什么觉得爸爸的画儿不太好？

2)　爸爸为什么说"喜欢吃糖，还要声明糖是苦的，嗯？"？

3)　契柯夫关于狗说的话，有什么意义 (yìyì: significance)？契柯夫说的跟罗丹说的意义一样吗？

4)　安然认为米晓玲有些什么长处 (chángchù: strong points)？什么短处 (duǎnchù: shortcomings)？她为什么最近跟米晓玲不那么好了？安静对这个有什么看法？

5)　妈妈要查康普顿是谁，这表现 (biǎoxiàn: to reveal) 出些什么？

6)　安然认为应该怎样评价一个人？

7)　最后那一幕 (mù: scene) 让我们看出祝文娟的哪一面？

S E G M E N T   VI

While Jing and Mother clear the table after a meal, Father is looking at Ran's essay.

安然： 爸，我這作文怎麼樣？

爸爸： 噢。 (hands the top page of the essay to Mother, who sits down slowly and starts to read it.)

安然： "噢"什麼呀？

爸爸： 不錯。

安然： 欸，就是。

媽媽： 你這寫的什麼呀？你怎麼寫起班長啦？老師不是挺喜歡她的？

爸爸： 班長沒什麼不能寫，又不是什麼<u>女皇</u><u>大人</u>。

In the kitchen, Ran and Jing are cleaning up.

安靜： 就<u>憑</u>你這作文，章老師還能喜歡你？

安然： 那是她的事兒。

安靜： 你呀，什麼時候才能學得聰明點兒呢？去去去。

安然： 姐，你今天怎麼了？

安靜： 反正這<u>陣兒</u>我希望你<u>老實</u>點兒。

安然： 我又怎麼了？

安靜： 我希望你，最好先別穿這件紅襯衫。

安然： 欸，這倒怪了。這不是你給我買的嗎？不是大家都說我穿這件衣服漂亮嗎？可你這麼一說，我非<u>連</u>穿它三天不可。考完了，<u>慶賀</u>一下兒。

---

1. 女皇	女皇	nǚhuáng	empress
2. 大人	大人	dàrén	great personage
^3. 憑	凭	píng	on the basis of...
^4. 陣兒	阵儿	zhènr	(colloquial) a period of time
*5. 老實	老实	lǎoshi	honest, well-behaved

66

SEGMENT VI

Scene 29 ───────────────

While Jing and Mother clear the table after a meal, Father is looking at Ran's essay.

安然： 爸，我这作文怎么样？

爸爸： 噢。 (hands the top page of the essay to Mother, who sits down slowly and starts to read it.)

安然： "噢"什么呀？

爸爸： 不错。

安然： 欸，就是。

妈妈： 你这写的什么呀？你怎么写起班长啦？老师不是挺喜欢她的？

爸爸： 班长沒什么不能写，又不是什么<u>女皇大人</u>。

Scene 30 ───────────────

In the kitchen, Ran and Jing are cleaning up.

安静： <u>就凭</u>你这作文，韦老师还能喜欢你？

安然： 那是她的事儿。

安静： 你呀，什么时候才能学得聪明点儿呢？去去去。

安然： 姐，你今天怎么了？

安静： 反正这<u>阵儿</u>我希望你<u>老实</u>点儿。

安然： 我又怎么了？

安静： 我希望你，最好先别穿这件红衬衫。

安然： 欸，这<u>倒</u>怪了。这不是你给我买的吗？不是大家都说我穿这件衣服漂亮吗？可你这么一说，我非<u>连</u>穿它三天不可。考完了，<u>庆贺</u>一下儿。

─────────────────────────────────

*6. 倒	倒	dào	an adverb conveying that reality is the opposite of expectations (cf. Grammatical Note VI.4.)
*7. 連	连	lián	successively, consecutively
^8. 慶賀	庆贺	qìnghè	to celebrate

安靜： 別穿，學校有反映。

安然： 怪事兒，一件衣服有什麼反映。

安靜： 你們不是要評選 "三好" 嗎？

安然： 哪天評選，我哪天穿。

安靜： 別穿，太紅。

Ran slowly walks into the living room as she sings, followed by Jing.

安然： "不要太多情，不要假正經，

我看你一眼是因爲你太滑稽呀，太滑稽！"

安靜： 你別覺得自己考得不錯就放肆，想想，你還用這話來諷刺米曉玲。

安然： "我看你一眼是……" (continues to sing in the background.)

安靜： 爸，媽，你們看然然。

Scene 31 ——————————

Mother walks into the parents' room where Father is already working at the desk.
She turns the light on for him.

媽媽： 欸，你別老遷就然然，她幹嘛寫這種作文？

爸爸： 我看挺好嘛。作文就是講心裡話，説真話。

媽媽： 現在有幾個人願意聽真話？ (爸爸： 我願意。) 有幾個人像你那麼傻？應該讓她懂
點兒人情世故，心眼兒別太實。

爸爸： 實點兒好。

媽媽： 好什麼？還像我們以前那樣？安靜那封信呢？

爸爸： 嗯，不是放在抽屜裡了？ (takes the letter out of a drawer.)

媽媽： 又是秦皇島三二三二信箱來的？

爸爸： 欸，我給她送去。

媽媽： 不，你叫她過來，我問問她。

---

*9. 反映	反映	fǎnyìng	(originally) to reflect; (PRC) to report, make known
^10. 評選	评选	píngxuǎn	to appraise and select or elect
^11. 放肆	放肆	fàngsì	unbridled, wanton
^12. 諷刺	讽刺	fěngcì	to satirize, be sarcastic
^13. 遷就	迁就	qiānjiù	to yield to, be overly lenient

安静：　别穿，学校有<u>反映</u>。

安然：　怪事儿，一件衣服有什么反映。

安静：　你们不是要<u>评选</u>"三好"吗？

安然：　哪天评选，我哪天穿。

安静：　别穿，太红。

Ran slowly walks into the living room as she sings, followed by Jing.

安然：　"不要太多情，不要假正经，

　　　　我看你一眼是因为你太滑稽呀，太滑稽！"

安静：　你别觉得自己考得不错就<u>放肆</u>，想想，你还用这话来<u>讽刺</u>米晓玲。

安然：　"我看你一眼是……"　(continues to sing in the background.)

安静：　爸，妈，你们看然然。

Scene 31 ──────────────

Mother walks into the parents' room where Father is already working at the desk.
She turns the light on for him.

妈妈：　欸，你别老<u>迁就</u>然然，她干嘛写这种作文？

爸爸：　我看挺好嘛。作文就是讲心里话，说真话。

妈妈：　现在有几个人愿意听真话？（爸爸：我愿意。）　有几个人象你那么傻？应该让她懂
　　　　点儿<u>人情</u><u>世故</u>，<u>心眼儿</u>别太<u>实</u>。

爸爸：　实点儿好。

妈妈：　好什么？还象我们以前那样？安静那封信呢？

爸爸：　嗯，不是放在抽屉里了？　(takes the letter out of a drawer.)

妈妈：　又是秦皇岛三二三二信箱来的？

爸爸：　欸，我给她送去。

妈妈：　不，你叫她过来，我问问她。

---

*14. 人情	人情	rénqíng	human feelings, human nature, human relationships (often followed by 世故); favor, "gift"
^15. 世故	世故	shìgù	ways of the world
^16. 心眼兒	心眼儿	xīnyǎnr	heart, mind
17. 實	实	shí	honest and sincere, guileless

In the girls' room, Ran is dancing to loud music. Father's voice calling Jing is barely audible.

爸爸：　静兒，静兒。
安静：　欸。
爸爸：　你來一下。

Jing gets up and goes to Father. Ran continues to dance, then turns off the music so she can eavesdrop on their conversation.

Scene 32 ─────────────

Meanwhile, in the parents' room...

安静：　他是<u>搞</u><u>化工</u>的。
爸爸：　怎麼<u>組稿</u>組到搞化工的人身上去啦？
安静：　上次，在省青年會上，我<u>採訪</u>了他。
媽媽：　他<u>形象</u>怎麼樣？你到他鼻子還到他眼睛？
安静：　他一<u>米</u>七八，我到他鼻子下。
媽媽：　他<u>經濟</u>條件怎麼樣？
安静：　呣，………

Ran has overheard the above conversation, and sadly realizes that her days with her sister are numbered. Sitting down at the desk, she looks up at the portrait of the two of them on the wall.

Scene 33 ─────────────

A few moments later, in the kitchen, Father is looking for something on the shelves. Ran is washing her own hair.

---

*18. 搞	搞	gǎo	(colloquial) to do, be engaged in
19. 化工	化工	huàgōng	chemical engineering
20. 組稿	組稿	zǔgǎo	to solicit or commission manuscripts
^21. 採訪	采访	cǎifǎng	to interview (for an article)

In the girls' room, Ran is dancing to loud music. Father's voice calling Jing is barely audible.

爸爸:　静儿，静儿。
安静:　欸。
爸爸:　你来一下。

Jing gets up and goes to Father. Ran continues to dance, then turns off the music so she can eavesdrop on their conversation.

Scene 32 ————————————

Meanwhile, in the parents' room...

安静:　他是<u>搞化工</u>的。
爸爸:　怎么<u>组稿</u>组到搞化工的人身上去啦?
安静:　上次，在省青年会上，我<u>采访</u>了他。
妈妈:　他<u>形象</u>怎么样? 你到他鼻子还到他眼睛?
安静:　他一<u>米</u>七八，我到他鼻子下。
妈妈:　他<u>经济</u>条件怎么样?
安静:　嗯，………

Ran has overheard the above conversation, and sadly realizes that her days with her sister are numbered. Sitting down at the desk, she looks up at the portrait of the two of them on the wall.

Scene 33 ————————————

A few moments later, in the kitchen, Father is looking for something on the shelves. Ran is washing her own hair.

---

^22. 形象	形象	xíngxiàng	physical form; vivid, true to form
*23. 米	米	mǐ	meter
*24. 經濟	经济	jīngjì	economics; financial

爸爸：　茶葉呢？

安然：　我姐姐知道。

爸爸：　你幹什麼？

安然：　從今天開始，我得練習自己洗頭髮啦。

Scene 34 ─────────────

On an athletic field at school, a girl runs up to Ran.

某女生：安然，安然，剛才，我在教務處聽說你們班有個同學在辦停學手續。

安然：　誰呀？

某女生：不知道。

Ran spots Zhu Wenjuan walking by on the other side of a fence and runs to her.
They talk across the fence as they walk.

安然：　祝文娟，咱們班誰退學了？

祝文娟：米曉玲啊。

安然：　爲什麼？

祝文娟：她想接她媽的班兒。

安然：　她媽不是還年輕嗎？

祝文娟：她學習不好，反正也考不上大學。

安然：　可她還沒畢業呢。

祝文娟：現在工作不好找，這個機會挺難得的。我走了。

For a moment, Ran becomes subdued, then runs off.

---

^25. 茶葉	茶叶	cháyè	tea leaves
^26. 教務處	教务处	jiàowùchù	dean's office, school administration office
^27. 停學	停学	tíngxué	to stop schooling, drop out of school

爸爸：　茶叶呢？

安然：　我姐姐知道。

爸爸：　你干什么？

安然：　从今天开始，我得练习自己洗头发啦。

Scene 34 —————————————

On an athletic field at school, a girl runs up to Ran.

某女生：安然，安然，刚才，我在教务处听说你们班有个同学在办停学手续。

安然：　谁呀？

某女生：不知道。

Ran spots Zhu Wenjuan walking by on the other side of a fence and runs to her. They talk across the fence as they walk.

安然：　祝文娟，咱们班谁退学了？

祝文娟：米晓玲啊。

安然：　为什么？

祝文娟：她想接她妈的班儿。

安然：　她妈不是还年轻吗？

祝文娟：她学习不好，反正也考不上大学。

安然：　可她还没毕业呢。

祝文娟：现在工作不好找，这个机会挺难得的。我走了。

For a moment, Ran becomes subdued, then runs off.

---

*28. 手續	手续	shǒuxù	procedures
^29. 退學	退学	tuìxué	to withdraw from school
^30. 接班兒	接班儿	jiēbānr	to take over a shift, take over a job
*31. 難得	难得	nándé	hard to come by

Scene 35 ────────────────

While a student chorus sings, Mi Xiaoling is alone tearfully gathering her things
and thoughts. An Ran runs into the classroom and finds Mi Xiaoling there. The
camera pans over various corners of the school while the chorus sings on. The two
girls communicate their feelings for each other, though both are too sad to speak.
Xiaoling gives Ran some stamps of swimmers.

合唱團：我們踏出了原野的小路，嗚⋯⋯
　　　　看見小樹上有許多新芽吐出，嗚⋯⋯
　　　　雖然匆匆、匆匆而過，
　　　　卻總也回頭，再看看每棵小樹。
　　　　一個新芽就是一個夢呀。
　　　　一個新芽就是一顆閃光的珍珠。

　　　　我們遙望這神秘的夜空，嗯⋯⋯
　　　　看見夜空上有無數星星閃爍，嗯⋯⋯
　　　　雖然是悠閑、悠閑而過，
　　　　卻總願把繁星、把繁星數了又數。
　　　　一顆星星就是一個夢呀，
　　　　一顆星星就是一顆閃光的珍珠。

^32.	踏	踏	tà	to step on
33.	原野	原野	yuányě	open country
34.	嗚	呜	wū	(onomatopoeia) here, just humming to carry a tune
35.	芽	芽	yá	sprout
^36.	吐	吐	tǔ	to spit, pour out, sprout
^37.	匆匆	匆匆	cōngcōng	hurriedly
*38.	卻	却	què	an adverb indicating an abrupt turn or twist
^39.	棵	棵	kē	M for trees

Scene 35 ─────────────────

While a student chorus sings, Mi Xiaoling is alone tearfully gathering her things and thoughts. An Ran runs into the classroom and finds Mi Xiaoling there. The camera pans over various corners of the school while the chorus sings on. The two girls communicate their feelings for each other, though both are too sad to speak. Xiaoling gives Ran some stamps of swimmers.

合唱团：我们踏出了原野的小路，呜……
　　　　看见小树上有许多新芽吐出，呜……
　　　　虽然匆匆、匆匆而过，
　　　　却总也回头，再看看每棵小树。
　　　　一个新芽就是一个梦呀。
　　　　一个新芽就是一颗闪光的珍珠。

　　　　我们遥望这神秘的夜空，嗯……
　　　　看见夜空上有无数星星闪烁，嗯……
　　　　虽然是悠闲、悠闲而过，
　　　　却总愿把繁星、把繁星数了又数。
　　　　一颗星星就是一个梦呀，
　　　　一颗星星就是一颗闪光的珍珠。

*40. 夢	梦	mèng	dream
^41. 閃光	闪光	shǎnguāng	to flash, sparkle
42. 珍珠	珍珠	zhēnzhū	pearl
^43. 神秘	神秘	shénmì	mysterious
44. 夜空	夜空	yèkōng	the night sky
*45. 無數	无数	wúshù	countless
46. 閃爍	闪烁	shǎnshuò	twinkling, sparkling
47. 悠閑	悠闲	yōuxián	leisurely and carefree
48. 繁星	繁星	fánxīng	the myriad stars

我們常常到<u>海灘</u>上<u>漫步</u>，嗚……

看見海上<u>奔騰</u>的<u>波峰浪谷</u>，嗚……

雖然是漫步、漫步而過，

卻總願唱着、唱着向大海<u>祝福</u>，

一聲祝願就是一個夢呀，

一聲祝願就是一顆閃光的珍珠。

我們剛踏入<u>人生</u>的旅途，嗚……

常<u>擔憂</u>，<u>純真</u>的心會感到<u>孤獨</u>，嗚……

雖然是路途、路途遙遙，

總會有朋友、有朋友和我<u>會晤</u>。

一個<u>童心</u>就是一個夢呀，

一個童心就是一顆閃光的珍珠。

---

^49. 海灘	海滩	hǎitān	seashore
50. 漫步	漫步	mànbù	to stroll
51. 奔騰	奔腾	bēnténg	to gallop, surge forward, roll on the waves
52. 波峰浪谷	波峰浪谷	bōfēng lànggǔ	the crests and valleys of waves
^53. 祝福	祝福	zhùfú	to bless, express good wishes
54. 祝願	祝愿	zhùyuàn	wish; to wish
*55. 人生	人生	rénshēng	life (human)

討論問題：

1)   安然寫的那篇作文有什麼特點？

2)   媽媽、安靜、和爸爸對安然這篇作文的看法怎麼不一樣？為什麼？

3)   安然和安靜為什麼為了那件紅襯衫吵起來了？為什麼安然又唱起那首歌來了？

4)   爸爸和媽媽關心不關心安靜有了"朋友"？ 他們到底關心什麼？

5)   安然為什麼開始自己洗頭髮了？

6)   為什麼米曉玲要退學了？安然對這件事有什麼感覺？

7)   電影中的那首歌有什麼意義？

我们常常到海滩上漫步，呜……

看见海上奔腾的波峰浪谷，呜……

虽然是漫步、漫步而过，

却总愿唱着、唱着向大海祝福，

一声祝愿就是一个梦呀，

一声祝愿就是一颗闪光的珍珠。

我们刚踏入人生的旅途，呜……

常担忧，纯真的心会感到孤独，呜……

虽然是路途、路途遥遥，

总会有朋友、有朋友和我会晤。

一个童心就是一个梦呀，

一个童心就是一颗闪光的珍珠。

---

^56. 旅途	旅途	lǚtú	journey
^57. 擔憂	担忧	dānyōu	to worry
^58. 純真	纯真	chúnzhēn	innocent, guileless
*59. 孤獨	孤独	gūdú	lonely, solitary
60. 路途	路途	lùtú	road, path, journey
61. 遙遙	遥遥	yáoyáo	long and far
^62. 會晤	会晤	huìwù	to meet (people)
63. 童心	童心	tóngxīn	"child's heart," i.e., childlike innocence

讨论问题：

1) 安然写的那篇作文有什么特点？

2) 妈妈、安静、和爸爸对安然这篇作文的看法怎么不一样？为什么？

3) 安然和安静为什么为了那件红衬衫吵起来了？为什么安然又唱起那首歌来了？

4) 爸爸和妈妈关心不关心安静有了"朋友"？　他们到底关心什么？

5) 安然为什么开始自己洗头发了？

6) 为什么米晓玲要退学了？安然对这件事有什么感觉？

7) 电影中的那首歌有什么意义？

SEGMENT VII

Scene 36 ————————————

In the An sisters' room, Ran puts the stamps of swimmers in her album, looking unusually subdued. Jing is reading in bed.

安靜：　然然，同學們最後總是要分開的，你也別太難過了，啊？
安然：　我想起過去的事兒，總覺得對不起她。我想請她到家裡來玩兒。
安靜：　那好啊。
安然：　我還想請她來吃飯。
安靜：　那倒沒必要。
安然：　你怎麼這麼説？你不是總批評我，説我對她不好嗎？
安靜：　那也用不着用吃飯的方式來表示友好哇。你可以送她件禮物。對，送她件禮物吧，啊？
安然：　不。我就請她吃飯。爲什麼你的同學、同事能來，我的同學就不能來？
安靜：　那是我們哪。
安然：　我們也是我們。
安靜：　你們還小。
安然：　我們還小？十五歲以上就是青年。
安靜：　那好吧。
安然：　啊。姐姐萬歲。　(hugs and kisses Jing without restraint.)
安靜：　哦呵呵。喔，喲，欸。

Scene 37 ————————————

Ran goes to Mother in the living room.

安然：　媽，媽啊。
媽媽：　嘎？

———————————————————————————————————

*1. 分開	分开	fēnkāi	to separate
*2. 難過	难过	nánguò	to feel bad
^3. 沒必要	沒必要	méi bìyào	it's not necessary
*4. 批評	批评	pīpíng	to criticize
*5. 用不着	用不着	yòngbuzháo	no need

78

SEGMENT VII

Scene 36 ——————————————

In the An sisters' room, Ran puts the stamps of swimmers in her album, looking unusually subdued.   Jing is reading in bed.

安静： 然然，同学们最后总是要<u>分开</u>的，你也别太难过了，啊？
安然： 我想起过去的事儿，总觉得对不起她。我想请她到家里来玩儿。
安静： 那好啊。
安然： 我还想请她来吃饭。
安静： 那倒<u>沒必要</u>。
安然： 你怎么这么说？你不是总<u>批评</u>我，说我对她不好吗？
安静： 那也用<u>不着</u>用吃饭的<u>方式</u>来<u>表示</u><u>友好</u>哇。你可以送她件礼物。对，送她件礼物吧，啊？
安然： 不。我就请她吃饭。为什么你的同学、同事能来，我的同学就不能来？
安静： 那是我们哪。
安然： 我们也是我们。
安静： 你们还小。
安然： 我们还小？十五岁以上就是<u>青年</u>。
安静： 那好吧。
安然： 啊。姐姐<u>万岁</u>。 (hugs and kisses Jing without restraint.)
安静： 哦呵呵。喔，哟，欻。

Scene 37 ——————————————

Ran goes to Mother in the living room.

安然： 妈，妈啊。
妈妈： 嘎？

---

^6. 方式	方式	fāngshì	method, way
*7. 表示	表示	biǎoshì	to express, indicate
^8. 友好	友好	yǒuhǎo	friendship
*9. 青年	青年	qīngnián	youth, young people
^10. …萬歲	…万岁	…wànsuì	long live (so and so), hooray for (someone)

安然：　我要請米曉玲吃飯。

媽媽：　這又是什麼新花樣？

安然：　米曉玲要工作了，要離開學校了。

媽媽：　離開學校又不是見不着面兒。

安然：　我要表示一下我的心情。

媽媽：　我看沒這個必要，別自找麻煩。你看媽媽，跟誰也不遠，跟誰也不近。我看透了。什麼朋友啊，友誼啊，都是瞎扯。別太輕信人。搞好自己的學習才是真的。你媽都活到五十來歲了，才明白這個道理，可惜晚了。

安然：　我要請。

媽媽：　要請自己請，我不管。考得怎麼樣？

安然：　挺好，平均九十四分兒。

媽媽：　成績單兒呢？

Ran gets her report card and hands it to Mother.

安然：　給，您就關心我的成績單兒。

媽媽：　哼。

Scene 38 ————————————

Ran and four male classmates are riding bikes and singing on a country road. Two of the boys approach a fruit vendor.

劉冬虎：這瓜不錯啊。

男生甲：嗯。行。

劉冬虎：買點兒吧。

^11. 花樣	花样	huāyàng	(colloquial) trick, gimmick, newfangled idea
^12. 見不着面	见不着面	jiànbuzháo miàn	(V不RE-O) unable to see each other (見面: to see each other)
*13. 心情	心情	xīnqíng	feelings, frame of mind
14. 自找麻煩	自找麻烦	zì zhǎo máfan	to look for trouble for oneself
^15. -透	-透	-tòu	(suffixed to a verb) ...through, fully, penetratingly
*16. 友誼	友谊	yǒuyì	friendship
^17. 扯	扯	chě	to chat, gossip; to tell a lie

安然：　我要请米晓玲吃饭。

妈妈：　这又是什么新花样？

安然：　米晓玲要工作了，要离开学校了。

妈妈：　离开学校又不是见不着面儿。

安然：　我要表示一下我的心情。

妈妈：　我看没这个必要，别自找麻烦。你看妈妈，跟谁也不远，跟谁也不近。我看透了。什么朋友啊，友谊啊，都是瞎扯。别太轻信人。搞好自己的学习才是真的。你妈都活到五十来岁了，才明白这个道理，可惜晚了。

安然：　我要请。

妈妈：　要请自己请，我不管。考得怎么样？

安然：　挺好，平均九十四分儿。

妈妈：　成绩单儿呢？

Ran gets her report card and hands it to Mother.

安然：　给，您就关心我的成绩单儿。

妈妈：　哼。

Scene 38 ————————————

Ran and four male classmates are riding bikes and singing on a country road. Two of the boys approach a fruit vendor.

刘冬虎：这瓜不错啊。

男生甲：嗯。行。

刘冬虎：买点儿吧。

ˆ18. 輕信	轻信	qīngxìn	to readily believe or trust
19. …才是真的	…才是真的	…cái shì zhēnde	only…is the real thing; only…can count for something
*20. 活	活	huó	to live, be alive
*21. 道理	道理	dàolǐ	principle, truth, reason, sense
*22. 可惜	可惜	kěxī	it's a pity
*23. 平均	平均	píngjūn	on the average
ˆ24. 成績單兒	成绩单儿	chéngjǐ-dānr	report card
*25. 關心	关心	guānxīn	to be concerned with
ˆ26. 瓜	瓜	guā	melon

The rest of them stop and wait for the two.

安然： 他們幹嘛呢？
男生乙：好像買瓜呢吧。

The vendor puts some fruit into Liu's bag. Liu hands over some money.

劉冬虎：喏，<u>大爺</u>，給您錢。
賣瓜的：嗯……行了，行了，夠了。
劉冬虎：夠了？
賣瓜的：夠了。
劉冬虎：走了，大爺。
賣瓜的：欸，好好。呵呵呵呵。

The vendor waves goodbye. They ride off.

男生甲：他們真買瓜去了。
男生乙：噯，吃瓜了。劉冬虎請客了。
男生丙：太好了。
男生丁：給。
男生甲：再來一個。
男生乙：給你。
男生丙：(hands a fruit to Ran.) 喏，給。
安然： 怎麼了？
男生甲：劉冬虎少給那<u>老頭兒</u>五毛錢。那老頭兒<u>算</u>不過<u>帳</u>來，還<u>沖</u>我們笑呢，真傻。呵呵。
安然： <u>討厭</u>。

Scene 39 ————————————

At the lake, we hear the following conversation while the camera pans across an expanse of reeds, the sky, and the water.

| 27. | 大爺 | 大爷 | dàye | "uncle" (a respectful form of address for an elderly man) |
| ˆ28. | 老頭兒 | 老头儿 | lǎotóur | (colloquial) old chap |

The rest of them stop and wait for the two.

安然：　他们干嘛呢？
男生乙：好象买瓜呢吧。

The vendor puts some fruit into Liu's bag. Liu hands over some money.

刘冬虎：喏，<u>大爷</u>，给您钱。
卖瓜的：嗯……行了，行了，够了。
刘冬虎：够了？
卖瓜的：够了。
刘冬虎：走了，大爷。
卖瓜的：欸，好好。呵呵呵呵。

The vendor waves goodbye. They ride off.

男生甲：他们真买瓜去了。
男生乙：嗳，吃瓜了。刘冬虎请客了。
男生丙：太好了。
男生丁：给。
男生甲：再来一个。
男生乙：给你。
男生丙：(hands a fruit to Ran.) 喏，给。
安然：　怎么了？
男生甲：刘冬虎少给那<u>老头儿</u>五毛钱。那老头儿<u>算</u>不过<u>帐</u>来，还<u>冲</u>我们笑呢，真傻。呵呵。
安然：　<u>讨厌</u>。

Scene 39 ──────────────

At the lake, we hear the following conversation while the camera pans across an expanse of reeds, the sky, and the water.

^29.	算…帐	算…帐	suàn...zhàng	to do accounts
30.	冲	冲	chòng	(colloquial) toward, facing
^31.	討厭	讨厌	tǎoyàn	disgusting! abominable!

男生甲：蘆葦，有種的嗎？

安然：　當然有。只有結種子，才算完成了植物生長的全過程。

男生乙：在地球上它算不了什麼。要是在太空航行，能讓植物結種子，可就不容易了。在航天
　　　　站裡，最早結種子的，是一種最不起眼的阿拉伯草，第一次，才收穫了二百粒種子。

男生丙：當然，那是太空啊。

安然：　太空怎麼了？不是也有人去了。

男生丁：這湖，也太小了。

男生甲：明年，我們要到哪兒去旅遊一下呢？

The camera now settles on the group, who are in a rowboat.

男生乙：欸，博士啊，世界上最大的湖在哪兒？

男生丙：你是指淡水湖還是鹹水湖？

男生甲：當然淡水湖嘛。是鹹水湖，還不如去海邊兒呢。

安然：　淡水湖好像是貝加爾湖最大。

男生甲：是嗎？

男生乙：它是淡水容量最大的。面積最大的，是北美的蘇必利爾湖。

男生甲：太遠了，去不了。

男生乙：你看，來這兒的人也不少嘛。

男生丁：當然，誰不知道這小小白洋淀啊。當年在這兒出了舉世聞名的雁翎隊呀。

---

32. 蘆葦	芦苇	lúwěi	reed
33. 種	种	zhǒng	seeds (usually 種子)
34. 結	结	jiē	to form (seeds)
*35. 完成	完成	wánchéng	to complete
^36. 植物	植物	zhíwù	plants, flora
*37. 過程	过程	guòchéng	process, course
^38. 地球	地球	dìqiú	globe
^39. 太空	太空	tàikōng	outer space
^40. 航行	航行	hángxíng	to travel on the ocean, in the air, or in outer space
41. 航天站	航天站	hángtiānzhàn	space station
^42. 不起眼	不起眼	bùqǐyǎn	unnoteworthy
43. 阿拉伯	阿拉伯	Ālābó	Arabia; Arabic
*44. 收穫	收获	shōuhuò	harvest
^45. 粒	粒	lì	M for granules or pellets

男生甲：<u>芦苇</u>，有<u>种</u>的吗？

安然：　当然有。只有<u>结</u>种子，才算<u>完成</u>了<u>植物</u>生长的全<u>过程</u>。

男生乙：<u>在地球上</u>它算不了什么。要是在<u>太空航行</u>，能让植物结种子，可就不容易了。在<u>航天站</u>里，最早结种子的，是一种最<u>不起眼</u>的阿拉伯草，第一<u>次</u>，才<u>收获</u>了二百<u>粒</u>种子。

男生丙：当然，那是太空啊。

安然：　太空怎么了？不是也有人去了。

男生丁：这湖，也太小了。

男生甲：明年，我们要到哪儿去<u>旅游</u>一下呢？

The camera now settles on the group, who are in a rowboat.

男生乙：欸，<u>博士</u>啊，世界上最大的湖在哪儿？

男生丙：你是<u>指淡水</u>湖还是<u>咸水</u>湖？

男生甲：当然淡水湖嘛。是咸水湖，还<u>不如</u>去海边儿呢。

安然：　淡水湖好象是<u>贝加尔</u>湖最大。

男生甲：是吗？

男生乙：它是淡水<u>容量</u>最大的。<u>面积</u>最大的，是北美的<u>苏必利尔</u>湖。

男生甲：太远了，去不了。

男生乙：你看，来这儿的人也不少嘛。

男生丁：当然，谁不知道这小小<u>白洋淀</u>啊。<u>当年</u>在这儿出了<u>举世闻名</u>的<u>雁翎队</u>呀。

---

*46. 旅遊	旅游	lǚyóu	to tour, travel
^47. 博士	博士	bóshì	Ph.D.
48. 指	指	zhǐ	to refer to
49. 淡水	淡水	dànshuǐ	fresh water (as opposed to salt water)
50. 鹹水	咸水	xiánshuǐ	salt water
*51. 不如	不如	bùrú	it would be best to...
52. 貝加爾	贝加尔	Bèijiāěr	Baikal (a lake in the former U.S.S.R.)
^53. 容量	容量	róngliàng	capacity
^54. 面積	面积	miànjī	surface area
55. 蘇比利爾	苏比利尔	Sūbǐlìěr	Superior (one of the five Great Lakes)
56. 白洋淀	白洋淀	Báiyángdiàn	a lake in Hebei province
*57. 當年	当年	dāngnián	in those years
58. 舉世聞名	举世闻名	jǔshì wénmíng	world renown
59. 雁翎隊	雁翎队	Yànlíngduì	the "Wild Goose Plume Band" (a communist guerrilla force)

Scene 40 ──────────────

Ran looks at peasants in boats doing their various tasks and is lost in thought.
The group rides home near the end of the day. Ran stops by the fruit vendor to
give him the money Liu Donghu cheated him out of earlier. The others stop and wait
at a distance.

安然：　大爺。

賣瓜的：欵。

劉冬虎：她幹嘛呢？

安然：　（thrusting money into the vendor's hand.）沒錯，您拿着…拿着吧。

賣瓜的：欵，夠了，……

安然：　再見。

賣瓜的：夠了。嘿，這<u>丫頭</u>，這丫頭。

Ran hops on her bike and rides past the boys.

安然：　（to the boys）討厭。

眾男生：呵呵呵。（All hop on their bikes and ride off.）

────────────────────

ˆ60. 丫頭　　　丫头　　　yātou　　　（colloquial, dialectal）"derogatory" or
　　　　　　　　　　　　　　　　　　endearing term of address for young girls

────────────────────

討論問題：

1)　媽媽和安靜對安然想請米曉玲吃飯這件事有什麼看法？為什麼？

2)　安然為什麼說"您就關心我的成績單兒"？　她為什麼對媽媽不滿意（mǎnyì: satisfied）？

3)　男同學們關於湖的大小那一段（duàn: segment）話表現（biǎoxiàn: to reveal）出些什麼？

4)　男同學們在買瓜的那一幕（mù: scene）中表現出些什麼？

5)　安然怎麼對待（duìdài: to deal with, treat）這件事？她那天一整（zhěng: whole）天都和男同學們
　　痛快（tòngkuai: to one's heart's content）地玩嗎？她還做了什麼？

Scene 40 ————————————

Ran looks at peasants in boats doing their various tasks and is lost in thought. The group rides home near the end of the day. Ran stops by the fruit vendor to give him the money Liu Donghu cheated him out of earlier. The others stop and wait at a distance.

安然：　大爷。
卖瓜的：欸。
刘冬虎：她干嘛呢？
安然：　（thrusting money into the vendor's hand.）沒错，您拿着…拿着吧。
卖瓜的：欸，够了，……
安然：　再见。
卖瓜的：够了。嘿，这<u>丫</u>头，这丫头。

Ran hops on her bike and rides past the boys.

安然：　（to the boys）讨厌。
众男生：呵呵呵。　（All hop on their bikes and ride off.）

————————————————————————————————

————————————————————————————————

讨论问题：

1)　妈妈和安静对安然想请米晓玲吃饭这件事有什么看法？为什么？

2)　安然为什么说"您就关心我的成绩单儿"？　她为什么对妈妈不满意 (mǎnyì: satisfied)？

3)　男同学们关于湖的大小那一段 (duàn: segment) 话表现 (biǎoxiàn: to reveal) 出些什么？

4)　男同学们在买瓜的那一幕 (mù: scene) 中表现出些什么？

5)　安然怎么对待 (duìdài: to deal with, treat) 这件事？她那天一整 (zhěng: whole) 天都和男同学们痛快 (tòngkuai: to one's heart's content) 地玩吗？她还做了什么？

SEGMENT VIII

Scene 41 ————————————

Father and Jing are busy cooking in the kitchen. Ran comes home with Mi Xiaoling.

安然：　爸，姐。米曉玲來啦。

爸爸：　啊，米曉玲。啊，哈哈哈。

安靜：　米曉玲，你好。

爸爸：　歡迎，歡迎。

安靜：　請坐。

爸爸：　裡邊兒坐，隨便玩兒啊。

Jing motions Mi Xiaoling to the couch, then sits across from her.

安靜：　坐那邊兒。

安然：　米曉玲，坐呀。

安靜：　米曉玲，喝水。

米曉玲：欵，行行行。

安靜：　你坐。

米曉玲：嗯。

安靜：　怎麼，馬上就<u>上班兒</u>嗎？

米曉玲：啊，就在我媽那家商店。

安靜：　啊，那家店我知道，<u>貨源</u>挺<u>豐富</u>的。

米曉玲：那當然啦，那是個老店。聽說，有幾十年的歷史了。

安靜：　嗯。

安然：　<u>到時候</u>我一定去看你。咱姐兒們。

安靜：　呵呵呵。

---

*1. 上班	上班	shàngbān	to go to work
2. 貨源	货源	huòyuán	supply of commodities

SEGMENT   VIII

Scene 41 ——————————

Father and Jing are busy cooking in the kitchen. Ran comes home with Mi Xiaoling.

安然：　爸，姐。米晓玲来啦。

爸爸：　啊，米晓玲。啊，哈哈哈。

安静：　米晓玲，你好。

爸爸：　欢迎，欢迎。

安静：　请坐。

爸爸：　里边儿坐，随便玩儿啊。

Jing motions Mi Xiaoling to the couch, then sits across from her.

安静：　坐那边儿。

安然：　米晓玲，坐呀。

安静：　米晓玲，喝水。

米晓玲：欸，行行行。

安静：　你坐。

米晓玲：嗯。

安静：　怎么，马上就<u>上班儿</u>吗？

米晓玲：啊，就在我妈那家商店。

安静：　啊，那家店我知道，<u>货源</u>挺<u>丰富</u>的。

米晓玲：那当然啦，那是个老店。听说，有几十年的历史了。

安静：　嗯。

安然：　<u>到时候</u>我一定去看你。咱姐儿们。

安静：　呵呵呵。

---

*3. 豐富　　　　丰富　　　　fēngfù　　　　rich, abundant
*4. 到時候　　　到时候　　　dào shíhou　　when the time comes

米曉玲：咱們老同學，<u>沒説的</u>。我們那兒<u>處理</u>水果<u>罐頭</u>特多，<u>草梅醬</u>才五毛錢一瓶。聽安然講，
　　　　大姐喜歡吃水果，……

安靜：　是啊，哦。我去<u>廚房</u>，你坐一會兒，啊。　(goes back into the kitchen.)

米曉玲：啊，行。您忙吧，安姐姐。

安然：　太棒了。有草梅醬我買個十瓶。

米曉玲：來什麼<u>新鮮</u>貨，我就給你打電話。

安然：　呵呵呵呵。

米曉玲：呵呵呵呵。

Xiaoling pauses and looks around the living room.

米曉玲：嗳，你們家東西真多呀。這都誰<u>佈置</u>的？

安然：　我爸爸。

The two girls stop in front of the easel.

米曉玲：這是一張畫兒，真大呀。

安然：　你知道它叫什麼名字嗎？

米曉玲：光有樹和樹葉兒，還沒畫人呢。畫上人，我就知道叫什麼名字了。

安然：　這<u>幅</u>畫，永遠也不會有人。不過，它已經有名字了。我把它叫作……

米曉玲：叫"落葉"，對吧？

安然：　不，叫"<u>吻</u>"。

米曉玲：叫什麼？叫……

安然：　"吻"。就是一個"口"字加一個"<u>勿</u>"字呀。

米曉玲：哎呀，安然，你可真行。你能説出這個字來。

安然：　這有什麼？你看，大地<u>養育</u>了這棵大樹，大地就是它的母親。　(Father enters with
　　　　a bowl of food in hand. Hearing Ran expound on his painting, he stops and

---

^5. 沒説的	沒说的	méishuōde	it goes without saying, of course
^6. 處理	处理	chǔlǐ	to dispose of, deal with, (PRC) sell (old, overstocked, or defective) goods at reduced prices
^7. 罐頭	罐头	guàntou	canned goods
8. 草梅	草梅	cǎoméi	strawberry
9. 醬	酱	jiàng	jam, sauce

米晓玲：咱们老同学，<u>没说的</u>。我们那儿<u>处理</u>水果<u>罐头</u>特多，<u>草梅酱</u>才五毛钱一瓶。听安然讲，
　　　　大姐喜欢吃水果，……

安静：　是啊，哦。我去<u>厨房</u>，你坐一会儿，啊。（goes back into the kitchen.）

米晓玲：啊，行。您忙吧，安姐姐。

安然：　太棒了。有草梅酱我买个十瓶。

米晓玲：来什么<u>新鲜</u>货，我就给你打电话。

安然：　呵呵呵呵。

米晓玲：呵呵呵呵。

Xiaoling pauses and looks around the living room.

米晓玲：嗳，你们家东西真多呀。这都谁<u>布置</u>的？

安然：　我爸爸。

The two girls stop in front of the easel.

米晓玲：这是一张画儿，真大呀。

安然：　你知道它叫什么名字吗？

米晓玲：光有树和树叶儿，还没画人呢。画上人，我就知道叫什么名字了。

安然：　这<u>幅</u>画，永远也不会有人。不过，它已经有名字了。我把它叫作……

米晓玲：叫"落叶"，对吧？

安然：　不，叫"<u>吻</u>"。

米晓玲：叫什么？叫……

安然：　"吻"。就是一个"口"字加一个"<u>勿</u>"字呀。

米晓玲：哎呀，安然，你可真行。你能说出这个字来。

安然：　这有什么？你看，大地<u>养育</u>了这棵大树，大地就是它的母亲。（Father enters with
　　　　a bowl of food in hand. Hearing Ran expound on his painting, he stops and

---

*10. 廚房	厨房	chúfáng	kitchen
*11. 新鮮	新鲜	xīnxian	fresh
^12. 佈置	布置	bùzhì	to arrange, decorate
^13. 幅	幅	fú	M for paintings
^14. 吻	吻	wěn	kiss; to kiss
^15. 勿	勿	wù	(literary) do not
^16. 養育	养育	yǎngyù	to nurture

listens attentively.) 夏天的大樹，把陰涼獻給大地，它的母親。到秋天，大樹開
始用金子一樣的顏色打扮自己，它們穿着盛裝，飄向大地，飄向它們的母親，去親吻
母親的胸膛。你看，母親也敞開胸膛，歡迎兒子的歸來。這就是兒子獻給母親最好的
禮物： 一個莊重，深厚的吻。米曉玲，你喜歡我爸爸這張畫兒嗎？

米曉玲：嗯。

爸爸： 嗯，米曉玲，來，吃飯。

Ran goes to the table, then turns again to Xiaoling, who has started to cry.

安然： 米曉玲，你怎麼了？

米曉玲：我……看你多好，懂這麼多。說得我都……其實，我並不想上班，你知道，我多後悔，
為什麼當初不好好兒學習。

安然： 這也不能全怪你。你的家務活兒確實太多了。

米曉玲：你知道，我多怕同學們到商店裡來呀。我站在櫃台，看見一個個背着書包，來買這
買那的，多神氣呀。

安然： 米曉玲，你別哭了，我去看你的時候，保證不背書包。 (in tears now.)

Jing goes to them, pats Ran on the head, then puts her arm around Xiaoling.

安靜： 米曉玲，別哭，快別哭了，啊？人在哪兒都一樣，都能幹出成績的。來，來，快別哭
了，啊？別哭別哭。

The An sisters take Xiaoling by her arms and go to the table.

---

^17. 陰涼	阴凉	yīnliáng	shady coolness; shady and cool
*18. 獻給	献给	xiàngěi	to present to, donate to
^19. 金子	金子	jīnzi	gold
20. 盛裝	盛装	shèngzhuāng	splendid attire
21. 飄向	飘向	piāoxiàng	to float or flutter toward
22. 親吻	亲吻	qīnwěn	to kiss
23. 胸膛	胸膛	xiōngtáng	chest, bosom
24. 敞開	敞开	chǎngkāi	to open wide
^25. 歸來	归来	guīlai	(N) return; to return
^26. 莊重	庄重	zhuāngzhòng	solemn
*27. 深厚	深厚	shēnhòu	deep

listens attentively.) 夏天的大树，把阴凉献给大地，它的母亲。到秋天，大树开始用金子一样的颜色打扮自己，它们穿着盛装，飘向大地，飘向它们的母亲，去亲吻母亲的胸膛。你看，母亲也敞开胸膛，欢迎儿子的归来。这就是儿子献给母亲最好的礼物： 一个庄重，深厚的吻。米晓玲，你喜欢我爸爸这张画儿吗？

米晓玲：嗯。

爸爸： 嗯，米晓玲，来，吃饭。

Ran goes to the table, then turns again to Xiaoling, who has started to cry.

安然： 米晓玲，你怎么了？

米晓玲：我……看你多好，懂这么多。说得我都……其实，我并不想上班，你知道，我多后悔，为什么当初不好好儿学习。

安然： 这也不能全怪你。你的家务活儿确实太多了。

米晓玲：你知道，我多怕同学们到商店里来呀。我站在柜台，看见一个个背着书包，来买这买那的，多神气呀。

安然： 米晓玲，你别哭了，我去看你的时候，保证不背书包。 (in tears now.)

Jing goes to them, pats Ran on the head, then puts her arm around Xiaoling.

安静： 米晓玲，别哭，快别哭了，啊？人在哪儿都一样，都能干出成绩的。来，来，快别哭了，啊？别哭别哭。

The An sisters take Xiaoling by her arms and go to the table.

---

*28. 並	并	bìng	(used with a negative) an adverb indicating contradiction with expectation or assumption (cf. Grammatical Note VIII.4.)
*29. 後悔	后悔	hòuhuǐ	to regret; remorse
*30. 當初	当初	dāngchū	in the beginning
*31. 怪	怪	guài	to blame; strange
^32. 家務活	家务活	jiāwùhuó	housework
^33. 櫃台	柜台	guìtái	counter
^34. 背	背	bēi	to carry on one's back
^35. 神氣	神气	shénqì	cocky demeanor; expression, manner
*36. 保證	保证	bǎozhèng	to guarantee

爸爸：　來來來，米曉玲，工作了。啊，是大人了。

安靜：　快別哭了，啊？快別哭了。

爸爸：　可以喝一杯葡萄酒啦。　(pours wine for Xiaoling.)

安靜：　對對。來。

安靜：　笑一笑，呵呵呵。

Scene 42 ——————————

In a rare moment, Father is alone in the quiet living room, gazing at his easel.
His contemplation is interrupted by Mother's home-coming.

媽媽：　小靜，屋裡人呢？快來接東西啊。　(Jing runs to the door.)　豆腐。

爸爸：　(to Mother) 怎麼樣？今天進展如何？

媽媽：　研究所明確表態，他們説我專業扔了太久了，他們提議我去小學當英語教師。

爸爸：　那你怎麼考慮？

媽媽：　那也要考核啊。我這個歲數，還去趕那個時髦？

Mother leaves Father in the living room and goes into the kitchen, where Jing is
straightening things up.

媽媽：　怎麼沒做晚飯？

安靜：　哦，給你留了飯菜。米曉玲來了。午飯吃得晚，我們也有點累。

媽媽：　我早説過，沒這個必要。那你們自找的。

安靜：　你還是媽媽。

37. 葡萄	葡萄	pútao	grape
^38. 豆腐	豆腐	dòufu	tofu, beancurd
^49. 進展	进展	jìnzhǎn	to make headway or progress
*40. 如何	如何	rúhé	(literary) 怎麼樣 (cf. Grammatical Note VIII.6.)
^41. 研究所	研究所	yánjiūsuǒ	research institute
*42. 明確	明确	míngquè	clear, definite, explicit
^43. 表態	表态	biǎotài	to declare one's position

爸爸：　来来来，米晓玲，工作了。啊，是大人了。

安静：　快别哭了，啊？快别哭了。

爸爸：　可以喝一杯葡萄酒啦。 (pours wine for Xiaoling.)

安静：　对对。来。

安静：　笑一笑，呵呵呵。

Scene 42 ——————————————

In a rare moment, Father is alone in the quiet living room, gazing at his easel.
His contemplation is interrupted by Mother's home-coming.

妈妈：　小静，屋里人呢？快来接东西啊。 (Jing runs to the door.) 豆腐。

爸爸：　(to Mother) 怎么样？今天进展如何？

妈妈：　研究所明确表态，他们说我专业扔了太久了，他们提议我去小学当英语教师。

爸爸：　那你怎么考虑？

妈妈：　那也要考核啊。我这个岁数，还去赶那个时髦？

Mother leaves Father in the living room and goes into the kitchen, where Jing is
straightening things up.

妈妈：　怎么沒做晚饭？

安静：　哦，给你留了饭菜。米晓玲来了。午饭吃得晚，我们也有点累。

妈妈：　我早说过，沒这个必要。那你们自找的。

安静：　你还是妈妈。

^44.	提議	提议	tíyì	to suggest, propose
^45.	考核	考核	kǎohé	to examine or assess (someone's proficiency)
^46.	趕時髦	赶时髦	gǎn shímáo	to follow the fashion, try to be "in the swim"
*47.	留	留	liú	to save, retain

媽媽：　你滾！ (Ran appears at the doorway.) 媽媽怎麼啦？媽媽就一定得是家庭婦女？
　　　　我還沒當夠哇。一當就是十年，滿腦子油鹽醬醋。還得跟着喊，舉着紅旗喊，舉着語
　　　　錄喊，喊得什麼都忘了，都丟了。

安靜：　誰讓你跟着喊嘛。

媽媽：　誰？你！

安靜：　我？

媽媽：　就是你！ (stomps out of the kitchen, sees Ran at the doorway as she
　　　　passes) 你們！

安然：　(chuckling sarcastically) 媽媽說得對，為了使你我不變修。

Hearing Ran, Mother comes back to scold her.

媽媽：　又是你，別以為你考得不錯就不知道天高地厚。我還有話跟你談，你來。

48. 滾	滾	gǔn	to roll; (scolding) "Roll!" "Get out of here!"
^49. 家庭婦女	家庭妇女	jiātíng fùnǚ	housewife
*50. 當	当	dāng	to be in the role of
*51. 滿…	满…	mǎn…	the entire...; the...is full of/filled with... (cf. Grammatical Note VIII.8.)
^52. 腦子	脑子	nǎozi	brains
53. 油鹽醬醋	油盐酱醋	yóu yán jiàng cù	"oil, salt, sauce, vinegar," i.e., all the trivial domestic matters (having to do with cooking)

討論問題：

1)　安然怎麼能把沒有人的一幅畫兒名為"吻"？你怎樣評價那幅畫兒？那幅畫兒和媽媽跟
　　安靜在第五段裡要爸爸畫的畫兒怎麼不同？

2)　米曉玲覺得自己快要開始的工作怎麼樣？她剛到安家的時候好像挺高興，後來為什麼哭了？

3)　媽媽的研究所表了什麼態？因此 (yīncǐ: therefore, due to this)，媽媽的心情怎樣？

4)　在那個時代，家庭婦女除了管家以外，還得做什麼？為什麼？

5)　媽媽現在覺得當"家庭婦女"怎麼樣？在這方面 (fāngmiàn: aspect)，安靜、安然了解不了解
　　媽媽？你對"家庭婦女"這個問題有什麼看法？

妈妈： 你滚！（Ran appears at the doorway.）妈妈怎么啦？妈妈就一定得是<u>家庭妇女</u>？
我还没<u>当</u>够哇。一当就是十年，<u>满脑子油盐酱醋</u>。还得跟着<u>喊</u>，<u>举</u>着红旗喊，举着<u>语</u>
<u>录</u>喊，喊得什么都忘了，都丢了。

安静： 谁让你跟着喊嘛。

妈妈： 谁？你！

安静： 我？

妈妈： 就是你！（stomps out of the kitchen, sees Ran at the doorway as she
passes）你们！

安然： （chuckling sarcastically）妈妈说得对，为了使你我不变<u>修</u>。

Hearing Ran, Mother comes back to scold her.

妈妈： 又是你，别以为你考得不错就不知道<u>天高地厚</u>。我还有话跟你谈，你来。

^54. 喊	喊	hǎn	to shout, yell
*55. 舉	举	jǔ	to raise
56. 語錄	语录	yǔlù	quotations (of a personage) (here, it refers specifically to the quotations of Mao - the "little red book")
^57. 修	修	xiū	revisionist
^58. 天高地厚	天高地厚	tiāngāo dìhòu	"the sky is high and the earth is thick," i.e., the immensity of the universe, the complexity of things

讨论问题：

1) 安然怎么能把沒有人的一幅画儿名为"吻"？你怎样评价那幅画儿？那幅画儿和妈妈跟
安静在第五段里要爸爸画的画儿怎么不同？

2) 米晓玲觉得自己快要开始的工作怎么样？她刚到安家的时候好象挺高兴，后来为什么哭了？

3) 妈妈的研究所表了什么态？因此（yīncǐ: therefore, due to this），妈妈的心情怎样？

4) 在那个时代，家庭妇女除了管家以外，还得做什么？为什么？

5) 妈妈现在觉得当"家庭妇女"怎么样？在这方面（fāngmiàn: aspect），安静、安然了解不了解
妈妈？你对"家庭妇女"这个问题有什么看法？

SEGMENT IX

Scene 43 ——————————

In the parents' room: Father at the desk, Ran sitting by the edge of the bed, swinging her leg, Mother on a chair facing her.

媽媽：　你説呀。

安然：　不是您説嗎？我聽着還不行？

Jing appears at the doorway.

媽媽：　我説？可以。 (Mother slaps Ran's crossed legs. Ran immediately straightens them up.) 別<u>悠蕩</u>着腿，沒<u>家教</u>的樣子。考完<u>體育</u>那天，你到哪兒去啦？

安然：　我<u>反對</u>你這樣<u>審問</u>我。

媽媽：　反對？反對也得問。別當我什麼都不知道。

安靜：　媽，你<u>既然</u>什麼都知道，幹嘛還<u>拿人一把</u>？

媽媽：　(to Jing) 我就知道你站她那一邊兒。欽，你是當姐姐的。 (to Ran) 開完<u>班會</u>不回家，去逛什麼白洋淀？！

安然：　考完了，累了，不能玩兒玩兒嗎？

媽媽：　為什麼偏要跟男生玩兒啊？就你一個女生。

爸爸：　別説了。

安然：　男生怎麼了？

媽媽：　那也應該跟我<u>打個招呼</u>，<u>何必</u>那麼<u>偷偷摸摸</u>的？

安然：　好哇，<u>原來</u>你這麼看我。我從來就不會偷偷摸摸。我<u>恨死</u>偷偷摸摸了！媽，我看不起你！ (stomps out of the door.)

_____

1. 悠蕩	悠荡	yōudàng	to swing or sway (back and forth)
^2. 家教	家教	jiājiào	"family education," proper upbringing
^3. 體育	体育	tǐyù	physical education
*4. 反對	反对	fǎnduì	to object, oppose
^5. 審問	审问	shěnwèn	to interrogate
*6. 既然	既然	jìrán	(MA) since, given the fact that... (cf. Grammatical Note IX.1.)
7. 拿人一把	拿人一把	ná rén yìbǎ	(idiom) to make things difficult for others
8. 班會	班会	bān-huì	class meeting

SEGMENT IX

Scene 43 ————————————

In the parents' room: Father at the desk, Ran sitting by the edge of the bed, swinging her leg, Mother on a chair facing her.

妈妈：　你说呀。

安然：　不是您说吗？我听着还不行？

Jing appears at the doorway.

妈妈：　我说？可以。(Mother slaps Ran's crossed legs. Ran immediately straightens them up.) 别悠荡着腿，没家教的样子。考完体育那天，你到哪儿去啦？

安然：　我反对你这样审问我。

妈妈：　反对？反对也得问。别当我什么都不知道。

安静：　妈，你既然什么都知道，干嘛还拿人一把？

妈妈：　(to Jing) 我就知道你站她那一边儿。欸，你是当姐姐的。(to Ran) 开完班会不回家，去逛什么白洋淀？！

安然：　考完了，累了，不能玩儿玩儿吗？

妈妈：　为什么偏要跟男生玩儿啊？就你一个女生。

爸爸：　别说了。

安然：　男生怎么了？

妈妈：　那也应该跟我打个招呼，何必那么偷偷摸摸的？

安然：　好哇，原来你这么看我。我从来就不会偷偷摸摸。我恨死偷偷摸摸了！妈，我看不起你！(stomps out of the door.)

---

^9. 逛	逛	guàng	to ramble, roam (for fun)
^10. 打招呼	打招呼	dǎ zhāohu	to notify, touch base (with someone); to greet someone
*11. 何必	何必	hébì	(adv.) why must (cf. Grammatical Note IX.3.)
^12. 偷偷摸摸	偷偷摸摸	tōutōumōmō	furtively, surreptitiously
*13. 原來	原来	yuánlái	(MA) originally; as it turns out (as if it's a revelation)
14. 恨死	恨死	hènsǐ	to hate intensely, detest

安靜： 欸，然然，然然！媽，你不對。

媽媽： (furiously fanning herself) 怎麼不對？

爸爸： 你不懂得<u>尊重</u>人。

媽媽： <u>專</u>找男生玩兒，你考慮過影響沒有？

爸爸： 什麼專找？我看你像上個<u>世紀</u>過來的。

安靜： 有個男孩我認識，就住咱們樓裡。

媽媽： 你們了解現在的孩子嗎？<u>複雜</u>着呢。

爸爸： 哼。安靜，去把然然叫回來。

安靜： 嗯。 (goes out, but stops momentarily outside the door and eavesdrops.)

爸爸： 咳，你又"複雜複雜"。你忘了那年你對小靜也是這麼説。

Jing closes the apartment door behind her as she leaves to find Ran.

Scene 44 ———————————

Through Jing's reminiscence, we see a flashback in which Mother catches the teenage
Jing talking with a boy and scolds her.

媽媽： 小靜，你幹什麼呢？你怎麼變複雜了。

Consequently, Jing rejects the boy's further efforts to approach her.

Scene 45 ———————————

Back to the present, Ran is with an ice cream vendor on the street.

安然： 這<u>糖精</u>放多了就<u>發苦</u>，真的，你們應該到北京去<u>取取經</u>。

冰糕販：對，有機會是應該到北京學習學習。<u>活到老，學到老</u>嘛。對吧，小同志？

^15. 尊重	尊重	zūnzhòng	to respect
^16. 專	专	zhuān	(to do something) exclusively or especially
*17. 世紀	世纪	shìjì	century
*18. 複雜	复杂	fùzá	complicated, complex
19. 糖精	糖精	tángjīng	saccharin
20. 發苦	发苦	fā kǔ	to develop a bitter taste

安静：　欸，然然，然然！妈，你不对。

妈妈：　(furiously fanning herself) 怎么不对？

爸爸：　你不懂得<u>尊</u>重人。

妈妈：　<u>专找男生玩儿</u>，你考虑过影响沒有？

爸爸：　什么专找？我看你象上个<u>世纪</u>过来的。

安静：　有个男孩我认识，就住咱们楼里。

妈妈：　你们了解现在的孩子吗？<u>复杂</u>着呢。

爸爸：　哼。安静，去把然然叫回来。

安静：　嗯。(goes out, but stops momentarily outside the door and eavesdrops.)

爸爸：　咳，你又"复杂复杂"。你忘了那年你对小静也是这么说。

Jing closes the apartment door behind her as she leaves to find Ran.

Scene 44 ————————————

Through Jing's reminiscence, we see a flashback in which Mother catches the teenage Jing talking with a boy and scolds her.

妈妈：　小静，你干什么呢？你怎么变复杂了。

Consequently, Jing rejects the boy's further efforts to approach her.

Scene 45 ————————————

Back to the present, Ran is with an ice cream vendor on the street.

安然：　这<u>糖</u>精放多了就<u>发苦</u>，真的，你们应该到北京去<u>取取经</u>。

冰糕贩：对，有机会是应该到北京学习学习。<u>活到老，学到老</u>嘛。对吧，小同志？

^21. 取經	取经	qǔjīng	(originally) to go on a pilgrimage to obtain Buddhist scriptures; to learn from someone else's expertise
22. 冰糕	冰糕	bīnggāo	ice cream
23. 活到老，學到老	活到老，学到老	huó dào lǎo, xué dào lǎo	"live until old, learn until old," i.e., one is never too old to learn

安然： 啊，哈哈哈哈。

Jing finds Ran in a merry state.

安靜： 然然，然然。你還在這兒笑。快回家去。走。 (The girls walk off.)
安然： 再見。
冰糕販：欸，回頭見。

Scene 46 ──────────────

While strolling home, the An sisters have a heart-to-heart talk.

安然： 爸爸對我和男生去玩兒的事怎麼看？
安靜： 你覺得呢？
安然： 我猜不透。大人的心，猜不透。
安靜： 你呀，要相信爸爸，也要相信你自己。幹嘛這麼沒精打彩的？打起精神來。

Scene 47 ──────────────

Back in their room...

安然： 其實，誰也不理解我。姐，我給你念一段我的日記。 (unlocks her desk drawer,
        gets out her diary, and reads a passage to Jing) "今天，到白洋淀玩兒，使我
        想到了很多。知識是無窮盡的，我發現有的男同學視野開闊，知識面很廣。我願意和
        他們在一起。用自己的眼睛去發現美，是一種幸福。可有的人為什麼這麼自私呢？這
        我指的是劉冬虎，他買瓜少給了農民的錢。今天，我是用自己的眼睛觀察大自然的，

---

*24. 回頭見	回头见	huítóu jiàn	(idiom) See you! Goodbye!
^25. 猜不透	猜不透	cāibutòu	(V不RE) unable to guess
*26. 相信	相信	xiāngxìn	to believe
^27. 沒精打彩	没精打采	méi jīng dǎ cǎi	listless, in low spirits, lackadaisical
^28. 打起精神	打起精神	dǎqǐ jīngshen	to perk up, cheer up, raise one's spirits
^29. 段	段	duàn	section, paragraph
*30. 知識	知识	zhīshi	knowledge
^31. 無窮盡	无穷尽	wúqióngjìn	limitless, boundless

安然：　啊，哈哈哈哈。

Jing finds Ran in a merry state.

安静：　然然，然然。你还在这儿笑。快回家去。走。 (The girls walk off.)
安然：　再见。
冰糕贩：欸，回头见。

Scene 46 ——————————————

While strolling home, the An sisters have a heart-to-heart talk.

安然：　爸爸对我和男生去玩儿的事怎么看？
安静：　你觉得呢？
安然：　我猜不透。大人的心，猜不透。
安静：　你呀，要相信爸爸，也要相信你自己。干嘛这么没精打采的？打起精神来。

Scene 47 ——————————————

Back in their room...

安然：　其实，谁也不理解我。姐，我给你念一段我的日记。 (unlocks her desk drawer,
　　　　gets out her diary, and reads a passage to Jing) "今天，到白洋淀玩儿，使我
　　　　想到了很多。知识是无穷尽的，我发现有的男同学视野开阔，知识面很广。我愿意和
　　　　他们在一起。用自己的眼睛去发现美，是一种幸福。可有的人为什么这么自私呢？这
　　　　我指的是刘冬虎，他买瓜少给了农民的钱。今天，我是用自己的眼睛观察大自然的，

32. 視野	视野	shìyě	field of vision
33. 開闊	开阔	kāikuò	open and wide
^34. 知識面	知识面	zhīshimiàn	breadth of knowledge
^35. 廣	广	guǎng	wide
^36. 幸福	幸福	xìngfú	happiness, well-being
*37. 自私	自私	zìsī	selfish
^38. 觀察	观察	guānchá	to observe
^39. 大自然	大自然	dàzìrán	mother nature

我也要學會用自己的<u>分析能力</u>，認識同學，認識朋友，自己的。"你明白我的意思嗎?

安靜:　明白。

安然:　你相信我嗎?

安靜:　相信。

安然:　可是，媽媽和韋老師都不相信我。 (puts away her diary.)

安靜:　你有過……不尊重老師的地方……?

安然:　就那=次上語文課，我<u>糾正</u>老師念錯的字。這事兒我跟你說過……

安靜:　嗯，我記得。後來，韋老師對你怎麼樣?

安然:　後來，她又當全班同學講，有的同學學習<u>目的</u>不明確，專愛<u>表現</u>自己什麼的。可我後
　　　　來查了字典，老師確實念錯了。

安靜:　以後她找你談過嗎?

安然:　沒有。可以後<u>班級</u>出<u>牆報</u>，她再也不找我了。以前這些事兒，都是由我來幹的。這
　　　　<u>大概</u>算是不尊重她。

安靜:　哼，這<u>根本</u>不叫不尊重。這叫……然然，你沒錯。我全明白。 (turns off the lamp
　　　　by Ran's bed) 睡吧，然然，你對這=次評選，有<u>把握</u>?

安然:　沒有。算了，不當。

安靜:　憑什麼不當? 就得爭取一下。你們哪天評選?

安然:　明天。 (Ran covers herself to go to sleep. But a moment later, she gets up
　　　　again, turns on her lamp, and gets her red blouse out of a drawer.) 姐，明
　　　　天我就穿這件衣服，好嗎?

安靜:　穿吧，這有什麼?

Ran goes back to bed. A moment later, the parents come to their door to peep in on
them.

媽媽:　睡了。

爸爸:　<u>沒心沒肺</u>。 (Both walk away chuckling.)

---

^40. 分析	分析	fēnxī	to analyze
*41. 能力	能力	nénglì	ability
^42. 糾正	纠正	jiūzhèng	to correct, rectify
43. 當	当	dāng	in the presence of...
*44. 目的	目的	mùdì	objective, goal, purpose
*45. 表現	表现	biǎoxiàn	to display, show off; expression, manifestation
^46. 班級	班级	bānjí	class, year in school

我也要学会用自己的<u>分析能力</u>，认识同学，认识朋友，自己的。"你明白我的意思吗？

安静： 明白。

安然： 你相信我吗？

安静： 相信。

安然： 可是，妈妈和韦老师都不相信我。(puts away her diary.)

安静： 你有过……不尊重老师的地方……？

安然： 就那次上语文课，我<u>纠正</u>老师念错的字。这事儿我跟你说过……

安静： 嗯，我记得。后来，韦老师对你怎么样？

安然： 后来，她又当全班同学讲，有的同学学习<u>目的</u>不明确，专爱<u>表现</u>自己什么的。可我后来查了字典，老师确实念错了。

安静： 以后她找你谈过吗？

安然： 沒有。可以后<u>班级</u>出<u>墙报</u>，她再也不找我了。以前这些事儿，都是由我来干的。这<u>大概</u>算是不尊重她。

安静： 哼，这<u>根本</u>不叫不尊重。这叫……然然，你沒错。我全明白。(turns off the lamp by Ran's bed) 睡吧，然然，你对这次评选，有<u>把握</u>？

安然： 沒有。算了，不当。

安静： 凭什么不当？就得争取一下。你们哪天评选？

安然： 明天。(Ran covers herself to go to sleep. But a moment later, she gets up again, turns on her lamp, and gets her red blouse out of a drawer.) 姐，明天我就穿这件衣服，好吗？

安静： 穿吧，这有什么？

Ran goes back to bed. A moment later, the parents come to their door to peep in on them.

妈妈： 睡了。

爸爸： <u>沒心沒肺</u>。(Both walk away chuckling.)

---

47. 牆報	墙报	qiángbào	"wall newspaper," essays and pictures posted on bulletin boards
*48. 大概	大概	dàgài	probably
*49. 根本	根本	gēnběn	fundamentally, basically, simply
^50. 把握	把握	bǎwò	assurance, certainty
51. 沒心沒肺	沒心沒肺	méi xīn méi fèi	"no heart or lungs," i.e., not having things weighing on one's heart

Ran gets up, wraps her blanket around herself and goes to Jing's bed.

安然：　姐，我睡不着。給我半片<u>利眠寧</u>吧，就吃半片。

安靜：　去吧，能睡着。數數字，啊？去。

安然：　不，我選不上倒沒什麼，可有的人會説，是我和男生一起玩兒，影響不好，所以沒選上。

安靜：　別想這麼多。別人愛怎麼説就怎麼説。你忘了，(lifts Ran's hair to reveal two moles by her right ear lobe) 你這兒長着個<u>冒號</u>，就是專門爲了聽別人的議論的，啊？去。 (nudges Ran back to bed.)

安然：　(in bed) 一、二、三、四、五、六、七、八、……

Scene 48 ————————

There is commotion in the hallway outside Jing's office. Several men are clamoring to get something from Editor Ma.

馬編輯：(to the clamoring men) 不行，不行，不行。…這是按人頭兒分的。…(enters the office, puts a piece of paper in front of Jing) 欸，<u>簽個字</u>吧，這是局裡組織電影<u>觀摩</u>，每人一張。我的這張給你。

安靜：　欸，馬老師，這……

馬編輯：我可不<u>主張</u>什麼<u>獨身</u>主義。

安靜：　馬老師，你看你。 (Ma leaves, thus avoiding Jing's further protestations.)

---

52. 利眠寧	利眠宁	lìmiánníng	"benefit sleep tranquillity," name of a sleeping pill
53. 冒號	冒号	màohào	colon (here, the two moles on An Ran's face that look like a colon)
^54. 簽字	签字	qiānzì	to sign one's name
^55. 觀摩	观摩	guānmó	to view (a film or performance) and learn from it (it is a privilege of intellectuals and artists to have access to certain films and performances which are not available to the public)

Ran gets up, wraps her blanket around herself and goes to Jing's bed.

安然：　姐，我睡不着。给我半片利眠宁吧，就吃半片。

安静：　去吧，能睡着。数数字，啊？去。

安然：　不，我选不上倒沒什么，可有的人会说，是我和男生一起玩儿，影响不好，所以沒选
　　　　上。

安静：　别想这么多。别人爱怎么说就怎么说。你忘了，(lifts Ran's hair to reveal two
　　　　moles by her right ear lobe) 你这儿长着个冒号，就是专门为了听别人的议论的，
　　　　啊？去。 (nudges Ran back to bed.)

安然：　(in bed) 一、二、三、四、五、六、七、八、……

Scene 48 ───────────────

There is commotion in the hallway outside Jing's office. Several men are clamoring
to get something from Editor Ma.

马编辑：(to the clamoring men) 不行，不行，不行。…这是按人头儿分的。…(enters the
　　　　office, puts a piece of paper in front of Jing) 欸，签个字吧，这是局里组织
　　　　电影观摩，每人一张。我的这张给你。

安静：　欸，马老师，这……

马编辑：我可不主张什么独身主义。

安静：　马老师，你看你。 (Ma leaves, thus avoiding Jing's further protestations.)

───────────────────────────────

*56.	主張	主张	zhǔzhāng	to advocate, be in favor of
57.	獨身	独身	dúshēn	unmarried, single
*58.	主義	主义	zhǔyì	doctrine, -ism (獨身主義: "doctrine of singlehood," "single-ism," celibacy)

Jing picks up the telephone, hesitates, puts it down, then finally picks it up
again and dials. At the other end...

韋老師：啊，什麼電影？

安靜：　是新譯制的外國片，每人就一張。我已經看過了。

韋老師：呵呵，那太好了……哦？欸，不用不用。中午我自己去取。啊，好好好，再見啊，
　　　　哦。

59. 譯製	译制	yìzhì	(of films) translated and dubbed (the original foreign language sound track dubbed into Chinese)
^60. 片	片	piān	film

討論問題：

1)　媽媽爲什麼“審問”安然？

2)　安然對媽媽的“審問”有什麼反應 (fǎnyìng: reaction)？

3)　爸爸和安然對媽媽的態度有什麼看法？爲什麼？

4)　安然“和男生去玩兒”的那天有了什麼收獲？你能不能從她的日記中看出來？

5)　安靜爲什麼又同意安然穿那件紅襯衫了？

6)　安然的“誰也不理解我”那句話説得對不對？到底誰“不理解”她？爲什麼？

7)　安然爲什麼睡不着？她真的怕選不上“三好生”嗎？

8)　爲什麼馬編輯把他的電影票給了安靜？爲什麼安靜把它給韋老師？你從她給韋老師打電話
　　的那一幕能看出什麼？

Jing picks up the telephone, hesitates, puts it down, then finally picks it up
again and dials. At the other end...

韦老师：啊，什么电影？

安静： 是新译制的外国片，每人就一张。我已经看过了。

韦老师：呵呵，那太好了……哦？欸，不用不用。中午我自己去取。啊，好好好，再见啊，
　　　　哦。

讨论问题：

1) 妈妈为什么"审问"安然？

2) 安然对妈妈的"审问"有什么反应 (fǎnyìng: reaction)？

3) 爸爸和安然对妈妈的态度有什么看法？为什么？

4) 安然"和男生去玩儿"的那天有了什么收获？你能不能从她的日记中看出来？

5) 安静为什么又同意安然穿那件红衬衫了？

6) 安然的"谁也不理解我"那句话说得对不对？到底谁"不理解"她？为什么？

7) 安然为什么睡不着？她真的怕选不上"三好生"吗？

8) 为什么马编辑把他的电影票给了安静？为什么安静把它给韦老师？你从她给韦老师打电话
　　的那一幕能看出什么？

SEGMENT X

Scene 49 ───────────────

Lunch time in Ran's classroom, noise and commotion reign. Ran is telling a funny story to a group. At the end of her story...

安然：　他<u>醒來</u>一看，打開<u>燈</u>一看，是個<u>小偷</u>……，他就笑了。他非常<u>平靜</u>地對小偷説："小偷先生，我白天在這兒都找不着錢，<u>難道</u>你晚上來了，就能找着嗎？"

Ran's listeners break out laughing. Liu Donghu walks up.

劉冬虎：安然，你來一下。

Liu and Ran walk toward their desks. Liu puts a note on Ran's desk. She opens it and find a half dollar bill. She smiles, then writes a note and puts it on Liu's desk. He opens it. It reads: 你的收獲<u>何止</u>五角錢。 He gives her an acknowledging smile...Ran and several girls are singing now...

眾女生：(singing) "外婆的<u>澎湖灣</u>，有我<u>許多</u>的<u>童年</u>幻想，……"

Scene 50 ───────────────

At Jing's office.

章老師：呵呵，你們這房子不小的啦。
安靜：　沒有吧。還好。你看，樓下有賣<u>西瓜</u>的。

───

*1. 醒來	醒来	xǐnglai	to awake
^2. 燈	灯	dēng	light, lamp
^3. 小偷	小偷	xiǎotōu	thief
^4. 平靜	平静	píngjìng	calm
*5. 難道	难道	nándào	(MA) (literally "difficult to say") You mean to say...? How can it be that...? (an adverb conveying surprise or disbelief) (cf. Grammatical Note X.1.)

110

SEGMENT X

Scene 49 ────────────

Lunch time in Ran's classroom, noise and commotion reign. Ran is telling a funny story to a group. At the end of her story...

安然：　他<u>醒</u>来一看，打开<u>灯</u>一看，是个<u>小偷</u>……，他就笑了。他非常<u>平静</u>地对小偷说："小偷先生，我白天在这儿都找不着钱，<u>难道</u>你晚上来了，就能找着吗？"

Ran's listeners break out laughing. Liu Donghu walks up.

刘冬虎：安然，你来一下。

Liu and Ran walk toward their desks. Liu puts a note on Ran's desk. She opens it and find a half dollar bill. She smiles, then writes a note and puts it on Liu's desk. He opens it. It reads: 你的收获<u>何止</u>五角钱。 He gives her an acknowledging smile...Ran and several girls are singing now...

众女生：(singing)"外婆的<u>澎湖湾</u>，有我<u>许多</u>的<u>童年</u><u>幻想</u>，……"

Scene 50 ────────────

At Jing's office.

韦老师：呵呵，你们这房子不小的啦。
安静：　沒有吧。还好。你看，楼下有卖<u>西瓜</u>的。

---

^6. 何止	何止	hézhǐ	(literary) (literally "how can it be only...?") far more than
7. 澎湖灣	澎湖湾	Pénghú Wān	"Penghu Bay" (place name)
*8. 許多	许多	xǔduō	很多
^9. 童年	童年	tóngnián	childhood
^10. 幻想	幻想	huànxiǎng	fantasy, illusion
^11. 西瓜	西瓜	xīgua	watermelon

The two are now at the window.

章老師：哦。

安靜：　天太熱了，我們幾個就下樓買西瓜吃。

章老師：今年西瓜不<u>甜</u>，不過，倒挺便宜的，哦？

安靜：　就是。你們快放假了吧？

章老師：可不？學生考完，評選完三好……呃……呵呵，欸，你們這房子，是<u>朝</u>北還是朝南啊？

安靜：　朝西。

章老師：哦，呵呵呵。

安靜：　所以下午特別熱。

安靜：　哦，（starts to pack her bag）呵，<u>忙不過來</u>，只好拿回家去<u>校對</u>。（motions to a pile of proofs）哦，這批<u>清樣</u>裡還有你那首詩呢。

章老師：哦，呵，是嗎？

安靜：　嗯。

章老師：哦，那，<u>印</u>好了，別忘了給我留幾本兒，哦？

安靜：　那當然。哦，這是給你的票。（hands Wei Wan two tickets.）

章老師：呵。

安靜：　拿着。

章老師：好好。

安靜：　這可是觀摩票，挺難<u>弄</u>的，你一定<u>抽</u>時間去看看。

章老師：那當然去了。呵，謝謝你。還沒忘了咱們老同學。呵呵呵。

Scene 51 ─────────────

In Ran's classroom, a list of students' names are on the blackboard.

章老師：還有誰要<u>發言</u>？王麗萍。

王麗萍：（stands up）嗯……祝文娟同學，確實表現很<u>突出</u>，總是和<u>和氣氣</u>的，從不<u>挑剔</u>別人，

ˆ12.	甜	甜	tián	sweet
13.	朝	朝	cháo	to face (a certain direction)
ˆ14.	忙不過來	忙不过来	máng bú guòlai	too busy to manage everything
ˆ15.	校對	校对	jiàoduì	to proofread
16.	清樣	清样	qīngyàng	final proof
ˆ17.	印	印	yìn	to print

The two are now at the window.

韦老师：哦。

安静：　天太热了，我们几个就下楼买西瓜吃。

韦老师：今年西瓜不<u>甜</u>，不过，倒挺便宜的，哦？

安静：　就是。你们快放假了吧？

韦老师：可不？学生考完，评选完三好……呃……呵呵，欸，你们这房子，是<u>朝</u>北还是朝南啊？

安静：　朝西。

韦老师：哦，呵呵呵。

安静：　所以下午特别热。

安静：　哦，（starts to pack her bag）呵，<u>忙不过来</u>，只好拿回家去<u>校对</u>。（motions to
　　　　a pile of proofs）哦，这批<u>清样</u>里还有你那首诗呢。

韦老师：哦，呵，是吗？

安静：　嗯。

韦老师：哦，那，<u>印</u>好了，别忘了给我留几本儿，哦？

安静：　那当然。哦，这是给你的票。（hands Wei Wan two tickets.）

韦老师：呵。

安静：　拿着。

韦老师：好好。

安静：　这可是观摩票，挺难<u>弄</u>的，你一定<u>抽</u>时间去看看。

韦老师：那当然去了。呵，谢谢你。还没忘了咱们老同学。呵呵呵。

Scene 51 ————————————

In Ran's classroom, a list of students' names are on the blackboard.

韦老师：还有谁要<u>发言</u>？王丽萍。

王丽萍：（stands up）嗯……祝文娟同学，确实表现很<u>突出</u>，总是和<u>和气气</u>的，从不<u>挑剔</u>别人，

^18. 弄	弄	nòng	(colloquial) to get, fetch; to fool with; to handle	
^19. 抽	抽	chōu	to take out (from in between)	
*20. 發言	发言	fāyán	to speak up, make a public statement	
^21. 突出	突出	tūchū	outstanding, prominent; to stick out	
*22. 和氣	和气	héqì	amiable, kind	
23. 挑剔	挑剔	tiāotì	nitpicky	

而且，團結同學，嗯……尊敬老師，對老師交給的工作，也能認真完成。就這些。

韋老師：嗯，剛才，許多同學都講了祝文娟的優點，羣眾的看法是<u>公正</u>的。<u>如果</u>沒有什麼別的意見，我們就<u>表決</u>。<u>同意</u>祝文娟為三好學生的，請舉手。 (counts the raised hands) 好，大家把手放下。只有六個同學不同意。全班四十八人，米曉玲走了，還<u>剩</u>四十七個，四十一票同意。好，祝文娟同學<u>當選</u>。請大家<u>鼓掌</u>。 (The class applauds.) <u>下面</u>，我們來談談安然同學的<u>情況</u>。請大家<u>發表</u>意見。你。

女生甲：(stands up) 嗯，怎麼說呢……安然同學學習成績是不錯，可總感覺有點兒……自<u>以為</u><u>了不起</u>。就說上次上語文課，她<u>居然</u>還<u>指導</u>老師。嗯，就這些。 (sits down.)

韋老師：宋振國。

宋振國：(stands up) 我感覺，那次上語文課的事，完全是一種<u>自我表現</u>。我認為，安然應該記住韋老師批評你的，要端正學習目的。 (sits down.)

韋老師：洪鈞。

洪鈞： (stands up) 我認為，對一個人的看法，不能夠<u>單</u>憑感覺，要<u>實事求是</u>。安然上次<u>指出</u>老師的錯，那就看她說得對不對。

韋老師：坐下。 (takes a couple of steps) 白云。

白云： (stands up) 那天，您讀了她考試的那篇作文，她寫的祝文娟，看得出她對祝文娟不服氣，<u>有意</u><u>貶低</u>班<u>幹</u>部以<u>證明</u>自己正確。 (sits down.)

韋老師：嗯。還有誰要發言？高力偉。

高力偉：(stands up) 那得看人家寫的是不是事實。就上回打架吧，要是祝文娟出來講話呢？ (sits down.)

韋老師：你。

女生乙：(stands up) 我相信，祝文娟是不會那樣兒做的。

---

^24. 公正	公正	gōngzhèng	fair, just
*25. 如果	如果	rúguǒ	if
^26. 表決	表決	biǎojué	to decide by vote, to vote
*27. 同意	同意	tóngyì	to agree, be in favor
^28. 剩	剩	shèng	to remain
^29. 當選	当选	dāngxuǎn	to be elected
^30. 鼓掌	鼓掌	gǔzhǎng	to applaud
^31. 下面	下面	xiàmian	below; next, following
*32. 情況	情况	qíngkuàng	situation, condition
*33. 發表	发表	fābiǎo	to publish, issue; to express an opinion
*34. 以為	以为	yǐwéi	to think, believe, consider (often erroneously)
^35. 了不起	了不起	liǎobuqǐ	terrific, extraordinary

而且，团结同学，嗯……尊敬老师，对老师交给的工作，也能认真完成。就这些。

韦老师：嗯，刚才，许多同学都讲了祝文娟的优点，群众的看法是<u>公正</u>的。<u>如果</u>没有什么别的意见，我们就<u>表决</u>。<u>同意</u>祝文娟为三好学生的，请举手。(counts the raised hands) 好，大家把手放下。只有六个同学不同意。全班四十八人，米晓玲走了，还<u>剩</u>四十七个，四十一票同意。好，祝文娟同学<u>当选</u>。请大家<u>鼓掌</u>。(The class applauds.) <u>下面</u>，我们来谈谈安然同学的<u>情况</u>。请大家<u>发表</u>意见。你。

女生甲：(stands up) 嗯，怎么说呢……安然同学学习成绩是不错，可总感觉有点儿……自<u>以为了不起</u>。就说上<u>次</u>上语文课，她<u>居然</u>还<u>指导</u>老师。嗯，就这些。(sits down.)

韦老师：宋振国。

宋振国：(stands up) 我感觉，那次上语文课的事，完全是一种<u>自我</u>表现。我认为，安然应该记住韦老师批评你的，要端正学习目的。(sits down.)

韦老师：洪钧。

洪钧：　(stands up) 我认为，对一个人的看法，不能够<u>单</u>凭感觉，<u>要实事求是</u>。安然上次<u>指出</u>老师的错，那就看她说得对不对。

韦老师：坐下。(takes a couple of steps) 白云。

白云：　(stands up) 那天，您读了她考试的那篇作文，她写的祝文娟，看得出她对祝文娟不<u>服气</u>，<u>有意贬低班干部</u>以<u>证明</u>自己正确。(sits down.)

韦老师：嗯。还有谁要发言？高力伟。

高力伟：(stands up) 那得看人家写的是不是事实。就上回打架吧，要是祝文娟出来讲话呢？(sits down.)

韦老师：你。

女生乙：(stands up) 我相信，祝文娟是不会那样儿做的。

*36. 居然	居然	jūrán	an adverb conveying surprise (at someone's audacity, etc.) (cf. Grammatical Note X.5.)
^37. 指導	指导	zhǐdǎo	to guide, instruct; guidance
38. 自我	自我	zìwǒ	self-, oneself; egotistical
^39. 單	单	dān	only, singly
^40. 實事求是	实事求是	shíshì qiú shì	to seek truth from facts
*41. 指出	指出	zhǐchū	to point out
^42. 服氣	服气	fúqì	to be convinced, accept criticism, admit error or defeat
^43. 有意	有意	yǒuyì	intentionally
44. 貶低	贬低	biǎndī	to belittle, depreciate
*45. 幹部	干部	gànbù	cadre, leader
*46. 證明	证明	zhèngmíng	to prove; evidence

某男生：(whispers to the boy next to him) <u>吃人家嘴短</u>。

眾學生：(having heard the above) 呵呵呵。

韋老師：(taps a desk to quiet down the class) 你們誰要發言？

某男生：(stands up) 幹嘛那麼相信祝文娟……就不相信安然呢？ (sits down.)

劉冬虎：(raises his hand, then stands up) 上次，我們去白洋淀玩兒，我們，我，少給了
　　　　賣瓜的<u>老鄉</u>五毛錢，安然<u>替</u>我給了。 (sits down while the class laughs.)

女生乙：(to her deskmate Zhu Wenjuan) 欸，你去沒去呀？

祝文娟：是安然和幾個男生一塊兒去的。

韋老師：王小容。

王小容：(stands up) 安然用功，<u>熱情</u>，願意幫助同學，她還幫我講過<u>數學難題</u>呢。不過，她
　　　　不知怎麼，有個<u>勁兒</u>，和別人不一樣。我也說不好，<u>比如說</u>她身上那件紅襯衫吧。
　　　　(All eyes turn to Ran.) 幹嘛要<u>別出心裁</u>呢？你看你的襯衫，和我們都不一樣。幹
　　　　嘛不<u>釘</u>扣子，還<u>繫</u>個<u>腰帶</u>呢？ (All eyes again turn to Ran.)

Teacher Wei returns to the blackboard and taps it to hush the class.

韋老師：<u>從以上</u>發言中可以看出，大家對安然是很關心的。提了很多<u>寶貴</u>的意見。安然以後要
　　　　注意<u>克服驕傲</u>情緒，注意<u>團結</u>同學，尊敬老師。當然啦，安然還是有很多優點的。她
　　　　學習好、有<u>毅力</u>、熱情、積極。我認爲，安然同學她還是夠三好條件的。 (Furor
　　　　breaks out in the classroom.) 現在大家表決。同意安然的，舉手。 (counts) 一、
　　　　二、三、四、五、六、七、八、九、十、十一，…… 張曉英， (Zhang is brushing
　　　　her hair with her fingers.) 你，是舉手了吧？

張曉英：啊，我<u>這就</u>舉手。 (raises her hand while the class laughs.)

47.	吃人家嘴短	吃人家嘴短	chī rěnjia zuǐ duǎn	"eating from others results in having a short mouth," i.e., unable to speak freely for having received a favor from someone
48.	老鄉	老乡	lǎoxiāng	"old" peasant ("old" is not necessarily to be taken literally); fellow townsman, fellow villager
*49.	替	替	tì	for (someone), in someone's stead
^50.	熱情	热情	rèqíng	warmhearted, enthusiastic, ardent
*51.	數學	数学	shùxué	mathematics
^52.	難題	难题	nántí	difficult problem or question, dilemma
^53.	勁兒	劲儿	jìnr	energy, vigor; air, manner, expression
*54.	比如說	比如说	bǐrú shuō	for example
55.	別出心裁	别出心裁	bié chū xīncái	to try to be different, adopt an original approach

某男生：(whispers to the boy next to him) <u>吃人家嘴短</u>。

众学生：(having heard the above) 呵呵呵。

韦老师：(taps a desk to quiet down the class) 你们谁要发言？

某男生：(stands up) 干嘛那么相信祝文娟……就不相信安然呢？ (sits down.)

刘冬虎：(raises his hand, then stands up) 上次，我们去白洋淀玩儿，我们，我，少给了
　　　　卖瓜的<u>老乡</u>五毛钱，安然<u>替</u>我给了。 (sits down while the class laughs.)

女生乙：(to her deskmate Zhu Wenjuan) 欸，你去没去呀？

祝文娟：是安然和几个男生一块儿去的。

韦老师：王小容。

王小容：(stands up) 安然用功，<u>热情</u>，愿意帮助同学，她还帮我讲过<u>数学</u>难题呢。不过，她
　　　　不知怎么，有个<u>劲儿</u>，和别人不一样。我也说不好，<u>比如</u>说她身上那件红衬衫吧。
　　　　(All eyes turn to Ran.) 干嘛要<u>别出心裁</u>呢？你看你的衬衫，和我们都不一样。干
　　　　嘛不<u>钉</u>扣子，还<u>系</u>个<u>腰带</u>呢？ (All eyes again turn to Ran.)

Teacher Wei returns to the blackboard and taps it to hush the class.

韦老师：从<u>以上</u>发言中可以看出，大家对安然是很关心的。提了很多<u>宝贵</u>的意见。安然以后要
　　　　<u>注意克服骄傲情绪</u>，注意团结同学，尊敬老师。当然啦，安然还是有很多优点的。她
　　　　学习好、有<u>毅力</u>、热情、积极。我认为，安然同学她还是够三好条件的。 (Furor
　　　　breaks out in the classroom.) 现在大家表决。同意安然的，举手。 (counts) 一、
　　　　二、三、四、五、六、七、八、九、十、十一，…… 张晓英， (Zhang is brushing
　　　　her hair with her fingers.) 你，是举手了吧？

张晓英：啊，我<u>这就</u>举手。 (raises her hand while the class laughs.)

---

^56. 釘	钉	dīng	to sew, tack, or nail on
57. 繫	系	jì	to tie
58. 腰带	腰带	yāodài	sash, belt
*59. 以上	以上	yǐshàng	the above, the preceding
^60. 寶貴	宝贵	bǎoguì	precious, valuable
^61. 克服	克服	kèfú	to overcome
^62. 驕傲	骄傲	jiāo'ào	arrogance, pride; arrogant, proud
^63. 情緒	情绪	qíngxù	feelings, mood, sentiments, morale
^64. 毅力	毅力	yìlì	stamina, willpower, determination
^65. 這就	这就	zhè jiù	at this, now then (without further delay or ado)

韋老師：(continues counting) 十二、十三、十四、十五、十六、十七、十八、十九、二十、

二一、二二、二三、二四，……大家把手放下。全班四十七人，一共二十四票，好，

<u>超過半數</u>，安然當選。(Class applauds.)

Teacher Wei writes "24" under An Ran's name on the board.

Scene 52 ──────────────

On the way home, the above scene replays in Ran's mind.

安然：   (voices in her mind) "一、二、三、四、五、六、七、八、九、十、十一，……張

曉英，你是舉手了吧？"

"我這就舉手。"

"哈哈哈哈。"

"十二、十三、十四、十五、十六、十七、十八、十九、二十、二一、二二、二三、

二四，全班四十七人，一共二十四票，好，超過半數，安然當選。"(applause.)

*66. 超過	超过	chāoguò	to exceed
^67. 半數	半数	bànshù	half (in number)

討論問題：

1) 安然和劉冬虎的關係有了什麼變化 (biànhuà: change, transformation)？

2) 韋老師去安靜的編輯室做什麼？為什麼她和安靜說了那麼些話？

3) 你覺得同學們都喜歡祝文娟嗎？為什麼那麼多同學投她的票 (tóu...piào: to vote)？

4) 韋老師對安然的評價公平 (gōngpíng: fair) 嗎？她這次對安然的態度怎麼樣？你想原因
    (yuányīn: reason) 是什麼？

5) 安然對當選 "三好生" 有什麼反應？

韦老师：(continues counting) 十二、十三、十四、十五、十六、十七、十八、十九、二十、二一、二二、二三、二四，……大家把手放下。全班四十七人，一共二十四票，好，<u>超过半数</u>，安然当选。 (Class applauds.)

Teacher Wei writes "24" under An Ran's name on the board.

Scene 52 ——————————

On the way home, the above scene replays in Ran's mind.

安然： (voices in her mind) "一、二、三、四、五、六、七、八、九、十、十一，……张晓英，你是举手了吧？"

"我这就举手。"

"哈哈哈哈。"

"十二、十三、十四、十五、十六、十七、十八、十九、二十、二一、二二、二三、二四，全班四十七人，一共二十四票，好，超过半数，安然当选。" (applause.)

讨论问题：

1) 安然和刘冬虎的关系有了什么变化 (biànhuà: change, transformation)？

2) 韦老师去安静的编辑室做什么？为什么她和安静说了那么些话？

3) 你觉得同学们都喜欢祝文娟吗？为什么那么多同学投她的票 (tóu...piào: to vote)？

4) 韦老师对安然的评价公平 (gōngpíng: fair) 吗？她这次对安然的态度怎么样？你想原因 (yuányīn: reason) 是什么？

5) 安然对当选"三好生"有什么反应？

Scene 53 ————————————

Ran approaches the store where Mi Xiaoling works, but turns around at the door, takes off her school bag, and walks up to a vendor with it.

安然： <u>大嬸兒</u>，您幫我看一下書包，我馬上就來。

女<u>攤販</u>：嗯，好。

安然： 謝謝。（turns and goes into the store.）

Inside the store.

米曉玲：（to a customer）一共三塊六毛五。

女顧客：欸。

米曉玲：您拿好了。

女顧客：再見啊。

米曉玲：再見。

男顧客甲：謝謝。

米曉玲：（to another customer）您要點兒什麼？

男顧客乙：我們想買點兒點心。

米曉玲：哦，您<u>牙口</u>不好，就買點兒<u>鬆軟</u>的點心吧。這種<u>蛋糕</u>就不錯，最<u>適合</u>老年人吃了。價
　　　　錢也便宜。

男顧客乙：那好，那就要兩<u>斤</u>吧。

米曉玲：欸。

While waiting for Xiaoling to have a free moment, Ran looks at the "opinion book" hanging on the wall, and finds some very complimentary comments by customers about Xiaoling.

——

1.	嬸兒	婶儿	shěnr	"auntie"
2.	攤販	摊贩	tānfàn	stall vendor
^3.	牙口	牙口	yákǒu	the condition of a person's teeth (usually elderly)

S E G M E N T   XI

Scene 53 ————————————

Ran approaches the store where Mi Xiaoling works, but turns around at the door,
takes off her school bag, and walks up to a vendor with it.

安然： 大婶儿，您帮我看一下书包，我马上就来。

女摊贩：嗯，好。

安然： 谢谢。 (turns and goes into the store.)

Inside the store.

米晓玲：(to a customer) 一共三块六毛五。

女顾客：欸。

米晓玲：您拿好了。

女顾客：再见啊。

米晓玲：再见。

男顾客甲：谢谢。

米晓玲：(to another customer) 您要点儿什么？

男顾客乙：我们想买点儿点心。

米晓玲：哦，您牙口不好，就买点儿松软的点心吧。这种蛋糕就不错，最适合老年人吃了。价
        钱也便宜。

男顾客乙：那好，那就要两斤吧。

米晓玲：欸。

While waiting for Xiaoling to have a free moment, Ran looks at the "opinion book"
hanging on the wall, and finds some very complimentary comments by customers about
Xiaoling.

——

^4.	鬆軟	松软	sōngruǎn	spongy and soft
^5.	蛋糕	蛋糕	dàn'gāo	cake
*6.	適合	适合	shìhé	suitable
^7.	斤	斤	jīn	a measure of weight a little over a pound

米曉玲：安然。你什麼時候來的？ (Ran goes to the counter.)　我這兩天可真想你啊。考完了？

安然：　嗯。你幹得不錯，這上頭儘是<u>表揚</u>你的。

米曉玲：咳，我不能跟你比呀，<u>未來</u>的大學生。不過，人嘛，總是要個好，跟你一樣，不會<u>溜鬚拍馬</u>。咱姐們兒，全得<u>靠</u>自己努力。咱姐們兒。<u>哎喲</u>，呵呵。我又說咱姐們兒了。 (puzzled at Ran's sullenness) 你怎麼了？你怎麼了？

安然：　你還記得嗎？

Scene 54 ————————————

A flashback:　At a rite of passage, a band plays rousing music as Ran and her fellow students with "red kerchiefs" remove their kerchiefs.

女老師：現在，你們<u>超齡退隊</u>了。這意味着你們長大了，進入了人生中一個新的<u>時期</u>，希望你們快快<u>成長</u>，<u>早日成長</u>為一名<u>優秀</u>的青年。最重要的，是要誠實，要<u>正直</u>。為<u>理想</u>去<u>奮鬥</u>，是件不容易的事情。有時候會<u>遇到挫折</u>，有時候會遇到<u>意想不到</u>的<u>困難</u>，……

Scene 55 ————————————

Ran is working at her desk.　Father, uncharacteristically dressed up, sits lovingly by her.

安然：　爸，您坐在這兒看我幹嘛？

爸爸：　嘿嘿嘿。

*8. 表揚	表扬	biǎoyáng	to commend, praise
*9. 未來	未来	wèilái	future, approaching
10. 溜鬚拍馬	溜须拍马	liū xū pāi mǎ	(colloquial) to fawn on, toady to, shamelessly flatter
*11. 靠	靠	kào	to rely on, lean on
12. 哎喲	哎哟	āiyō	an expletive
^13. 超齡	超龄	chāolíng	to exceed the age limit; overage
^14. 退隊	退队	tuìduì	to withdraw or retire from the ranks
*15. 時期	时期	shíqī	era, period
*16. 成長	成长	chéngzhǎng	to mature

米晓玲：安然。你什么时候来的？ (Ran goes to the counter.)　我这两天可真想你啊。考完了？

安然：　　姆。你干得不错，这上头尽是<u>表扬</u>你的。

米晓玲：咳，我不能跟你比呀，<u>未来</u>的大学生。不过，人嘛，总是要个好，跟你一样，不会<u>溜须拍马</u>。咱姐们儿，全得<u>靠</u>自己努力。咱姐们儿。<u>哎哟</u>，呵呵。我又说咱姐们儿了。 (puzzled at Ran's sullenness) 你怎么了？　你怎么了？

安然：　　你还记得吗？

Scene 54 ─────────────

A flashback: At a rite of passage, a band plays rousing music as Ran and her fellow students with "red kerchiefs" remove their kerchiefs.

女老师：现在，你们<u>超龄退队</u>了。这意味着你们长大了，进入了人生中一个新的<u>时期</u>，希望你们快快<u>成长</u>，<u>早日</u>成长为一名<u>优秀</u>的青年。最重要的，是要诚实，要<u>正直</u>。为<u>理想</u>去<u>奋斗</u>，是件不容易的事情。有时候会<u>遇到挫折</u>，有时候会遇到<u>意想不到</u>的<u>困难</u>，……

Scene 55 ─────────────

Ran is working at her desk. Father, uncharacteristically dressed up, sits lovingly by her.

安然：　　爸，您坐在这儿看我干嘛？

爸爸：　　嘿嘿嘿。

*17. 早日	早日	zǎorì	at an early date, soon
*18. 優秀	优秀	yōuxiù	splendid, fine, outstanding, excellent
^19. 正直	正直	zhèngzhí	upright, forthright
*20. 理想	理想	lǐxiǎng	ideal
*21. 奮鬥	奋斗	fèndòu	to strive, struggle
*22. 遇到	遇到	yùdào	to encounter
^23. 挫折	挫折	cuòzhé	setback
*24. 意想不到	意想不到	yìxiǎng budào	unexpected
*25. 困難	困难	kùnnan	difficulty

媽媽：　(calls from the kitchen for Jing, who just came home.) 小靜，回來啦？快，正
　　　　好，幫我做菜。咱們家今天是<u>雙喜臨門</u>，你妹妹評上三好生啦，你爸爸的畫被選到北
　　　　京去了。

安靜：　真的？

媽媽：　啊。

Overhearing all this, Ran puts her arms on Father's shoulders.

安然：　爸爸，<u>怪不得</u>您這麼高興。

爸爸：　呵呵，欸，跟你一樣，三好生。

安然：　(ruefully) 我跟您可不一樣。

爸爸：　怎麼，你不高興？

安然：　不知道。我也說不好。

安然：　爸，您等今天，等了好<u>久</u>了吧？十年？

爸爸：　一生！孩子。(Jing walks in.) 欸，來。(taking off his jacket and rolling
　　　　up his sleeves, to himself) 幫着媽媽做事。我要做咱們家的三好生。嘿嘿。

安靜：　<u>祝賀</u>你，爸爸。

爸爸：　哈哈。

安靜：　呵呵呵。

爸爸：　呵呵呵。(goes to the kitchen.)

安靜：　小然然，也祝賀你。(kisses Ran) 呵呵，我給你洗幾個蘋果去，啊？

After Jing runs off, Ran looks at a stack of proofs in Jing's bag, and finds the
poem by Teacher Wei.

安然：　(yelling) 姐姐，安靜！

Jing, Father, and Mother come out of the kitchen to face a fuming Ran.

安靜：　怎麼了？

| 26. | 雙喜 | 双喜 | shuāngxǐ | double happiness |
| 27. | 臨門 | 临门 | línmén | "to arrive at the gate," i.e., to descend upon a household (雙喜臨門 is a four-character idiom) |

妈妈： (calls from the kitchen for Jing, who just came home.) 小静，回来啦？快，正
好，帮我做菜。咱们家今天是双喜临门，你妹妹评上三好生啦，你爸爸的画被选到北
京去了。

安静： 真的？

妈妈： 啊。

Overhearing all this, Ran puts her arms on Father's shoulders.

安然： 爸爸，怪不得您这么高兴。

爸爸： 呵呵，欸，跟你一样，三好生。

安然： (ruefully) 我跟您可不一样。

爸爸： 怎么，你不高兴？

安然： 不知道。我也说不好。

安然： 爸，您等今天，等了好久了吧？十年？

爸爸： 一生！孩子。(Jing walks in.) 欸，来。(taking off his jacket and rolling
up his sleeves, to himself) 帮着妈妈做事。我要做咱们家的三好生。嘿嘿。

安静： 祝贺你，爸爸。

爸爸： 哈哈。

安静： 呵呵呵。

爸爸： 呵呵呵。(goes to the kitchen.)

安静： 小然然，也祝贺你。(kisses Ran) 呵呵，我给你洗几个苹果去，啊？

After Jing runs off, Ran looks at a stack of proofs in Jing's bag, and finds the
poem by Teacher Wei.

安然： (yelling) 姐姐，安静！

Jing, Father, and Mother come out of the kitchen to face a fuming Ran.

安静： 怎么了？

---

*28.	怪不得	怪不得	guàibudé	(MA) no wonder
*29.	久	久	jiǔ	long time
^30.	祝贺	祝贺	zhùhè	to congratulate

安然：　這是怎麼回事兒？看看這是什麼詩！什麼"駕着時代的火箭，我在遙望"，作者韋婉。多響亮的名字。你這個大編輯，是怎麼發現這個大詩人的！

安靜：　然然，你不懂這是怎麼回事。

安然：　我懂。我不是小孩兒了。我什麼都懂。現在我明白了，為什麼韋老師動員大家選我。這種恩賜，就是從這兒來的。 (throws down the proofs and weeps.)

媽媽：　然然，你別想得太多，評上三好是你自己的努力呀。

安然：　(sobbing) 不對，我評三好，不是為了你們高興、你們滿意。我渴望得到一種理解和信任，可是我今天沒得到，什麼也沒得到。你們知道嗎？ (runs out of the apartment.)

媽媽：　這個家呀，沒個安寧。 (returns to the kitchen.)

爸爸：　小靜啊，你怎麼也學會這個？

Scene 56 —————————————

Ran is crying in the stairway outside the Ans' apartment. Liu Donghu walks up to her.

劉冬虎：安然，你怎麼了？今天選三好，我舉你的手了。 (hands Ran some melon seeds) 喏，你吃點兒瓜子兒吧。安然，我正要告訴你一件事兒。你知道嗎？我爸…和我媽分開過了，法院…… 把我判給我媽了。

安然：　那你……

劉冬虎：我就要搬到姥姥家去住，下星期轉學了。

安然：　那你常到你爸爸這邊兒來玩兒吧。

劉冬虎：安然，你怎麼了？

安然：　你搬走那天我去送你。

劉冬虎：不用了。 (leaves.)

31.	駕	驾	jià	to drive (a vehicle)
^32.	響亮	响亮	xiǎngliàng	loud and clear, resounding
^33.	動員	动员	dòngyuán	to mobilize (people)
34.	恩賜	恩赐	ēncì	favor, charity; to bestow favor or charity
*35.	滿意	满意	mǎnyì	satisfied
^36.	渴望	渴望	kěwàng	to yearn for
*37.	信任	信任	xìnrèn	to trust; trust, confidence

安然：　这是怎么回事儿？看看这是什么诗！什么"<u>驾着</u>时代的火箭，我在<u>遥望</u>"，作者韦婉。
　　　　多<u>响亮</u>的名字。你这个大编辑，是怎么发现这个大诗人的！

安静：　然然，你不懂这是怎么回事。

安然：　我懂。我不是小孩儿了。我什么都懂。现在我明白了，为什么韦老师<u>动员</u>大家选我。
　　　　这种<u>恩赐</u>，就是从这儿来的。 (throws down the proofs and weeps.)

妈妈：　然然，你别想得太多，评上三好是你自己的努力呀。

安然：　(sobbing) 不对，我评三好，不是为了你们高兴、你们<u>满意</u>。我<u>渴望</u>得到一种理解和
　　　　<u>信任</u>，可是我今天没得到，什么也没得到。你们知道吗？ (runs out of the
　　　　apartment.)

妈妈：　这个家呀，没个<u>安宁</u>。 (returns to the kitchen.)

爸爸：　小静啊，你怎么也学会这个？

Scene 56 ————————————

Ran is crying in the stairway outside the Ans' apartment. Liu Donghu walks up to
her.

刘冬虎：安然，你怎么了？今天选三好，我举你的手了。 (hands Ran some melon seeds) 喏，
　　　　你吃点儿瓜子儿吧。安然，我正要告诉你一件事儿。你知道吗？我爸…和我妈分开过
　　　　了，<u>法院</u>…… 把我<u>判</u>给我妈了。

安然：　那你……

刘冬虎：我就要<u>搬</u>到<u>姥姥</u>家去住，下星期<u>转学</u>了。

安然：　那你常到你爸爸这边儿来玩儿吧。

刘冬虎：安然，你怎么了？

安然：　你搬走那天我去送你。

刘冬虎：不用了。 (leaves.)

^38. 安宁	安宁	ānníng	peace, tranquillity
*39. 法院	法院	fǎyuàn	court
^40. 判	判	pàn	to adjudicate
*41. 搬	搬	bān	to move
42. 姥姥	姥姥	lǎolao	(colloquial) maternal grandmother
^43. 轉學	转学	zhuǎnxué	to transfer schools

Scene 57 ─────────────────

Later, in her room, Jing reads a letter, then frantically packs.

安靜： 哎喲，爸，媽。 (Jing runs to her parents in the living room. Ran is also
there, eating.) 我得<u>趕緊</u>出去一下。我得去買票，還要去火車站。我，我得趕緊去
<u>請假</u>。

爸爸： 欸，小靜，你別着急。他信上說什麼？

安靜： 他信上說，遇到了困難，我得趕緊去幫幫他。

爸爸： 什麼困難？

媽媽： 你慢慢兒說。

安靜： 他…他…他的孩子病了。

媽媽： 你說什麼？什麼孩子？誰的孩子？

安靜： 他的孩子。他和他<u>妻子</u>的孩子。

爸爸： 他妻子？那不…是個女的嗎？

安靜： 死了。

媽媽： 孩子多大？

安靜： 四歲。

Father reaches for something and accidentally drops it. Jing rushes to pick it up,
but is stopped by Father's harsh scolding.

爸爸： 你別管，我有手。

Jing shrinks back.

爸爸： 安靜，你！小靜！

安靜： 爸爸，這個情況，我本來應該早告訴你們的。可是現在，……等我回來再說不行嗎？

爸爸： 我要你把東西放下，放下！ (stomps off.)

Though remaining silent, Ran has observed all this and is apprehensive.

---

^44. 趕緊	赶紧	gǎnjǐn	to hurry
^45. 請假	请假	qǐngjià	to request a leave of absence
*46. 妻子	妻子	qīzi	wife

Scene 57 ——————————————————

Later, in her room, Jing reads a letter, then frantically packs.

安静：　哎哟，爸，妈。（Jing runs to her parents in the living room. Ran is also there, eating.）我得赶紧出去一下。我得去买票，还要去火车站。我，我得赶紧去请假。

爸爸：　欸，小静，你别着急。他信上说什么？

安静：　他信上说，遇到了困难，我得赶紧去帮帮他。

爸爸：　什么困难？

妈妈：　你慢慢儿说。

安静：　他…他…他的孩子病了。

妈妈：　你说什么？什么孩子？谁的孩子？

安静：　他的孩子。他和他妻子的孩子。

爸爸：　他妻子？那不…是个女的吗？

安静：　死了。

妈妈：　孩子多大？

安静：　四岁。

Father reaches for something and accidentally drops it. Jing rushes to pick it up, but is stopped by Father's harsh scolding.

爸爸：　你别管，我有手。

Jing shrinks back.

爸爸：　安静，你！小静！

安静：　爸爸，这个情况，我本来应该早告诉你们的。可是现在，……等我回来再说不行吗？

爸爸：　我要你把东西放下，放下！（stomps off.）

Though remaining silent, Ran has observed all this and is apprehensive.

——

討論問題：

1) 為什麼安然把書包放在大嬸兒那兒了？

2) 米曉玲在點心店工作的情況說明了什麼？為什麼電影中插入 (chārù: to insert) 了他們退隊的那一幕？

3) 爸爸為什麼看着安然？為什麼大家都高興而安然好像不太高興呢？

4) 安然為什麼忽然 (hūrán: suddenly) 大發脾氣 (fā píqi: to vent one's temper)？一家人對這事有什麼看法？

5) 劉冬虎告訴安然什麼事？安然有什麼反應 (fǎnyìng: reaction)？劉冬虎兩次問她"你怎麼了？"，她為什麼沒回答？

6) 爸爸、媽媽發現安靜的什麼事？是怎麼發現的？他們的反應怎麼樣？跟第六段中怎麼不同？

讨论问题：

1) 为什么安然把书包放在大姊儿那儿了？

2) 米晓玲在点心店工作的情况说明了什么？为什么电影中插入 (chārù: to insert) 了他们退队的那一幕？

3) 爸爸为什么看着安然？为什么大家都高兴而安然好象不太高兴呢？

4) 安然为什么忽然 (hūrán: suddenly) 大发脾气 (fā píqi: to vent one's temper)？一家人对这事有什么看法？

5) 刘冬虎告诉安然什么事？安然有什么反应 (fǎnyìng: reaction)？刘冬虎两次问她"你怎么了？"，她为什么没回答？

6) 爸爸、妈妈发现安静的什么事？是怎么发现的？他们的反应怎么样？跟第六段中怎么不同？

SEGMENT XII

Scene 58 ─────────────

Sobbing, Jing goes out in the night to be alone. Ran trails her. Later, as Jing walks up the stairs on her way home, she hears someone below.

安靜：　誰？誰呀？
安然：　我。
安靜：　這麼晚了，上哪兒去啦？
安然：　我到同學家問件事兒。

Scene 59 ─────────────

Ran's whole class is doing a big cleanup of their classroom. Wang Hongwei plays pingpong as Ran approaches carrying a basin of water.

安然：　王紅衞，別打了。老不<u>幹活兒</u>。

Ran takes the basin to a window, which Zhu Wenjuan is already wiping.

祝文娟：安然，我想和你談談。
安然：　談什麼？
祝文娟：我有很多<u>缺點</u>。
安然：　你指什麼？
祝文娟：我有時候<u>膽兒小</u>，<u>過份愛面子</u>，……
安然：　祝文娟，我<u>一直</u>想問你，你對我作文裡提的那件事怎麼看？我最近也在考慮一個問題，不是每件事兒都應該寫進作文裡的。

ˆ1. 幹活兒	干活儿	gànhuór	(colloquial) 工作，做事
*2. 缺點	缺点	quēdiǎn	shortcoming
ˆ3. 膽小	胆小	dǎnxiǎo	timid, cowardly
*4. 過份	过分	guòfèn	excessive; excessively

SEGMENT XII

Scene 58 ————————————

Sobbing, Jing goes out in the night to be alone. Ran trails her. Later, as Jing walks up the stairs on her way home, she hears someone below.

安静： 谁？谁呀？
安然： 我。
安静： 这么晚了，上哪儿去啦？
安然： 我到同学家问件事儿。

Scene 59 ————————————

Ran's whole class is doing a big cleanup of their classroom. Wang Hongwei plays pingpong as Ran approaches carrying a basin of water.

安然： 王红卫，别打了。老不<u>干活儿</u>。

Ran takes the basin to a window, which Zhu Wenjuan is already wiping.

祝文娟：安然，我想和你谈谈。
安然： 谈什么？
祝文娟：我有很多<u>缺点</u>。
安然： 你指什么？
祝文娟：我有时候<u>胆儿小</u>，<u>过分爱面子</u>，……
安然： 祝文娟，我<u>一直</u>想问你，你对我作文里提的那件事怎么看？我最近也在<u>考虑</u>一个问题，不是每件事儿都应该写进作文里的。

---

*5. 面子	面子	miànzi	"face," reputation, prestige
*6. 一直	一直	yìzhí	all along
*7. 考慮	考虑	kǎolù	to consider

In the front of the classroom, a boy is pointing to the blackboard with the names of those elected 三好生。

男生甲：欸，同學們，請看光榮榜了啊。

Ran goes to the board and adds "明年再爭取" next to her name.

男生乙：(tossing a rag) 欸，接着。
男生丙：欸，欸，欸。看那黑板嘞。

Furor breaks out as everyone turns to look at the board.

男生甲：欸欸欸欸，諸位，諸位，這可是咱們頭號新聞啊。不受名利的誘惑。
男生丁：這可真是咱們班的大能人啊。
某女生：(gesturing to 男生丁 to get his feet off a table) 嘿，下來，下來。人家剛擦的。
祝文娟：別鬧了，快點兒幹活吧，好早點兒回家。

Scene 60 ─────────────

In the teachers' office.

韋老師：怎麼，你覺得你不夠嗎？
安然：　不，我認為我夠。這學期我一直是按照自己理解的三好條件做的。
韋老師：那你為什麼還要這樣做？這是大家給你的榮譽啊。
安然：　韋老師，您認為大家真的願意給我這個榮譽嗎？
韋老師：那當然，你的選票超過了半數。
安然：　那是因為，您動員了大家。其實，您並不喜歡我。

---

^8. 光榮榜	光荣榜	guāngróng-bǎng	honor roll
*9. 黑板	黑板	hēibǎn	blackboard
^10. 諸位	诸位	zhūwèi	(honorific) everyone; you all
^11. 頭號新聞	头号新闻	tóuhào xīnwén	headline news
^12. 名利	名利	mínglì	fame and gain
^13. 誘惑	诱惑	yòuhuò	enticement, temptation; to entice, tempt

In the front of the classroom, a boy is pointing to the blackboard with the names
of those elected 三好生。

男生甲：欸，同学们，请看光荣榜了啊。

Ran goes to the board and adds "明年再争取" next to her name.

男生乙：(tossing a rag) 欸，接着。
男生丙：欸，欸，欸。看那黑板嘞。

Furor breaks out as everyone turns to look at the board.

男生甲：欸欸欸欸，诸位，诸位，这可是咱们头号新闻啊。不受名利的诱惑。
男生丁：这可真是咱们班的大能人啊。
某女生：(gesturing to 男生丁 to get his feet off a table) 嘿，下来，下来。人家刚擦
　　　　的。
祝文娟：别闹了，快点儿干活吧，好早点儿回家。

Scene 60 ─────────────────

In the teachers' office.

韦老师：怎么，你觉得你不够吗？
安然：　不，我认为我够。这学期我一直是按照自己理解的三好条件做的。
韦老师：那你为什么还要这样做？这是大家给你的荣誉啊。
安然：　韦老师，您认为大家真的愿意给我这个荣誉吗？
韦老师：那当然，你的选票超过了半数。
安然：　那是因为，您动员了大家。其实，您并不喜欢我。

*14. 擦	擦	cā	to wipe, mop
*15. 鬧	闹	nào	to make a ruckus
*16. 按照	按照	ànzhào	according to
^17. 榮譽	荣誉	róngyù	honor, credit, glory
^18. 選票	选票	xuǎnpiào	vote

韋老師：呵，你想得太多了。安然，你<u>一向</u>是很<u>單純</u>的，可不能把事情想得太複雜了，啊？回
　　　　去吧。

安然：　不是我想的，是我用自己的眼睛發現的。

韋老師：你先回去吧。　(Ran leaves.)

男教員：<u>後生可畏</u>啊。

女教員：她叫安然吧，我教過她，上課最愛提問題了。

韋老師：呵，<u>個性</u>太強了。

Scene 61 ─────────────

Having cleared the air about the 三好生 election, Ran is relieved and back to her
normal jolly self. Coming home, she runs into a little girl in the stairway.

小朋友：安然姐姐，還你書。

安然：　看完了？

小朋友：看完了。安徒生童話真好看。

安然：　你喜歡，我再借你幾本兒，都是他寫的。

小朋友：那好吧。欸，安然姐姐，他姓安，你也姓安，他是你的<u>親戚</u>吧。

安然：　啊，哈哈哈。他是外國人，已經死了好久了。

小朋友：唉，真可惜。人為什麼要死呢？

安然：　你長大就知道了。

小朋友：嗯，嗯。

Scene 62 ─────────────

Mother, Father, and Jing are sitting in the dark in the girls' room. Ran enters
and turns on a light.

爸爸：　(pointing to a train ticket for Jing) 這是車票，放這兒了。你這次到他那兒去，
　　　　就是先去一<u>趟</u>，你自己要<u>冷靜</u>。(Mother gets up and leaves.) 我們的話還沒談完
　　　　呢！(Father walks out.)

---

*19.	一向	一向	yíxiàng	all along, consistently in the past
^20.	單純	单纯	dānchún	simple, pure, innocent
21.	後生可畏	后生可畏	hòushēng kěwèi	"a youth is to be regarded with respect or awe"

韦老师：呵，你想得太多了。安然，你一向是很单纯的，可不能把事情想得太复杂了，啊？回
　　　　去吧。

安然：　不是我想的，是我用自己的眼睛发现的。

韦老师：你先回去吧。（Ran leaves.）

男教员：后生可畏啊。

女教员：她叫安然吧，我教过她，上课最爱提问题了。

韦老师：呵，个性太强了。

Scene 61 ——————————————

Having cleared the air about the 三好生 election, Ran is relieved and back to her
normal jolly self. Coming home, she runs into a little girl in the stairway.

小朋友：安然姐姐，还你书。

安然：　看完了？

小朋友：看完了。安徒生童话真好看。

安然：　你喜欢，我再借你几本儿，都是他写的。

小朋友：那好吧。欸，安然姐姐，他姓安，你也姓安，他是你的亲戚吧。

安然：　啊，哈哈哈。他是外国人，已经死了好久了。

小朋友：唉，真可惜。人为什么要死呢？

安然：　你长大就知道了。

小朋友：嗯，嗯。

Scene 62 ——————————————

Mother, Father, and Jing are sitting in the dark in the girls' room. Ran enters
and turns on a light.

爸爸：　（pointing to a train ticket for Jing）这是车票，放这儿了。你这次到他那儿去，
　　　　就是先去一趟，你自己要冷静。（Mother gets up and leaves.）我们的话还没谈完
　　　　呢！（Father walks out.）

---

*22. 個性	个性	gèxìng	character, individuality, personality
*23. 親戚	亲戚	qīnqi	relative
^24. 趟	趟	tàng	M for trips
*25. 冷静	冷静	lěngjìng	cool-headed, level-headed, sober-minded

The two sisters sit sullenly on their own beds, across from each other. After a long silence...

安靜：　然然，你還生我的氣嗎？你看，爸爸不理解我，我也不理解你。

安然：　姐，你説我長大了嗎？

安靜：　當然，十五歲以上就是青年。

安然：　那你以前有事兒爲什麼瞞着我？不夠朋友。

安靜：　瞞你？

安然：　秦皇島三二三二信箱。姐，什麼時候走？

安靜：　明天。

安然：　決定了？

安靜：　決定了。

安然：　姐，明天我去送你。 (Jing sobs. Ran sits down next to her.) 姐，你別哭了，一切會好的，真的，會好的。就是再也沒人給我洗頭髮了。 (They sob in each others' arms.) 姐姐！

Meanwhile, in the parents' room, Mother looks longingly at a photo of her two daughters.

媽媽：　唉！

Father pats Mother's hand to comfort her.

Scene 63 ─────────────────

Next morning, the two sisters walk toward the train station. The film ends with its theme song:

　　　我們踏出了原野的小路，嗚……
　　　看見小樹上有許多新芽吐出，嗚……
　　　雖然是忽忽、忽忽而過，

───

^26. 瞞　　　　瞞　　　mán　　　　to conceal the truth from (someone)
^27. 不夠朋友　不够朋友　búgòu péngyou　not enough of a true friend

The two sisters sit sullenly on their own beds, across from each other. After a long silence...

安静： 然然，你还生我的气吗？你看，爸爸不理解我，我也不理解你。

安然： 姐，你说我长大了吗？

安静： 当然，十五岁以上就是青年。

安然： 那你以前有事儿为什么瞒着我？不够朋友。

安静： 瞒你？

安然： 秦皇岛三二三二信箱。姐，什么时候走？

安静： 明天。

安然： 决定了？

安静： 决定了。

安然： 姐，明天我去送你。(Jing sobs. Ran sits down next to her.) 姐，你别哭了，一切会好的，真的，会好的。就是再也没人给我洗头发了。(They sob in each others' arms.) 姐姐！

Meanwhile, in the parents' room, Mother looks longingly at a photo of her two daughters.

妈妈： 唉！

Father pats Mother's hand to comfort her.

Scene 63 ——————————

Next morning, the two sisters walk toward the train station. The film ends with its theme song:

> 我们踏出了原野的小路，呜……
> 看见小树上有许多新芽吐出，呜……
> 虽然是匆匆、匆匆而过，

---

*28. 决定　　决定　　juédìng　　to decide, determine
*29. 一切　　一切　　yíqiè　　everything

卻總也回頭，再看看每棵小樹。

一個新芽就是一個夢呀。

一個新芽就是一顆閃光的珍珠。

我們常常到海灘上漫步，嗚……

看見海上奔騰的波峰浪谷，嗚……

雖然是漫步、漫步而過，

卻總願唱着、唱着向大海祝福，

一聲祝願就是一個夢呀，

一聲祝願就是一顆閃光的珍珠。

我們剛踏入人生的旅途，嗚……

常擔憂，純真的心會感到孤獨，嗚……

雖然是路途、路途遙遙，

卻總會有朋友、有朋友和我會晤。

一個童心就是一個夢呀，

一個童心就是一顆閃光的珍珠。

--完--

討論問題：

1) 安然為什麼要看着安靜而不讓她知道呢？這表現出她們姐妹的關係怎麼樣？

2) 安然和祝文娟的對話說明了什麼？你想，她們能成為朋友嗎？

3) 為什麼那個男生把安然做的那件事叫做"頭號新聞"？ 同學們對這件事有什麼不同的反應？

4) 安然覺得她應該選上"三好生"嗎？她為什麼要把她的名字劃掉 (huàdiào: to strike out)？

5) 老師們對安然的行為 (xíngwéi: behavior) 有什麼反應？為什麼那位男教員說"後生可畏啊"？

6) 哪兒出現 (chūxiàn: to appear) 過"安徒生童話"，"你長大就知道了"， 和"秦皇島三二三二信箱"？ 這些話為什麼在第六十一、二幕又出現了呢？

7) 爸爸對安靜去看她男朋友的態度有了什麼變化？

8) 安靜、安然倆坐着，怎麼好像又生氣又難過？最後她們的關係有了什麼變化？

9) 媽媽為什麼最後"哎"了一聲？這一個情景 (qíngjǐng: scenario) 表現出什麼？

10) 以 (yǐ: by, with) 那首歌結束 (jiéshù: to conclude) 這部電影起了什麼作用？那首歌上次出現的時候又起了什麼作用？

11) 聽着這首歌，看着安然和安靜漸漸 (jiànjian: gradually) 遠去，你想到些什麼呢？

却总也回头，再看看每棵小树。

一个新芽就是一个梦呀。

一个新芽就是一颗闪光的珍珠。

我们常常到海滩上漫步，呜……

看见海上奔腾的波峰浪谷，呜……

虽然是漫步、漫步而过，

却总愿唱着、唱着向大海祝福，

一声祝愿就是一个梦呀，

一声祝愿就是一颗闪光的珍珠。

我们刚踏入人生的旅途，呜……

常担忧，纯真的心会感到孤独，呜……

虽然是路途、路途遥遥，

却总会有朋友、有朋友和我会晤。

一个童心就是一个梦呀，

一个童心就是一颗闪光的珍珠。

--完--

_____

讨论问题：

1) 安然为什么要看着安静而不让她知道呢？这表现出她们姐妹的关系怎么样？

2) 安然和祝文娟的对话说明了什么？你想，她们能成为朋友吗？

3) 为什么那个男生把安然做的那件事叫做"头号新闻"？ 同学们对这件事有什么不同的反应？

4) 安然觉得她应该选上"三好生"吗？她为什么要把她的名字划掉 (huàdiào: to strike out)？

5) 老师们对安然的行为 (xíngwéi: behavior) 有什么反应？为什么那位男教员说"后生可畏啊"？

6) 哪儿出现 (chūxiàn: to appear) 过"安徒生童话"，"你长大就知道了"， 和"秦皇岛三二三二信箱"？ 这些话为什么在第六十一、二幕又出现了呢？

7) 爸爸对安静去看她男朋友的态度有了什么变化？

8) 安静、安然俩坐着，怎么好象又生气又难过？最后她们的关系有了什么变化？

9) 妈妈为什么最后"哎"了一声？这一个情景 (qíngjǐng: scenario) 表现出什么？

10) 以 (yǐ: by, with) 那首歌结束 (jiéshù: to conclude) 这部电影起了什么作用？那首歌上次出现的时候又起了什么作用？

11) 听着这首歌，看着安然和安静渐渐 (jiànjiàn: gradually) 远去，你想到些什么呢？

PRIORITY VOCABULARY IN COMPLEX FORM

Codes used in annotations: * top priority vocabulary
^ secondary priority vocabulary

Title:

Top Priority Vocabulary:

少女　　　襯衫　　　人物

Secondary Priority Vocabulary:

原著　　　紐扣　　　導演　　　編輯

Segment I:

Top Priority Vocabulary:

追	餓死	風	吹	頭髮	變	農民
人家	扔	可憐	換	輔導	緊	禮貌
歷史	結婚	比方	夫妻	咱們	愛情	實在
記錄	沒事兒	害怕	進行	總	複習	眼睛
印象	了解					

Secondary Priority Vocabulary:

哦	螞蟻	呀	雪花	飄	啊	甲
乙	欸	好意思	精彩	木刻	熊貓	指
怪	女士	防	塗	怎麼	抓	挺
古文	套	吵嘴	意味	老	身上	幹嘛
玩意兒	肚子	沉悶	怎麼了	期末	思考	憤怒
流淚	憂慮	評	稀罕			

Segment II:

Top Priority Vocabulary:

讀	按	進入	之	認真	必須	態度
精力	管	不舒服	丟掉	專業	被	檢查
儘	照顧	優點	紀念	發現	物理	作業
許	準	畢業	下鄉	教育		

143

Secondary Priority Vocabulary:

查	翻	班	大能人	順便	高一	難度
更加	講解	端正	謙虛	謹慎	家訪	欺負
幹	過剩	哪兒	滋味	賞識	倒霉	洗頭
抽煙	偷着	伺候	關鍵	嘛	爭取	郵票
週年	哎呀	本兒	參考	這麼回事	部隊	部門

Segment III:

Top Priority Vocabulary:

其實	聰明	成人	關係	反正	語文	作者
同志	早就	翻譯	勸	積極	政治	條件
到底	世界	感覺	準確	民族		

Secondary Priority Vocabulary:

專門	形容	羣眾	成績	不便	重複	還有
接觸	接着	朴素	打扮	扣子	跡象	引起
作為	協助	篇	稿子	瞎	上	業餘
髒	順手	看待	地地道道	校友	聚會	家
辦事員	創造	眾	童話	完蛋	太陽	詩
清醒	場合	反射	宇宙	旗	甩開	

Segment IV:

Top Priority Vocabulary:

收	贏	講課	褲子	議論	美滿	看法
一天到晚	良心	抱	躲	外語	提	理解
藍	說不定	嘴	發音	請教	可不	

Secondary Priority Vocabulary:

棒	搗亂	傻	當成	美術家	背後	虐待
幹校	煩惱	雲	熱愛	祖國	於	遺傳
基因	起作用	咳嗽	牛	舌頭	別扭	叫住
向	耐心	硬	虛心	光	打架	理
廢話						

Segment V:

Top Priority Vocabulary:

時代	選	強	苦	存在	戴	丈夫
技術	假	受	影響	票	科學	力量
作文	評價	完整	團結	未必	認為	誠實

Secondary Priority Vocabulary:

跳動	樹林	說明性	糖	拔	聲明	嗯
追求	一輩子	狗	給予	名言	眼鏡	灌輸
自個兒	吃虧	遍	秘密	寶貝	鎖	激情
謊	偏要	演	主角	殺	由	生
正派	跳水	腿	領教	千真萬確	傢伙	不要臉
多情	正經	看一眼	滑稽	亂七八糟	省得	流氓
時刻	打抱不平	確實	跟…好	短篇	人類	禮物
真理	辭海	熟悉	精確	概括	顯然	班長
尊敬	文具					

Segment VI:

Top Priority Vocabulary:

老實	倒	連	反映	人情	搞	米
經濟	手續	難得	卻	夢	無數	人生
孤獨						

Secondary Priority Vocabulary:

憑	陣兒	慶賀	評選	放肆	諷刺	遷就
世故	心眼兒	採訪	形象	茶葉	教務處	停學
退學	接班兒	踏	吐	忽忽	棵	閃光
神秘	海灘	祝福	旅途	擔憂	純真	會晤

Segment VII:

Top Priority Vocabulary:

分開	難過	批評	用不着	表示	青年	心情
友誼	活	道理	可惜	平均	關心	完成
過程	收獲	旅遊	不如	當年		

Secondary Priority Vocabulary:

沒必要	方式	友好	萬歲	花樣	見不着面兒	透
扯	輕信	成績單兒	瓜	老頭兒	算帳	討厭
植物	地球	太空	航行	不起眼	粒	博士
容量	面積	丫頭				

Segment VIII:

Top Priority Vocabulary:

上班	豐富	到時候	廚房	新鮮	獻給	深厚
並	後悔	當初	怪	保證	如何	明確
留	當	滿	舉			

Secondary Priority Vocabulary:

沒説的	處理	罐頭	佈置	幅	吻	勿
養育	陰涼	金子	歸來	莊重	家務活	櫃台
背	神氣	豆腐	進展	研究所	表態	提議
考核	趕時髦	家庭婦女	腦子	喊	修	天高地厚

Segment IX:

Top Priority Vocabulary:

反對	既然	何必	原來	世紀	回頭見	複雜
相信	知識	自私	能力	目的	表現	大概
根本	主張	主義				

Secondary Priority Vocabulary:

家教	體育	審問	逛	打招呼	偷偷摸摸	尊重
專	取經	猜不透	沒精打彩	打起精神	段	無窮盡
知識面	廣	幸福	觀察	大自然	分析	糾正
班級	把握	簽字	觀摩	片		

Segment X:

Top Priority Vocabulary:

醒來	難道	許多	發言	和氣	如果	同意
情況	發表	以為	居然	指出	幹部	證明
替	數學	比如說	以上	超過		

Secondary Priority Vocabulary:

燈	小偷	平靜	何止	童年	幻想	西瓜
甜	忙不過來	校對	印	弄	抽	突出
公正	表決	剩	當選	鼓掌	下面	了不起
指導	單	實事求是	服氣	有意	熱情	難題
勁兒	釘	寶貴	克服	驕傲	情緒	毅力
這就	半數					

Segment XI:

Top Priority Vocabulary:

適合	表揚	未來	靠	時期	成長	早日
優秀	理想	奮鬥	遇到	意想不到	困難	怪不得
久	滿意	信任	法院	搬	妻子	

Secondary Priority Vocabulary:

牙口	鬆軟	蛋糕	斤	超齡	退隊	正直
挫折	祝賀	響亮	動員	渴望	安寧	判
轉學	趕緊	請假				

Segment XII:

Top Priority Vocabulary:

缺點	過份	面子	一直	考慮	黑板	擦
鬧	按照	一向	個性	親戚	冷靜	決定
一切						

Secondary Priority Vocabulary:

幹活兒	膽小	光榮榜	諸位	頭號新聞	名利	誘惑
榮譽	選票	單純	趟	瞞	不夠朋友	

PRIORITY VOCABULARY IN SIMPLIFIED FORM

Codes used in annotations: * top priority vocabulary
^ secondary priority vocabulary

Title:

Top Priority Vocabulary:

少女	衬衫	人物

Secondary Priority Vocabulary:

原著	纽扣	导演	编辑

Segment I:

Top Priority Vocabulary:

追	饿死	风	吹	头发	变	农民
人家	扔	可怜	换	辅导	紧	礼貌
历史	结婚	比方	夫妻	咱们	爱情	实在
记录	没事儿	害怕	进行	总	复习	眼睛
印象	了解					

Secondary Priority Vocabulary:

哦	蚂蚁	呀	雪花	飘	啊	甲
乙	欤	好意思	精彩	木刻	熊猫	指
怪	女士	防	涂	怎么	抓	挺
古文	套	吵嘴	意味	老	身上	干嘛
玩意儿	肚子	沉闷	怎么了	期末	思考	愤怒
流泪	忧虑	评	稀罕			

Segment II:

Top Priority Vocabulary:

读	按	进入	之	认真	必须	态度
精力	管	不舒服	丢掉	专业	被	检查
尽	照顾	优点	纪念	发现	物理	作业
许	准	毕业	下乡	教育		

Secondary Priority Vocabulary:

查	翻	班	大能人	顺便	高一	难度
更加	讲解	端正	谦虚	谨慎	家访	欺负
干	过剩	哪儿	滋味	赏识	倒霉	洗头
抽烟	偷着	伺候	关键	嘛	争取	邮票
周年	哎呀	本儿	参考	这么回事	部队	部门

Segment III:

Top Priority Vocabulary:

其实	聪明	成人	关系	反正	语文	作者
同志	早就	翻译	劝	积极	政治	条件
到底	世界	感觉	准确	民族		

Secondary Priority Vocabulary:

专门	形容	群众	成绩	不便	重复	还有
接触	接着	朴素	打扮	扣子	迹象	引起
作为	协助	篇	稿子	瞎	上	业余
脏	顺手	看待	地地道道	校友	聚会	家
办事员	创造	众	童话	完蛋	太阳	诗
清醒	场合	反射	宇宙	旗	甩开	

Segment IV:

Top Priority Vocabulary:

收	赢	讲课	裤子	议论	美满	看法
一天到晚	良心	抱	躲	外语	提	理解
蓝	说不定	嘴	发音	请教	可不	

Secondary Priority Vocabulary:

棒	捣乱	傻	当成	美术家	背后	虐待
干校	烦恼	云	热爱	祖国	于	遗传
基因	起作用	咳嗽	牛	舌头	别扭	叫住
向	耐心	硬	虚心	光	打架	理
废话						

Segment V:

Top Priority Vocabulary:

时代	选	强	苦	存在	戴	丈夫
技术	假	受	影响	票	科学	力量
作文	评价	完整	团结	未必	认为	诚实

Secondary Priority Vocabulary:

跳动	树林	说明性	糖	拔	声明	嗯
追求	一辈子	狗	给予	名言	眼镜	灌输
自个儿	吃亏	遍	秘密	宝贝	锁	激情
谎	偏要	演	主角	杀	由	生
正派	跳水	腿	领教	千真万确	家伙	不要脸
多情	正经	看一眼	滑稽	乱七八糟	省得	流氓
时刻	打抱不平	确实	跟…好	短篇	人类	礼物
真理	辞海	熟悉	精确	概括	显然	班长
尊敬	文具					

Segment VI:

Top Priority Vocabulary:

老实	倒	连	反映	人情	搞	米
经济	手续	难得	却	梦	无数	人生
孤独						

Secondary Priority Vocabulary:

凭	阵儿	庆贺	评选	放肆	讽刺	迁就
世故	心眼儿	采访	形象	茶叶	教务处	停学
退学	接班儿	踏	吐	匆匆	棵	闪光
神秘	海滩	祝福	旅途	担忧	纯真	会晤

Segment VII:

Top Priority Vocabulary:

分开	难过	批评	用不着	表示	青年	心情
友谊	活	道理	可惜	平均	关心	完成
过程	收获	旅游	不如	当年		

Secondary Priority Vocabulary:

沒必要	方式	友好	万岁	花样	见不着面儿	透
扯	轻信	成绩单儿	瓜	老头儿	算帐	讨厌
植物	地球	太空	航行	不起眼	粒	博士
容量	面积	丫头				

Segment VIII:

Top Priority Vocabulary:

上班	丰富	到时候	厨房	新鲜	献给	深厚
并	后悔	当初	怪	保证	如何	明确
留	当	满	举			

Secondary Priority Vocabulary:

沒说的	处理	罐头	布置	幅	吻	勿
养育	阴凉	金子	归来	庄重	家务活	柜台
背	神气	豆腐	进展	研究所	表态	提议
考核	赶时髦	家庭妇女	脑子	喊	修	天高地厚

Segment IX:

Top Priority Vocabulary:

反对	既然	何必	原来	世纪	回头见	复杂
相信	知识	自私	能力	目的	表现	大概
根本	主张	主义				

Secondary Priority Vocabulary:

家教	体育	审问	逛	打招呼	偷偷摸摸	尊重
专	取经	猜不透	沒精打彩	打起精神	段	无穷尽
知识面	广	幸福	观察	大自然	分析	纠正
班级	把握	签字	观摩	片		

Segment X:

Top Priority Vocabulary:

醒来	难道	许多	发言	和气	如果	同意
情况	发表	以为	居然	指出	干部	证明
替	数学	比如说	以上	超过		

Secondary Priority Vocabulary:

灯	小偷	平静	何止	童年	幻想	西瓜
甜	忙不过来	校对	印	弄	抽	突出
公正	表决	剩	当选	鼓掌	下面	了不起
指导	单	实事求是	服气	有意	热情	难题
劲儿	钉	宝贵	克服	骄傲	情绪	毅力
这就	半数					

Segment XI:

Top Priority Vocabulary:

适合	表扬	未来	靠	时期	成长	早日
优秀	理想	奋斗	遇到	意想不到	困难	怪不得
久	满意	信任	法院	搬	妻子	

Secondary Priority Vocabulary:

牙口	松软	蛋糕	斤	超龄	退队	正直
挫折	祝贺	响亮	动员	渴望	安宁	判
转学	赶紧	请假				

Segment XII:

Top Priority Vocabulary:

缺点	过份	面子	一直	考虑	黑板	擦
闹	按照	一向	个性	亲戚	冷静	决定
一切						

Secondary Priority Vocabulary:

干活儿	胆小	光荣榜	诸位	头号新闻	名利	诱惑
荣誉	选票	单纯	趟	瞒	不够朋友	

VOCABULARY INDEX

Codes: Roman numeral - segment number
Arabic numeral - item number
C - Credits and Cast of Characters (p. 2)
* - vocabulary item of primary importance
^ - vocabulary item of secondary importance

A

a	^啊	^啊	I.16
Ālābó	阿拉伯	阿拉伯	VII.43
á	嘎	嘎	I.60
āi, ài	唉	唉	I.21
āiyā	^哎呀	^哎呀	II.63
āiyō	哎哟	哎哟	XI.12
ài	嗳	嗳	I.47
Ai Qīng	艾青	艾青	III.72
àiqíng	*爱情	*爱情	I.69
ānníng	^安宁	^安宁	XI.38
Āntúshēng	安徒生	安徒生	III.65
àn	*按	*按	II.06
ànzhào	*按照	*按照	XII.16

B

bá	^拔	^拔	V.13
bǎ lùzi zǒuzhèng	把路子 走正	把路子 走正	III.29
bǎwò	^把握	^把握	IX.50
bái máo nǚ	白毛女	白毛女	I.09
Báiyángdiàn	白洋淀	白洋淀	VII.56
bān	*搬	*搬	XI.41
bān	^班	^班	II.09
bān-huì	班會	班会	IX.08
bānjí	^班級	^班级	IX.46
bānzhǎng	^班長	^班长	V.97
bànshìyuán	^辦事員	^办事员	III.53
bànshù	^半數	^半数	X.67
bǎngzi	膀子	膀子	III.93
bàng	^棒	^棒	IV.01
bǎobèi	^寶貝	^宝贝	V.37

bǎoguì	^寶貴	^宝贵	X.60
bǎoyòu	保佑	保佑	IV.29
bǎozhèng	*保證	*保证	VIII.36
bào	*抱	*抱	IV.21
bēi	^背	^背	VIII.34
bèihòu	^背後	^背后	IV.11
bèi	*被	*被	II.39
Bèijiāěr	貝加爾	贝加尔	VII.52
bēnténg	奔騰	奔腾	VI.51
běnr	^本兒	^本儿	II.66
bǐfang	*比方	*比方	I.62
bǐrú shuō	*比如説	*比如说	X.54
bìxū	*必須	*必须	II.20
bìyè	*畢業	*毕业	II.71
biānjí	^編輯	^编辑	C.12
biǎndī	貶低	贬低	X.44
biàn	^遍	^遍	V.35
biàn	*變	*变	I.18
biàn			
biǎojué	^表決	^表决	X.26
biǎoshì	*表示	*表示	VII.07
biǎotài	^表態	^表态	VIII.43
biǎoxiàn	*表現	*表现	IX.45
biǎoyáng	*表揚	*表扬	XI.08
bié chū xīncái	別出 心裁	別出 心裁	X.55
bièniu	^別扭	^別扭	IV.51
bīnggāo	冰糕	冰糕	IX.22
bīnggùnr	冰棍兒	冰棍儿	I.71
bìng	*並	*并	VIII.28
bōfēng lànggǔ	波峰 浪谷	波峰 浪谷	VI.52
bóshì	^博士	^博士	VII.47
búbiàn	^不便	^不便	III.14

153

búgòu péngyou	^不夠 朋友	^不够 朋友	XII.27
búyàoliǎn	^不要臉	^不要脸	V.62
bùqǐyǎn	^不起眼	^不起眼	VII.42
bùrú	*不如	*不如	VII.51
bùshūfu	*不舒服	*不舒服	II.34
bùduì	^部隊	^部队	II.75
bùmén	^部門	^部门	II.78
bùzhì	^佈置	^布置	VIII.12

C

cā	*擦	*擦	XII.14
cāibutòu	^猜不透	^猜不透	IX.25
… cái shì zhēnde	…才是 真的	…才是 真的	VII.19
cǎifǎng	^採訪	^采访	VI.21
cānkǎo	^參考	^参考	II.68
cǎoméi	草梅	草梅	VIII.08
chá	^查	^查	II.07
cháyè	^茶葉	^茶叶	VI.25
chǎnshù	闡述	阐述	III.74
chǎnghé	^場合	^场合	III.77
chǎngkāi	敞開	敞开	VIII.24
chāoguò	*超過	*超过	X.66
chāolíng	^超齡	^超龄	XI.13
cháo	朝	朝	X.13
chǎozuǐ	^吵嘴	^吵嘴	I.63
chě	^扯	^扯	VII.17
chénmèn	^沉悶	^沉闷	I.82
chènshān	*襯衫	*衬衫	C.07
chéngjī	^成績	^成绩	III.11
chéngjī-dānr	^成績 單兒	^成绩 单儿	VII.24
chéngrén	*成人	*成人	III.06
chéngzhǎng	*成長	*成长	XI.16
chéngshí	*誠實	*诚实	V.108
chīkuī	^吃虧	^吃亏	V.34
chī lǎo běnr	吃老 本兒	吃老 本儿	IV.26
chī rénjia zuǐ duǎn	吃人家 嘴短	吃人家 嘴短	X.47
chídùn	遲鈍	迟钝	V.54
chìchéng	赤誠	赤诚	III.88
chóngfù	^重複	^重复	III.15

chòng	沖	冲	VII.30
chōu	^抽	^抽	X.19
chōujīn	抽筋	抽筋	V.56
chōutì	抽屜	抽屉	V.39
chōuyān	^抽煙	^抽烟	II.43
chúfáng	*廚房	*厨房	VIII.10
chǔlǐ	^處理	^处理	VIII.06
chuàngzào	^創造	^创造	III.56
chuī	*吹	*吹	I.11
chúnzhēn	^純真	^纯真	VI.58
Cíhǎi	^辭海	^辞海	V.89
cízǎo	辭藻	辞藻	V.42
cìhou	^伺候	^伺候	II.48
cìyǔ	賜予	赐予	V.83
cōngcōng	^匆匆	^匆匆	VI.37
cōngming	*聰明	*聪明	III.04
cóngshēng	叢生	丛生	IV.63
cúnzài	*存在	*存在	V.23
cuòzhé	^挫折	^挫折	XI.23

D

dǎbàn	^打扮	^打扮	III.22
dǎ bàobùpíng	^打抱 不平	^打抱 不平	V.75
dǎjià	^打架	^打架	IV.64
dǎ mǎnfēn	打滿分	打满分	III.81
dǎqǐ jīngshen	^打起 精神	^打起 精神	IX.28
dǎ zhāohu	^打招呼	^打招呼	IX.10
dàgài	*大概	*大概	IX.48
dà néngrén	^大能人	^大能人	II.10
dàrén	大人	大人	VI.02
dàye	大爺	大爷	VII.27
dàzìrán	^大自然	^大自然	IX.39
dāizhì	呆滯	呆滞	I.93
dài	*戴	*戴	V.30
dān	^單	^单	X.39
dānchún	^單純	^单纯	XII.20
dānrén-	^單人-	^单人-	I.59
dānshù	單數	单数	IV.31
dānyōu	^擔憂	^担忧	VI.57
dǎnxiǎo	^膽小	^胆小	XII.03
dànshuǐ	淡水	淡水	VII.49
dàn'gāo	^蛋糕	^蛋糕	XI.05

dāng	當	当	IX.43
dāng	*當	*当	VIII.50
dāngchéng	^當成	^当成	IV.09
dāngchū	*當初	*当初	VIII.30
dāngguānr	當官兒	当官儿	III.52
dāngnián	*當年	*当年	VII.57
dāngxuǎn	*當選	^当选	X.29
dǎoluàn	^搗亂	^捣乱	IV.03
dǎoyǎn	^導演	^导演	C.09
dǎoméi	^倒霉	^倒霉	II.41
dào	*倒	*倒	VI.06
dàodǐ	*到底	*到底	III.59
dào shíhou	*到時候	*到时候	VIII.04
dàolǐ	*道理	*道理	VII.21
dēng	^燈	^灯	X.02
dìdìdàodào	^地地道道	^地地道道	III.47
dìqiú	^地球	^地球	VII.38
dīng	^釘	^钉	X.56
diūdiào	*丟掉	*丢掉	II.36
dòngyuán	^動員	^动员	XI.33
dòufu	^豆腐	^豆腐	VIII.38
dú	*讀	*读	II.05
dúshēn	獨身	独身	IX.57
dùzi	^肚子	^肚子	I.77
duānzhèng	^端正	^端正	II.21
duǎnpiān	^短篇	^短篇	V.80
duàn	^段	^段	IX.29
duōqíng	^多情	^多情	V.63
duǒ	*躲	*躲	IV.22

E

ē, é, ě, è	^欸	^欸	I.24
Éméi	峨眉	峨眉	C.02
èsǐ	*餓死	*饿死	I.05
ēncì	恩賜	恩赐	XI.34

F

fābiǎo	*發表	*发表	X.33
fā kǔ	發苦	发苦	IX.20
fāxiàn	*發現	*发现	II.59
fāyán	*發言	*发言	X.20
fāyīn	*發音	*发音	IV.53

fǎyuàn	*法院	*法院	XI.39
fān	^翻	^翻	II.08
fānyì	*翻譯	*翻译	III.50
fánnǎo	^煩惱	^烦恼	IV.35
fánxīng	繁星	繁星	VI.48
fǎnduì	*反對	*反对	IX.04
fǎnshè	^反射	^反射	III.79
fǎnyìng	*反映	*反映	VI.09
fǎnzhèng	*反正	*反正	III.09
-fàn	-販	-贩	I.19
fāngshì	^方式	^方式	VII.06
fáng	^防	^防	I.44
fàngsì	^放肆	^放肆	VI.11
fèihuà	^廢話	^废话	IV.66
fēnkāi	*分開	*分开	VII.01
fēnxī	^分析	^分析	IX.40
fèndòu	*奮鬥	*奋斗	XI.21
fènnù	^憤怒	^愤怒	I.92
fēng	*風	*风	I.10
fēngfù	*豐富	*丰富	VIII.03
fēnglì	鋒利	锋利	III.87
fěngcì	^諷刺	^讽刺	VI.12
fūqī	*夫妻	*夫妻	I.65
fúqì	^服氣	^服气	X.42
fú	^幅	^幅	VIII.13
fǔdǎo	*輔導	*辅导	I.49
fùxí	*複習	*复习	I.88
fùzá	*複雜	*复杂	IX.18

G

gāi	該	该	IV.13
gàikuò	^概括	^概括	V.95
gǎnjǐn	^趕緊	^赶紧	XI.44
gǎn shímáo	^趕時髦	^赶时髦	VIII.46
gǎnjué	*感覺	*感觉	III.75
gàn	^幹	^干	II.28
gànbù	*幹部	*干部	X.45
gànhuór	^幹活兒	^干活儿	XII.01
gànmá	^幹嘛	^干嘛	I.72
gànxiào	^幹校	^干校	IV.24
gāoyā-xiàn	高壓線	高压线	V.08
gāo yī	^高一	^高一	II.13
gǎo	*搞	*搞	VI.18
gǎozi	^稿子	^稿子	III.32

gēcí	歌詞	歌词	III.13
gētán	歌壇	歌坛	III.39
gèxìng	*個性	*个性	XII.22
gēn...hǎo	^跟…好	^跟…好	V.78
gēnběn	*根本	*根本	IX.49
gèngjiā	^更加	^更加	II.16
gōngzhèng	^公正	^公正	X.24
gǒu	^狗	^狗	V.22
gòu jiěmenr	夠姐	够姐	
	們兒	们儿	V.77
gūdú	*孤獨	*孤独	VI.59
gǔwén	^古文	^古文	I.54
gǔzhǎng	^鼓掌	^鼓掌	X.30
gù	故	故	II.01
guā	^瓜	^瓜	VII.26
guāzǐ	瓜子	瓜子	I.29
guài	*怪	*怪	VIII.31
guài	^怪	^怪	I.39
guàibudé	*怪不得	*怪不得	XI.28
guānchá	^觀察	^观察	IX.38
guānmó	^觀摩	^观摩	IX.55
guānjiàn	^關鍵	^关键	II.51
guānxi	*關係	*关系	III.08
guānxīn	*關心	*关心	VII.25
guǎn	*管	*管	II.31
guànshū	^灌輸	^灌输	V.32
guàntou	^罐頭	^罐头	VIII.07
guāng	^光	^光	IV.60
guāngróng-bǎng	^光榮榜	^光荣榜	XII.08
guǎng	^廣	^广	IX.35
guàng	^逛	^逛	IX.09
guīlai	^歸來	^归来	VIII.25
guìtái	^櫃台	^柜台	VIII.33
guìzi	櫃子	柜子	V.81
gǔn	滾	滚	VIII.48
guòchéng	*過程	*过程	VII.37
guòfèn	*過分	*过份	XII.04
guòshèng	^過剩	^过剩	II.30

H

ha	哈	哈	I.33
hai	咳	咳	I.83
háiyǒu	^還有	^还有	III.16

hǎitān	^海灘	^海滩	VI.49
hàipà	*害怕	*害怕	I.84
hǎn	^喊	^喊	VIII.54
hángtiānzhàn	航天站	航天站	VII.41
hángxíng	^航行	^航行	VII.40
hǎoyìsi	^好意思	^好意思	I.30
hē	呵	呵	I.79
hébì	*何必	*何必	IX.11
hézhǐ	^何止	^何止	X.06
héqì	*和氣	*和气	X.22
hétao	核桃	核桃	I.15
hēi	嘿	嘿	I.35
hēibǎn	*黑板	*黑板	XII.09
hènsǐ	恨死	恨死	IX.14
hng!	哼	哼	II.33
hòuhuǐ	*後悔	*后悔	VIII.29
hòushēng kěwèi	後生 可畏	后生 可畏	XII.21
huāyàng	^花樣	^花样	VII.11
huáji	^滑稽	^滑稽	V.67
huà	化	化	I.78
huàgōng	化工	化工	VI.19
huàn	*換	*换	I.41
huànxiǎng	^幻想	^幻想	X.10
huángdǎnxìng gānyán	黃膽性 肝炎	黄胆性 肝炎	I.43
huáng máo	黃毛	黄毛	I.08
huánghuò	惶惑	惶惑	V.24
huǎng	^謊	^谎	V.43
huítóu jiàn	*回頭見	*回头见	IX.24
huìwù	^會晤	^会晤	VI.62
huó	*活	*活	VII.20
huó dào lǎo, xué dào lǎo	活到老, 學到老	活到老, 学到老	IX.23
huǒjiàn	火箭	火箭	III.85
huòyuán	貨源	货源	VIII.02

J

jījí	*積極	*积极	III.55
jīmáo suànpí	雞毛 蒜皮	鸡毛 蒜皮	IV.18
jīqíng	^激情	^激情	V.40
jīxiàng	^跡象	^迹象	III.25
jīyīn	^基因	^基因	IV.45

K

L

T

tāshi	踏實	踏实	II.17
tà	^踏	^踏	VI.32
tái	檯	台	V.06
tàidu	*態度	*态度	II.22
tàikōng	^太空	^太空	VII.39
tàiyáng	^太陽	^太阳	III.69
tānfàn	攤販	摊贩	XI.02
táng	^糖	^糖	V.12
tángjīng	糖精	糖精	IX.19
tàng	^趟	^趟	XII.24
tǎoyàn	^討厭	^讨厌	VII.31
tào	^套	^套	I.57
tí	*提	*提	IV.33
tíyì	^提議	^提议	VIII.44
tǐyù	^體育	^体育	IX.03
tì	*替	*替	X.49
tiāngāo dìhòu	^天高地厚	^天高地厚	VIII.58
tián	^甜	^甜	X.12
tiāotì	挑剔	挑剔	X.23
tiáojiàn	*條件	*条件	III.58
tiàodòng	^跳動	^跳动	V.03
tiàoshuǐ	^跳水	^跳水	V.53
Tiě Níng	鐵凝	铁凝	C.05
tíngxué	^停學	^停学	VI.27
tǐng	^挺	^挺	I.52
tónghuà	^童話	^童话	III.66
tóngnián	^童年	^童年	X.09
tóngxīn	童心	童心	VI.63
tóngyì	*同意	*同意	X.27
tóngzhì	*同志	*同志	III.43
tōutōumōmō	^偷偷摸摸	^偷偷摸摸	IX.12
tōuzhe	^偷着	^偷着	II.46
tóufa	*頭髮	*头发	I.17
tóuhào xīnwén	^頭號新聞	^头号新闻	XII.11
-tòu	^-透	^-透	VII.15
tūchū	^突出	^突出	X.21
tú	^塗	^涂	I.45
tǔ	^吐	^吐	VI.36
tuánjié	*團結	*团结	V.98
tuǐ	^腿	^腿	V.55
tuìduì	^退隊	^退队	XI.14
tuìxué	^退學	^退学	VI.29
tuōlājī	拖拉機	拖拉机	V.07

W

wàipó	外婆	外婆	IV.25
wàixiào	外校	外校	V.103
wàiyǔ	*外語	*外语	IV.27
wánchéng	*完成	*完成	VII.35
wándàn	^完蛋	^完蛋	III.67
wánzhěng	*完整	*完整	V.93
wányìr	^玩意兒	^玩意儿	I.75
...wànsuì	^...萬歲	^...万岁	VII.10
wǎng xīnli qù	往心裡去	往心里去	III.30
wèibì	*未必	*未必	V.101
wèilái	*未來	*未来	XI.09
wénjù	^文具	^文具	V.104
wěn	^吻	^吻	VIII.14
wū	嗚	呜	VI.34
wúqióngjìn	^無窮盡	^无穷尽	IX.31
wúshù	*無數	*无数	VI.45
wǔdòu	武門	武斗	IV.23
wǔxiāng	五香	五香	I.28
wù	^勿	^勿	VIII.15
wùlǐ	*物理	*物理	II.64

X

xī	嘻	嘻	I.26
xīgua	^西瓜	^西瓜	X.11
xīhan	^稀罕	^稀罕	I.98
xīkè	稀客	稀客	III.19
xízuò	習作	习作	III.01
xǐtóu	^洗頭	^洗头	II.42
xiā	^瞎	^瞎	III.33
xiàba	下巴	下巴	I.81
xiàmian	^下面	^下面	X.31
xiàxiāng	*下鄉	*下乡	II.74
xiánshuǐ	鹹水	咸水	VII.50
xiǎnrán	^顯然	^显然	V.96
xiàngěi	*獻給	*献给	VIII.18
xiāngjiāo	香蕉	香蕉	III.62
xiāngxìn	*相信	*相信	IX.26

xiǎngliàng	^響亮	^响亮	XI.32
xiàng	^向	^向	IV.55
xiǎotōu	^小偷	^小偷	X.03
xiàoyǒu	^校友	^校友	III.48
xiézhù	^協助	^协助	III.28
xīnqíng	*心情	*心情	VII.13
xīnyǎnr	^心眼兒	^心眼儿	VI.16
xīnxian	*新鮮	*新鲜	VIII.11
xīnxiù	新秀	新秀	III.40
xìnrèn	*信任	*信任	XI.37
xíngróng	^形容	^形容	III.05
xíngxiàng	^形象	^形象	VI.22
xǐnglai	*醒來	*醒来	X.01
xìngfú	^幸福	^幸福	IX.36
xiōngtáng	胸膛	胸膛	VIII.23
xióngmāo	^熊貓	^熊猫	I.34
xiū	^修	^修	VIII.57
xūxīn	^虛心	^虚心	IV.59
xǔ	*許	*许	II.67
xǔduō	*許多	*许多	X.08
xuǎn	*選	*选	V.09
xuǎnpiào	^選票	^选票	XII.18
xuéshé	學舌	学舌	V.26
xuěhuā	^雪花	^雪花	I.12

Y

ya	^呀	^呀	I.06
yātou	^丫頭	^丫头	VII.60
yá	芽	芽	VI.35
yákǒu	^牙口	^牙口	XI.03
yánjiūsuǒ	^研究所	^研究所	VIII.41
yǎn	^演	^演	V.46
yǎnjing	*眼睛	*眼睛	I.90
yǎnjìng	^眼鏡	^眼镜	V.31
Yànlíngduì	雁翎隊	雁翎队	VII.59
yǎngyù	^養育	^养育	VIII.16
yāodài	腰帶	腰带	X.58
yáowàng	遙望	遥望	III.89
yáoyáo	遙遙	遥遥	VI.61
yèkōng	夜空	夜空	VI.44
yèyú	^業餘	^业余	III.37
yíbèizi	^一輩子	^一辈子	V.20
yíqiè	*一切	*一切	XII.29

yìtiān dàowǎn	*一天 到晚	*一天 到晚	IV.17
yíxiàng	*一向	*一向	XII.19
yìzhí	*一直	*一直	XII.06
yí	噯	噯	IV.06
yíchuán	^遺傳	^遗传	IV.44
yǐ	乙	乙	I.27
yǐshàng	*以上	*以上	X.59
yǐwéi	*以為	*以为	X.34
yìlì	^毅力	^毅力	X.64
yìlùn	*議論	*议论	IV.12
yìwèi	^意味	^意味	I.64
yìxiǎng budào	*意想 不到	*意想 不到	XI.24
yìzhì	譯製	译制	IX.59
yīnliáng	^陰涼	^阴凉	VIII.17
yǐnqǐ	^引起	^引起	III.26
yìn	^印	^印	X.17
yìnxiàng	*印象	*印象	I.99
yíng	*贏	*赢	IV.05
yǐngxiǎng	*影響	*影响	V.71
yìng	^硬	^硬	IV.58
yō	喲	喲	IV.36
yòngbuzháo	*用不着	*用不着	VII.05
yōudàng	悠蕩	悠荡	IX.01
yōuxián	悠閑	悠闲	VI.47
yōulù	^憂慮	^忧虑	I.95
yōudiǎn	*優點	*优点	II.53
yōuxiù	*優秀	*优秀	XI.18
yóu	^由	^由	V.50
yóu yán jiàng cù	油鹽 醬醋	油盐 酱醋	VIII.53
yóupiào	^郵票	^邮票	II.56
yǒuhǎo	^友好	^友好	VII.08
yǒuyì	*友誼	*友谊	VII.16
yǒuyì	^有意	^有意	X.43
yòuhuò	^誘惑	^诱惑	XII.13
yú	^於	^于	IV.42
yǔlù	語錄	语录	VIII.56
yǔwén	*語文	*语文	III.34
yǔzhòu	^宇宙	^宇宙	III.90
yùdào	*遇到	*遇到	XI.22
yuánlái	*原來	*原来	IX.13
yuányě	原野	原野	VI.33

yuánzhù	^原著	^原著	C.04
yuē	曰	曰	II.02
yún	^雲	^云	IV.38

Z

zácǎo	雜草	杂草	IV.62
zánmen	*咱們	*咱们	I.66
zāng	^髒	^脏	III.41
zǎo	棗	枣	I.03
zǎojiù	*早就	*早就	III.44
zǎorì	*早日	*早日	XI.17
zěnme	^怎麼	^怎么	I.48
zěnmele	^怎麼了	^怎么了	I.85
zhàngfu	*丈夫	*丈夫	V.48
zhàochāo	照抄	照抄	II.70
zhàogu	*照顧	*照顾	II.50
zhèbu	這不	这不	II.76
zhè jiù	^這就	^这就	X.65
zhème huí shì	^這麼 回事	^这么 回事	II.73
zhēnjiǔ	針灸	针灸	V.57
zhēnlǐ	^真理	^真理	V.86
zhēnzhū	珍珠	珍珠	VI.42
zhènr	^陣兒	^阵儿	VI.04
zhēngqǔ	^爭取	^争取	II.55
zhèngjing	^正經	^正经	V.65
zhèngpài	^正派	^正派	V.52
zhèngyìgǎn	正義感	正义感	V.107
zhèngzhí	^正直	^正直	XI.19
zhèngmíng	*證明	*证明	X.46
zhèngzhì	*政治	*政治	III.57
zhī	枝	枝	I.74
zhī	*之	*之	II.14
zhīshi	*知識	*知识	IX.30
zhīshimiàn	^知識面	^知识面	IX.34
zhíwù	^植物	^植物	VII.36
zhí	執	执	III.86
zhǐ	指	指	VII.48
zhǐ	^指	^指	I.36
zhǐchū	*指出	*指出	X.41
zhǐdǎo	^指導	^指导	X.37
zhìpiān-chǎng	製片廠	制片厂	C.03
zhǒng	種	种	VII.33
zhòng-, -zhòng	^眾	^众	III.60

Zhōu Lì	周力	周力	C.10
zhōunián	^週年	^周年	II.61
zhūwèi	^諸位	^诸位	XII.10
zhǔjiǎo	^主角	^主角	V.47
zhǔyì	*主義	*主义	IX.58
zhǔzhāng	*主張	*主张	IX.56
zhùfú	^祝福	^祝福	VI.53
zhùhè	^祝賀	^祝贺	XI.30
zhùyuàn	祝願	祝愿	VI.54
zhùyá	蛀牙	蛀牙	V.15
zhuā	^抓	^抓	I.50
zhuān	^專	^专	IX.16
zhuānmén	^專門	^专门	III.03
zhuānyè	*專業	*专业	II.37
zhuǎnxué	^轉學	^转学	XI.43
zhuāngzhòng	^莊重	^庄重	VIII.26
zhuī	*追	*追	I.01
zhuīqiú	^追求	^追求	V.19
zhǔn	*準	*准	II.69
zhǔnquè	*準確	*准确	III.80
zhuōliè	拙劣	拙劣	V.29
zīwèi	^滋味	^滋味	II.38
zìgěr	^自個兒	^自个儿	V.33
zìsī	*自私	*自私	IX.37
zìwǒ	自我	自我	X.38
zì zhǎo máfan	自找 麻煩	自找 麻烦	VII.14
zǒng	*總	*总	I.87
zǔgǎo	組稿	组稿	VI.20
zǔguó	^祖國	^祖国	IV.40
zuǐ	*嘴	*嘴	IV.47
zūnjìng	^尊敬	^尊敬	V.99
zūnzhòng	^尊重	^尊重	IX.15
Zuǒluó	佐羅	佐罗	I.80
zuòwéi	^作為	^作为	III.27
zuòwén	*作文	*作文	V.90
zuòyè	*作業	*作业	II.65
zuòzhě	*作者	*作者	III.38

LIST OF FIRST CHARACTERS IN THE VOCABULARY INDEX

IN COMPLEX FORM

The lead characters of all entries in the vocabulary index are listed here. Characters are ordered by number of strokes and, within each stroke-number grouping, by the configuration of the first stroke of each character. Thus a character whose pronunciation is not known can first be looked up here, then entries beginning with this character can be found in the alphabetically ordered vocabulary index on the preceding pages.

一畫

一	yí
乙	yǐ

二畫

十	shí
人	rén
力	lì
了	liǎo

三畫

丫	yā
之	zhī
三	sān
下	xià
丈	zhàng
大	dà
才	cái
上	shàng
千	qiān
久	jiǔ
小	xiǎo
女	nǚ

四畫

火	huǒ
方	fāng
文	wén
心	xīn
天	tiān

夫	fū
木	mù
五	wǔ
不	bú
友	yǒu
太	tài
牙	yá
比	bǐ
少	shào
日	yuē
公	gōng
分	fēn
手	shǒu
牛	niú
化	huà
片	piān
斤	jīn
反	fǎn
勿	wù
引	yǐn
幻	huàn

五畫

半	bàn
主	zhǔ
必	bì
平	píng
未	wèi
世	shì
古	gǔ
本	běn
正	zhèng
扔	rēng

可	kě
打	dǎ
由	yóu
甲	jiǎ
目	mù
叫	jiào
生	shēng
白	bái
瓜	guā
甩	shuǎi
外	wài
用	yòng
以	yǐ
民	mín

六畫

宇	yǔ
安	ān
米	mǐ
忙	máng
冰	bīng
扣	kòu
艾	ài
地	dì
老	lǎo
考	kǎo
西	xī
存	cún
成	chéng
有	yǒu
早	zǎo
光	guāng

吐	tǔ
同	tóng
吃	chī
回	huí
丟	diū
舌	shé
向	xiàng
自	zì
印	yìn
名	míng
多	duō
收	shōu
如	rú
好	hǎo

七畫

冷	lěng
完	wán
沉	chén
沖	chòng
判	pàn
決	jué
沒	méi
良	liáng
形	xíng
戒	jiè
弄	nòng
克	kè
豆	dòu
赤	chì
更	gèng
夾	jiá
扯	chě

抓	zhuā
技	jì
把	bǎ
批	pī
呆	dāi
吹	chuī
困	kùn
貝	bèi
別	bié, biè
吻	wěn
吵	chǎo
呀	ya
見	jiàn
利	lì
佐	zuǒ
伺	cì
佈	bù
何	hé
作	zuò
身	shēn
肚	dù
防	fáng

八畫

油	yóu
並	bìng
波	bō
法	fǎ
夜	yè
於	yú
放	fàng
怪	guài
青	qīng

武 wǔ	活 huó	**十畫**	航 háng	眼 yǎn
玩 wán	突 tū		胸 xiōng	喏 nuò
表 biǎo	恨 hèn	丶	脈 mò	ノ
芽 yá	契 qì	海 hǎi	留 liú	殺 shā
協 xié	一	害 hài	針 zhēn	梨 lí
其 qí	珍 zhēn	家 jiā	能 néng	甜 tián
取 qǔ	故 gù	容 róng	閃 shǎn	透 tòu
幸 xìng	查 chá	記 jì	退 tuì	動 dòng
枝 zhī	苦 kǔ	旅 lǚ	純 chún	假 jiǎ
花 huā	政 zhèng	討 tǎo	紐 niǔ	悠 yōu
奔 bēn	相 xiāng	高 gāo	陣 zhèn	貨 huò
妻 qī	耐 nài	祖 zǔ		停 tíng
拔 bá	研 yán	神 shén	**十一畫**	偷 tōu
拙 zhuō	面 miàn	祝 zhù		偏 piān
到 dào	按 àn	一	丶	條 tiáo
抽 chōu	勁 jìn	班 bān	密 mì	逛 guàng
抱 bào	指 zhǐ	秦 qín	淡 dàn	夠 gòu
拖 tuō	挑 tiāo	馬 mǎ	粒 lì	猜 cāi
拉 lā	丨	草 cǎo	清 qīng	乚
丨	省 shěng	根 gēn	深 shēn	參 cān
呣 m	虐 nüè	真 zhēn	部 bù	習 xí
呵 hē	背 bēi, bèi	茶 chá	許 xǔ	欸 ē, é, ě, è
明 míng	咦 yí	起 qǐ	康 kāng	強 qiáng
哎 āi	品 pǐn	原 yuán	這 zhè	蛋 dàn
ノ	冒 mào	套 tào	情 qíng	組 zǔ
受 shòu	咳 hai, ké	挫 cuò	被 bèi	陰 yīn
金 jīn	哈 ha	校 xiào, jiào	一	
爭 zhēng	咱 zán	核 hé	執 zhí	**十二畫**
和 hé	思 sī	挺 tǐng	理 lǐ	
物 wù	科 kē	唉 āi, ài	基 jī	丶
知 zhī	怎 zěn	哦 ó, ò	採 cǎi	渴 kě
往 wǎng	看 kàn	峨 é	莊 zhuāng	滋 zī
狗 gǒu	重 chóng	恩 ēn	連 lián	尊 zūn
周 zhōu	香 xiāng	哼 hng	專 zhuān	童 tóng
服 fú	信 xìn	哪 nǎ	教 jiào	評 píng
乚	保 bǎo	時 shí	票 piào	惶 huáng
居 jū	段 duàn	ノ	雪 xuě	視 shì
阿 ā	卻 què	拿 ná	盛 shèng	一
糾 jiū	後 hòu	釘 dīng	接 jiē	替 tì
孤 gū	風 fēng	缺 quē	丨	博 bó
	忽 cōng	秘 mì	處 chǔ	朝 cháo
九畫	乚	倔 jué	蛀 zhù	棵 kē
	既 jì	追 zhuī	哈 shá	棒 bàng
丶	眉 méi	倒 dǎo, dào	販 fàn	植 zhí
美 měi	姥 lǎo	個 gè	啦 la	超 chāo
首 shǒu	紀 jì	修 xiū	啊 a	棗 zǎo
流 liú			畢 bì	場 chǎng
洗 xǐ			眾 zhòng	期 qī
				欺 qī

雲	˙yún	萬	wàn	語	yǔ	遷	qiān	噢	o
黃	huáng	落	luò	認	rèn	確	què	瞞	mán
雁	yàn	葡	pú	說	shuō	憂	yōu	丿	
硬	yìng	鼓	gǔ	聚	jù	撒	sā	積	jī
提	tí	感	gǎn	夢	mèng	賞	shǎng	儘	jǐn
換	huàn	搗	dǎo	歌	gē	嘻	xī	學	xué
敞	chǎng	搞	gǎo	緊	jǐn	嘴	zuǐ	膨	péng
丨		搬	bān	趕	gǎn	瞎	xiā	獨	dú
虛	xū	丨		輔	fǔ	嘮	láo	乀	
幅	fǔ	當	dāng	輕	qīng	賜	cì	選	xuǎn
貶	biǎn	業	yè	摸	mō	嘿	hēi	遲	chí
喊	hǎn	嗓	sǎng	丨		影	yǐng		
單	dān	遇	yù	嘞	lei	數	shù	**十七畫**	
喲	yō	嘎	á	嘛	ma	踏	tā, tà		
黑	hēi	嗚	wū	團	tuán	丿		丶	
丿		跡	jǐ	領	lǐng	劍	jiàn	謙	qiān
創	chuàng	嗯	ń, ň, ǹ	算	suàn	鋒	fēng	謊	huǎng
短	duǎn	照	zhào	種	zhǒng	餓	è	講	jiǎng
稀	xī	跟	gēn	製	zhì	稿	gǎo	一	
剩	shèng	路	lù	管	guǎn	篇	piān	檢	jiǎn
無	wú	跳	tiào	膀	bǎng	靠	kào	聲	shēng
郵	yóu	農	nóng	遙	yáo	駕	jià	聰	cōng
傢	jiā	過	guò	腿	tuǐ	編	biān	戴	dài
順	shùn	丿		乀		練	liàn	臨	lín
進	jìn	亂	luàn	熊	xióng			擦	cā
週	zhōu	愛	ài	態	tài	**十六畫**		丨	
乀		會	huì					顆	kē
發	fā	傻	shǎ	**十五畫**		丶		還	hái
開	kāi	躲	duǒ			激	jī	繁	fán
結	jiē, jié	僅	jǐn	丶		憑	píng	丿	
給	jǐ	腰	yāo	澎	péng	燈	dēng	優	yōu
		腦	nǎo	養	yǎng	導	dǎo	舉	jǔ
十三畫		乀		審	shěn	糖	táng	膽	dǎn
		羣	qún	穀	yì	諷	fěng	乀	
丶		經	jīng	熟	shú	親	qīn	牆	qiáng
溜	liū			廢	fèi	辦	bàn	總	zǒng
塗	tú	**十四畫**		諸	zhū	褲	kù		
煩	fán			適	shì	一		**十八畫**	
滑	huá	丶		廚	chú	醒	xǐng		
準	zhǔn	演	yǎn	廣	guǎng	樸	pǔ	丶	
道	dào	精	jīng	慶	qìng	樹	shù	謹	jǐn
誠	chéng	榮	róng	請	qǐng	頭	tóu	雜	zá
意	yì	實	shí	憤	fèn	奮	fèn	禮	lǐ
新	xīn	滾	gǔn	複	fù	歷	lì	一	
該	gāi	滿	mǎn	一		擔	dān	鬆	sōng
詩	shī	漫	màn	鬧	nào	丨		櫃	guì
遍	biàn	旗	qí	賣	mài	噯	ài	藍	lán
一		端	duān	熱	rè	螞	mǎ	轉	zhuǎn
概	gài	誘	yòu	趟	tàng	遺	yí	檯	tái
幹	gàn							叢	cóng
								丿	
								翻	fān
								鎖	suǒ
								雞	jī
								歸	guī
								雙	shuāng

⌐ 豐	fēng		靈	líng
醬	jiàng		罐	guàn
嬸	shěn		觀	guān

十九畫

證	zhèng
攀	pān
繫	jì
難	nán
羅	luó
辭	cí
簽	qiān
關	guān

二十畫

寶	bǎo
議	yì
譯	yì
贏	yíng
蘆	lú
飄	piāo
勸	quàn
蘋	píng
蘇	sū
獻	xiàn
鹹	xián
嚷	rǎng
闡	chǎn

二十一 - 二十四畫

灌	guàn
蠟	là
鐵	tiě
響	xiǎng
讀	dú
變	biàn
襯	chèn
驕	jiāo
攤	tān
顯	xiǎn
髒	zāng
體	tǐ

LIST OF FIRST CHARACTERS IN THE VOCABULARY INDEX

IN SIMPLIFIED FORM

The lead characters of all entries in the vocabulary index are listed here. Characters are ordered by number of strokes and, within each stroke-number grouping, by the configuration of the first stroke of each character. Thus a character whose pronunciation is not known can first be looked up here, then entries beginning with this character can be found in the alphabetically ordered vocabulary index on the preceding pages.

一画
一 yí
乙 yǐ

二画
十 shí
人 rén
力 lì
了 liǎo

三画
广 guǎng
丫 yā
之 zhī
于 yú
三 sān
干 gàn
下 xià
丈 zhàng
大 dà
万 wàn
才 cái
上 shàng
千 qiān
个 gè
久 jiǔ
小 xiǎo
习 xí
女 nǚ
马 mǎ

四画
火 huǒ
方 fāng
文 wén
心 xīn
认 rèn
天 tiān
夫 fū
专 zhuān
无 wú
开 kāi
云 yún
木 mù
五 wǔ
历 lì
不 bú
友 yǒu
太 tài
牙 yá
比 bǐ
少 shào
曰 yuē
贝 bèi
见 jiàn
公 gōng
分 fēn
丰 fēng
手 shǒu
牛 niú
仅 jǐn
化 huà
片 piān
斤 jīn

反 fǎn
勿 wù
风 fēng
双 shuāng
劝 quàn
引 yǐn
办 bàn
幻 huàn
以 yǐ

五画
半 bàn
头 tóu
主 zhǔ
闪 shǎn
记 jì
议 yì
必 bì
讨 tǎo
礼 lǐ
平 píng
未 wèi
世 shì
古 gǔ
本 běn
正 zhèng
布 bù
扔 rēng
可 kě
打 dǎ
业 yè
归 guī
由 yóu
甲 jiǎ

目 mù
叫 jiào
丛 cóng
生 shēng
白 bái
瓜 guā
甩 shuǎi
外 wài
用 yòng
处 chǔ
台 tái
民 mín
发 fā
纠 jiū

六画
宇 yǔ
冲 chòng
并 bìng
灯 dēng
安 ān
米 mǐ
决 jué
关 guān
讲 jiǎng
庄 zhuāng
冰 bīng
庆 qìng
忙 máng
许 xǔ
讽 fěng
农 nóng

过 guò
夹 jiá
动 dòng
艾 ài
协 xié
朴 pǔ
地 dì
老 lǎo
考 kǎo
西 xī
存 cún
成 chéng
有 yǒu
扣 kòu
执 zhí
毕 bì
团 tuán
光 guāng
当 dāng
吐 tǔ
同 tóng
吃 chī
回 huí
早 zǎo
丢 diū
杀 shā
众 zhòng
创 chuàng
会 huì
舌 shé
迁 qiān
向 xiàng
优 yōu
自 zì

后	hòu
印	yìn
名	míng
多	duō
争	zhēng
杂	zá
观	guān
尽	jǐn
导	dǎo
收	shōu
如	rú
好	hǎo
纪	jì

七画

冷	lěng
完	wán
沉	chén
判	pàn
没	méi
这	zhè
忧	yōu
评	píng
良	liáng
证	zhèng
译	yì
形	xíng
戒	jiè
弄	nòng
进	jìn
克	kè
豆	dòu
赤	chì
声	shēng
却	què
更	gèng
场	chǎng
苏	sū
还	hái
扯	chě
抓	zhuā
技	jì
把	bǎ
批	pī

呆	dāi
吹	chuī
困	kùn
别	bié, biè
吻	wěn
吵	chǎo
呀	ya
时	shí
邮	yóu
利	lì
钉	dīng
针	zhēn
乱	luàn
佐	zuǒ
伺	cì
何	hé
作	zuò
身	shēn
体	tǐ
肚	dù
条	tiáo
劲	jìn
鸡	jī
灵	líng
迟	chí
防	fáng
纽	niǔ
阵	zhèn
阴	yīn
纯	chún

八画

油	yóu
波	bō
法	fǎ
单	dān
实	shí
审	shěn
学	xué
宝	bǎo
夜	yè
废	fèi
变	biàn

放	fàng
怪	guài
闹	nào
诚	chéng
视	shì
该	gāi
诗	shī
衬	chèn
青	qīng
武	wǔ
玩	wán
表	biǎo
芽	yá
枣	zǎo
卖	mài
芦	lú
其	qí
取	qǔ
幸	xìng
枝	zhī
花	huā
松	sōng
苹	píng
奔	bēn
态	tài
奋	fèn
妻	qī
拔	bá
拙	zhuō
连	lián
担	dān
到	dào
抽	chōu
抱	bào
拖	tuō
转	zhuǎn
紧	jǐn
拉	lā
嗯	m
贩	fàn
贬	biǎn
呜	wū
罗	luó
呵	hē
明	míng

哎	āi
受	shòu
金	jīn
采	cǎi
制	zhì
和	hé
物	wù
知	zhī
货	huò
凭	píng
往	wǎng
忽	cōng
狗	gǒu
周	zhōu
周(週)	zhōu
服	fú
参	cān
居	jū
阿	ā
驾	jià
组	zǔ
孤	gū
经	jīng
练	liàn

九画

美	měi
首	shǒu
涂	tú
养	yǎng
举	jǔ
流	liú
洗	xǐ
活	huó
突	tū
总	zǒng
亲	qīn
恨	hèn
诱	yòu
语	yǔ
说	shuō
契	qì
珍	zhēn
故	gù

查	chá
苦	kǔ
树	shù
柜	guì
政	zhèng
相	xiāng
耐	nài
研	yán
面	miàn
咸	xián
按	àn
指	zhǐ
挑	tiāo
轻	qīng
省	shěng
虐	nüè
背	bēi, bèi
临	lín
咦	yí
品	pǐn
蚂	mǎ
响	xiǎng
显	xiǎn
冒	mào
咳	hai, ké
哈	ha
咱	zán
思	sī
哟	yō
剑	jiàn
科	kē
种	zhǒng
复	fù
怎	zěn
看	kàn
重	chóng
香	xiāng
顺	shùn
信	xìn
保	bǎo
段	duàn
独	dú
胆	dǎn
既	jì
眉	méi

姥 lǎo
骄 jiāo
结 jiē, jié
给 jǐ

十画

海 hǎi
烦 fán
害 hài
家 jiā
家(傢) jiā
容 róng
迹 jī
旅 lǚ
高 gāo
准 zhǔn
祖 zǔ
诸 zhū
读 dú
神 shén
祝 zhù
请 qǐng
班 bān
秦 qín
草 cǎo
荣 róng
根 gēn
真 zhēn
茶 chá
起 qǐ
赶 gǎn
原 yuán
套 tào
挫 cuò
校 xiào, jiào
核 hé
挺 tǐng
换 huàn
热 rè
唉 āi, ài
哦 ó, ò
峨 é

恩 ēn
哼 hng
哪 nǎ
拿 ná
铁 tiě
爱 ài
缺 quē
适 shì
积 jī
选 xuǎn
秘 mì
倔 jué
追 zhuī
倒 dǎo, dào
修 xiū
航 háng
胸 xiōng
脉 mò
脑 nǎo
饿 è
留 liú
脏 zāng
能 néng
难 nán
退 tuì

十一画

密 mì
淡 dàn
粒 lì
清 qīng
深 shēn
部 bù
康 kāng
阐 chǎn
情 qíng
被 bèi
理 lǐ
基 jī
检 jiǎn
教 jiào
票 piào
雪 xuě
梦 mèng

盛 shèng
捣 dǎo
接 jiē
辅 fǔ
虚 xū
蛀 zhù
唅 shá
唠 láo
啦 la
啊 a
眼 yǎn
喏 nuò
领 lǐng
梨 lí
甜 tián
透 tòu
假 jiǎ
悠 yōu
停 tíng
偷 tōu
偏 piān
逛 guàng
够 gòu
猜 cāi
欸 ē, é, ě, è
强 qiáng
蛋 dàn
婶 shěn

十二画

渴 kě
滋 zī
尊 zūn
童 tóng
惶 huáng
愤 fèn
谦 qiān
谎 huǎng
裤 kù
替 tì
博 bó
朝 cháo
棵 kē
棒 bàng

植 zhí
超 chāo
期 qī
欺 qī
黄 huáng
雁 yàn
确 què
硬 yìng
厨 chú
提 tí
敞 chǎng
赏 shǎng
幅 fú
赐 cì
喊 hǎn
黑 hēi
锋 fēng
短 duǎn
稀 xī
剩 shèng
锁 suǒ
编 biān

十三画

溜 liū
酱 jiàng
滑 huá
道 dào
满 mǎn
数 shù
意 yì
新 xīn
谨 jǐn
遍 biàn
概 gài
献 xiàn
落 luò
葡 pú
鼓 gǔ
蓝 lán
感 gǎn
摊 tān
搞 gǎo
搬 bān

嗓 sǎng
遇 yù
嘎 á
嗳 ài
遗 yí
嗯 n, ň, ǹ
照 zhào
跟 gēn
路 lù
跳 tiào
辞 cí
签 qiān
傻 shǎ
躲 duǒ
腰 yāo
群 qún

十四画

演 yǎn
精 jīng
滚 gǔn
漫 màn
旗 qí
端 duān
聚 jù
墙 qiáng
歌 gē
摸 mō
嘞 lei
颗 kē
蜡 là
嘛 ma
遥 yáo
算 suàn
管 guǎn
膀 bǎng
腿 tuǐ
熊 xióng

十五画

澎 péng
毅 yì
熟 shú

一 聪   cōng
飘   piāo
趟   tàng
撒   sā
丨 嘻   xī
嘴   zuǐ
瞎   xiā
嘿   hēi
影   yǐng
踏   tā, tà
瞒   mán
丿 稿   gǎo
篇   piān
靠   kào

十六画

激   jī
糖   táng
醒   xǐng
噢   o
膨   péng

十七 - 二十四画

赢   yíng
戴   dài
擦   cā
繁   fán
翻   fān
攀   pān
嚷   rǎng
灌   guàn
罐   guàn

红衣少女

二. 句型解釋及練習

Part II: Grammatical Notes and Exercises

CONTENTS OF PART II: GRAMMATICAL NOTES AND EXERCISES

PREFACE TO GRAMMATICAL NOTES AND EXERCISES

The grammatical notes, example sentences and exercises in this volume are designed to enhance the student's understanding of the dialogues in this film and of the authentic Chinese language in general, and to aid the student in gaining active control of the discourse patterns and key vocabulary items used in the film. In many cases notes and examples go beyond the dialogues in the film, placing the vocabulary and discourse patterns in the larger linguistic context. Many of the items selected for study here are neither purely grammatical patterns nor simple lexical items, as the syntactic and semantic aspects of the language are inextricably interwoven. This semantic-syntactic interdependence, with added dimensions of context sensitivity and emotional connotation, is much more prominent in colloquial speech than in expository prose, and dictionary definitions and textbook explanations are often inadequate to convey the full meaning and nuance of the utterance in its context. In such cases our explanations and examples need to be fleshed out and brought to life by a teacher with native-level proficiency in the language presenting the examples orally, with appropriate intonation, facial expressions, and body language.

This part is divided into the same twelve segments as *Part I: Script and Vocabulary Annotations*. Each segment contains, on the average, eight discourse patterns. In identifying the patterns to be included, a wide net was cast in order to accommodate students from different textbook backgrounds. Certain high-frequency patterns that are especially difficult for students to absorb, even though they appear in all the basic textbooks, are deliberately included in this volume for "recycling." Individual instructors should feel free to select from the list of discourse patterns to cover in class and to weed out those that seem superfluous for their students.

Within each segment, each discourse pattern is first labeled by a pattern heading, followed in the same line by the contextual example from the film. The pattern is then explained in English and further clarified by two examples (例句) placing the pattern in contexts beyond the film. To help students carry their "passive knowledge" of these patterns into "active usage," exercises of three different kinds are provided under each pattern: 造句, creating sentences using the given pattern; 填充, filling in blanks, either with the given vocabulary or in free form; and 改寫, paraphrasing the given sentence using the given pattern.

Aside from the exercises under each pattern, each segment ends with a set of inclusive translation exercises (翻譯) in which the patterns are represented in random order to foster their active use. In the translations, each sentence should contain at least one of the discourse patterns introduced in the segment.

In all the exercises, an attempt has been made to reinforce the student's newly acquired key vocabulary and to place the discourse patterns and vocabulary in a larger linguistic context beyond that of the film. If there is sufficient class time, all of these exercises, but particularly 填充 and 改寫, as well as the 討論問題 in Part I, can best be done orally to further the student's spoken language proficiency.

1) (是)… 的   不吃飯要餓死的！   (Part I, p. 4)

This is an instance of the 是…的 pattern with the 是 omitted. The pattern is used to focus on a certain aspect of the sentence or to convey emphasis. In the above example, the latter is intended. The omission of 是, which does not change the meaning, occurs frequently in colloquial speech.

例句：   1) 喝冷水會不舒服的！
            2) 吃了藥，病就會好的。

造句 - Create your own sentence, using this pattern. This exercise is inserted after example sentences under all patterns which students should learn to use actively as well as to understand. If appropriate, provide sufficient context so the meaning of your sentence is clear.

填充 - Translate the English words or short phrases into Chinese; fill in the remaining blanks with words that logically fit the contexts, incorporating the Chinese words in parentheses at the end of each sentence as well as this sentence pattern. Read the completed sentences for comprehension.

     1) 多吃那 ("plaything"), (stomach) _____ (不舒服)。
     2) (Shed tears) 以後，(eyes) ____ (紅)。
     3) 下雪了，(rather, quite) ___ (冷)。
     4) 這隻 (panda) _____ (木刻)。

2) 那…   那為什麼會餓死？   (p. 4)

那 at the beginning of a sentence means "in that case, that being the case, then..." The sentence in which 那 occurs may be a statement or a question. In context, the 那 sentence always follows a statement of a fact or situation.

例句：   1) 那為什麼會流淚？
            2) 那她怎麼會不害怕呢？

造句：

填充 - Translate the English words or short phrases into Chinese; fill in the remaining blanks with words that logically fit the contexts, using this sentence pattern. Read the completed sentences for comprehension.

     1)   A： 本來打算和她一塊兒 (review) 功課的，可是現在她不來了。
         B： _____？

SEGMENT I

1) (是)⋯ 的   不吃饭要饿死的！   (Part I, p. 5)

This is an instance of the 是⋯的 pattern with the 是 omitted. The pattern is used to focus on a certain aspect of the sentence or to convey emphasis. In the above example, the latter is intended. The omission of 是, which does not change the meaning, occurs frequently in colloquial speech.

例句：   1) 喝冷水会不舒服的！
         2) 吃了药，病就会好的。

造句 - Create your own sentence, using this pattern. This exercise is inserted after example sentences under all patterns which students should learn to use actively as well as to understand. If appropriate, provide sufficient context so the meaning of your sentence is clear.

填充 - Translate the English words or short phrases into Chinese; fill in the remaining blanks with words that logically fit the contexts, incorporating the Chinese words in parentheses at the end of each sentence as well as this sentence pattern. Read the completed sentences for comprehension.

    1) 多吃那 ("plaything"), (stomach) _____ (不舒服)。
    2) (Shed tears) 以后，(eyes) ____ (红)。
    3) 下雪了，(rather, quite) ____ (冷)。
    4) 这只 (panda) _____ (木刻)。

2) 那⋯   那为什么会饿死？   (p. 5)

那 at the beginning of a sentence means "in that case, that being the case, then..." The sentence in which 那 occurs may be a statement or a question. In context, the 那 sentence always follows a statement of a fact or situation.

例句：   1) 那为什么会流泪？
         2) 那她怎么会不害怕呢？

造句：

填充 - Translate the English words or short phrases into Chinese; fill in the remaining blanks with words that logically fit the contexts, using this sentence pattern. Read the completed sentences for comprehension.

    1)   A： 本来打算和她一块儿 (review) 功课的，可是现在她不来了。
         B： _____？

2) A： 他的 (history) 一直很好，可這次沒考好。

　　B： _____ ?

3) A： 那對 (husband and wife) 老是 (bicker, quarrel)，沒什麼 (love).

　　B： __ 他們原來為什麼要 (marry) 呢？

4) A： 多吃核桃 (hair) 會 (become) 黑的。

　　B： __ 你怎麼不 ____ 呢？

3) 還 V   還笑，好意思。 (p. 8)

還, meaning "yet" or "even," is sometimes used in scolding someone whose behavior or action is inappropriate for the situation at hand.

例句： 1) 是你自己的錯，還哭！
　　　　2) 還唱，真難聽！

填充： 1) 姐妹 (quarrel) 了，她們的母親對她們說：" ____ , _____ 。"
　　　　2) 弟弟打了哥哥，可他自己哭了。媽媽說："弟弟，_____ , _____ 。"
　　　　3) 那個 (peasant) 來得太晚了，公共汽車剛走。他趕快地 (chase) 上去。旁邊的人說：
　　　　　 " ____ , _____ 。"
　　　　4) 這學期他一點兒書都沒讀。到了 (end of semester) 他想請一位同學給他 (tutor)。
　　　　　 這位同學不高興地說：" _____ , _____ 。"

4) 多/多麼…   多精彩的木刻。 (p. 8)

The closest English equivalent to this exclamatory pattern is "How...!" The shorter form 多, rather than 多麼, is frequently used in colloquial speech, as exemplified by the above example. The exclamatory remark may also end with the particle 啊 to convey an even greater exclamatory tone.

例句： 1) 你看，多憂慮的眼睛。
　　　　2) 聽，多有意思的音樂。

造句：

填充： 1) 這部 (film) 很有意思。
　　　　2) 那篇 (ancient literature) 真難懂。
　　　　3) 這隻 (panda) 太可愛了。
　　　　4) 這對 (husband and wife) 很 (pitiful).

改寫 - Reword the completed sentences in the preceding exercise, using this pattern.

2) A： 他的 (history) 一直很好，可这次沒考好。
    B： ＿＿＿＿＿＿＿＿＿ ？

3) A： 那对 (husband and wife) 老是 (bicker, quarrel)，沒什么 (love)。
    B： ＿ 他们原来为什么要 (marry) 呢？

4) A： 多吃核桃 (hair) 会 (become) 黑的。
    B： ＿ 你怎么不 ＿＿＿ 呢？

3) 还 V   还笑，好意思。 (p. 9)

还, meaning "yet" or "even," is sometimes used in scolding someone whose behavior or action is inappropriate for the situation at hand.

例句： 1) 是你自己的错，还哭！
       2) 还唱，真难听！

填充： 1) 姐妹 (quarrel) 了，她们的母亲对她们说："＿＿＿，＿＿＿＿＿。"
       2) 弟弟打了哥哥，可他自己哭了。妈妈说："弟弟，＿＿＿＿，＿＿＿＿。"
       3) 那个 (peasant) 来得太晚了，公共汽车刚走。他赶快地 (chase) 上去。旁边的人说：
           "＿＿＿＿，＿＿＿＿。"
       4) 这学期他一点儿书都没读。到了 (end of semester) 他想请一位同学给他 (tutor)。
           这位同学不高兴地说："＿＿＿＿＿，＿＿＿＿。"

4) 多/多么…   多精彩的木刻。 (p. 9)

The closest English equivalent to this exclamatory pattern is "How...!" The shorter form 多, rather than 多么, is frequently used in colloquial speech, as exemplified by the above example. The exclamatory remark may also end with the particle 啊 to convey an even greater exclamatory tone.

例句： 1) 你看，多忧虑的眼睛。
       2) 听，多有意思的音乐。

造句：

填充： 1) 这部 (film) 很有意思。
       2) 那篇 (ancient literature) 真难懂。
       3) 这只 (panda) 太可爱了。
       4) 这对 (husband and wife) 很 (pitiful)。

改写 - Reword the completed sentences in the preceding exercise, using this pattern.

5) 可   她媽對她學習抓得可緊呢！(p. 10)

The adverb 可 has two meanings: a) It can be a synonym of 可是, in which case it is a movable adverb just like 可是, and can occur before or after the subject. b) It can also mean "indeed, certainly," in which case it is not a movable adverb, and must follow the subject and immediately precede the verb phrase. The second meaning is intended in the example above.

例句：   1) 他對朋友可好呢。
     2) 我複習功課可認真啦。

造句：

填充：   1) 那個 (wood sculpture) 真 (splendid).
     2) 八十年代的新 (peasant) 真有意思.
     3) 這次歷史 (end of semester) 考試真難啊。

改寫 - Reword the following sentence and the completed sentences in the preceding exercise, using this pattern: 北方的冬天太冷了。

6) V 起 (O) (來)   講起三國演義來…… (p. 10)

The 起來 in this pattern functions as the complement attached to the preceding verb. If the verb has an object, it would be placed between 起 and 來, e.g. 下起雪來, 唱起歌來. As verb complement, 起來 has two meanings: a) "To begin...," e.g. 你怎麼抽起煙來了？ "How come you've begun to smoke?" A variation of this is SV-起來 "to begin to become SV, to be becoming SV," e.g. 他好起來了。 "He is getting well." b) "When it comes to," e.g. 他喝起來酒來，真不得了。 "When he gets to drinking, he is really something (he drinks a great deal)." The latter usage is intended in the above example.

例句：   1) 唱起歌來，聲音可大呢。
     2) 思考起來，像個大人似的。

造句 - Create sentences, incorporating the vocabulary items given and this pattern.
    1) 輔導學生   認真
    2) 寫小說   有意思
    3) 吵嘴   利害
    4) 畫畫兒   什麼都忘了

5) 可   她妈对她学习抓得可紧呢！ (p. 11)

The adverb 可 has two meanings: a) It can be a synonym of 可是, in which case it is a movable adverb just like 可是, and can occur before or after the subject. b) It can also mean "indeed, certainly," in which case it is not a movable adverb, and must follow the subject and immediately precede the verb phrase. The second meaning is intended in the example above.

例句：   1) 他对朋友可好呢。
          2) 我复习功课可认真啦。

造句：

填充：   1) 那个 (wood sculpture) 真 (splendid).
          2) 八十年代的新 (peasant) 真有意思.
          3) 这次历史 (end of semester) 考试真难啊。

改写 - Reword the following sentence and the completed sentences in the preceding exercise, using this pattern: 北方的冬天太冷了。

6) V 起 (O) (来)   讲起三国演义来…… (p. 11)

The 起来 in this pattern functions as the complement attached to the preceding verb. If the verb has an object, it would be placed between 起 and 来, e.g. 下起雪来, 唱起歌来. As verb complement, 起来 has two meanings: a) "To begin...," e.g. 你怎么抽起烟来了？ "How come you've begun to smoke?" A variation of this is SV-起来 "to begin to become SV, to be becoming SV," e.g. 他好起来了。 "He is getting well." b) "When it comes to," e.g. 他喝起来酒来，真不得了。 "When he gets to drinking, he is really something (he drinks a great deal)." The latter usage is intended in the above example.

例句：   1) 唱起歌来，声音可大呢。
          2) 思考起来，象个大人似的。

造句 - Create sentences, incorporating the vocabulary items given and this pattern.
          1) 辅导学生   认真
          2) 写小说   有意思
          3) 吵嘴   利害
          4) 画画儿   什么都忘了

7) …的   讲起三国演义来一套一套的…… (p. 11)

In colloquial Chinese, one way to describe something (a person, a matter, a phenomenon, etc.) is to use a descriptive predicate made by adding 的 to a phrase or a stock expression. Thus 一套一套的 means "in a well-organized, set by set, manner."

例句：   1) 他吃饭一大碗一大碗的。
          2) 他爱唱歌，一首接一首的。

填充, incorporate this pattern into the completed sentences:
          1) 他爱讲故事，＿＿＿＿＿ (一个又一个)。
          2) 他写的毛笔字 ＿＿＿＿ (漂亮)。
          3) 祝文娟复习起功课来 ＿＿＿＿ (认真)。
          4) 这对夫妻吵起嘴来 ＿＿＿＿ (打，骂)。

8) 为 O (V)   那就为你自己？ (p. 11)

为 can be the main verb of a sentence meaning "for, for the sake of" as in the above example, or it can be a coverb in the context of 为 O V "to V for the sake of...." Note that when 为 is used in this sense, it is pronounced in the fourth tone and not the second tone as in 以为.

例句：   1) 我不能老为你洗衣服啊！
          2) 你就知道为你自己。

造句 - Create sentences, incorporating the vocabulary items given and this pattern.
          1) 洗头发
          2) 做饭
          3) 辅导古文
          4) 做物理作业

9) O 不能/可/应该…   话不能这么说。 (p. 11)

This is an injunction against doing something. But to tone down the harshness of it, the sentence is cast in the "notional passive" form in the following way: the logical subject 你 is omitted from the standard pattern "你不能/可/应该 VP," and the object is shifted to the topic position in front of the sentence in order to focus on it. The same effect is achieved in English by using passive voice. E.g., "You shouldn't tell others about that matter." vs. "That matter shouldn't be told to others."

例句：   1) 事情不应该这么做。
          2) 这种酒不能多喝。

造句：

改寫：　例：別老讓姐姐幫你洗頭髮。　　　　頭髮不能老讓姐姐幫你洗。
1) 不要那樣寫毛筆字。
2) 別喝太多的冷水。
3) 吃太多糖不好。
4) 別扔掉這個西瓜。

10)　V 上　　　　　　　　媽怎麼會愛上爸的？　(p. 12)

The 上 in this pattern is a resultative verb, one meaning of which is similar to the resultative verb 起 ("to begin, to start up, to up and...," cf. pattern 6 above). A second meaning of the resultative verb 上, which does not overlap with the meaning of 起, is "attachment," in either the literal (e.g. 貼上郵票) or the figurative (e.g. 愛上了她) sense. Both meanings are present in the above example.

例句：　1) 我愛上工作了。
2) 才十三歲，怎麼抽上煙了？

填充：　1) 韋老師開始寫 (poetry) 了。
2) 那對夫妻又開始 (quarrel) 了。
3) 媽媽開始愛 (wood sculpture) 了。
4) 外國朋友也開始愛 (panda) 了。

改寫 - Reword the completed sentences in the preceding exercise, using this pattern.

11)　就(是)　　　　　　　　佐羅就漂亮。　(p. 12)

就(是) in this context can be translated as "just" or "simply," indicating that there is no ambivalence in the fact or situation. In some cases, 就(是) implies that the subject is determined or stubborn about doing something. In the above example, the 是 in 就是 is omitted, as is often done in colloquial speech (cf. Grammatical Note II.11.).

例句：　1) 我就喜歡看小說嘛。
2) 妹妹就是不聽話。

造句：

填充, incorporate this pattern into the completed sentences:
1) 安然喜歡那件 (red blouse)，她說：＿＿＿＿＿。

造句：

改写：　例：别老让姐姐帮你洗头发。　　　　　头发不能老让姐姐帮你洗。
　　　　1) 不要那样写毛笔字。
　　　　2) 别喝太多的冷水。
　　　　3) 吃太多糖不好。
　　　　4) 别扔掉这个西瓜。

10)　V 上　　　　　　　　　　　妈怎么会爱上爸的？　(p. 13)

The 上 in this pattern is a resultative verb, one meaning of which is similar to the resultative verb 起 ("to begin, to start up, to up and...," cf. pattern 6 above). A second meaning of the resultative verb 上, which does not overlap with the meaning of 起, is "attachment," in either the literal (e.g. 贴上邮票) or the figurative (e.g. 爱上了她) sense. Both meanings are present in the above example.

例句：　1) 我爱上工作了。
　　　　2) 才十三岁，怎么抽上烟了？

填充：　1) 韦老师开始写 (poetry) 了。
　　　　2) 那对夫妻又开始 (quarrel) 了。
　　　　3) 妈妈开始爱 (wood sculpture) 了。
　　　　4) 外国朋友也开始爱 (panda) 了。

改写 - Reword the completed sentences in the preceding exercise, using this pattern.

11)　就(是)　　　　　　　　　　佐罗就漂亮。 (p. 13)

就(是) in this context can be translated as "just" or "simply," indicating that there is no ambivalence in the fact or situation. In some cases, 就(是) implies that the subject is determined or stubborn about doing something. In the above example, the 是 in 就是 is omitted, as is often done in colloquial speech (cf. Grammatical Note II.11.).

例句：　1) 我就喜欢看小说嘛。
　　　　2) 妹妹就是不听话。

造句：

填充, incorporate this pattern into the completed sentences:
　　　　1) 安然喜欢那件 (red blouse)，她说：＿＿＿＿＿＿。

2) 安靜 (understands) 她妹妹。她自信地說：_____。

3) 劉冬虎不願意 (review) 功課，他說：_____。

4) 爸爸、媽媽不願意姐姐和 (peasant) (marry). 可是姐姐說：_____。

12) …，…也…　　　　　　　　你不願意聽，我也要説！ (p. 14)

This is a two-clause expression meaning "even if..., (still)..." The tricky thing here is that the key to this pattern, 也, occurs in the second clause in Chinese, whereas the key words "even if" occur in the first clause in English. In addition to 也 in the second clause, the adverb 就是 may be used in the first clause, in which case the relationship between the two clauses would be even more explicit. E.g. 你就是不願意聽，我也要説！

例句：　1) 你不愛聽，我也要唱。

　　　　2) 你不愛喝茶，我也要你喝。

造句：

填充, incorporate this pattern into the completed sentences:

　　　　1) 你功課再好，_____ (認真複習)。

　　　　2) 你再累，_____ (完成工作)。

　　　　3) 現在你不喜歡畫畫兒，_____ (畫完)。

　　　　4) 我不喜歡物理，可是爲了考試，_____ (複習)。

13) 不是…嗎？　　　　　　　　她不是你的小學同學嗎？ (p. 14)

This is a rhetorical question meaning "isn't it...?" and implying that it is indeed the case, but at the same time urging the other person to confirm or recognize the fact. This pattern can also be used to "enclose" two phrases, as in 你不是總批評我，説我對她不好嗎？ (Cf. Part I, p. 78.)

例句：　1) 你不是比我大一歲嗎？

　　　　2) 那對夫妻不是不吵嘴了嗎？

造句：

填充：　1) 他有個 (tutoring) 老師，怎麼還是沒考好？

　　　　2) 你已經 (review) 過了 (ancient literature), 對不對？

　　　　3) 那個 (wood-carved) (panda), 扔了 (rather) 可惜的。

2) 安静 (understands) 她妹妹。她自信地说：＿＿＿＿＿。

3) 刘冬虎不愿意 (review) 功课，他说：＿＿＿＿＿。

4) 爸爸、妈妈不愿意姐姐和 (peasant) (marry). 可是姐姐说：＿＿＿＿。

12) …，…也…　　　　　　　你不愿意听，我也要说！ (p. 15)

This is a two-clause expression meaning "even if..., (still)..." The tricky thing here is that the key to this pattern, 也, occurs in the second clause in Chinese, whereas the key words "even if" occur in the first clause in English. In addition to 也 in the second clause, the adverb 就是 may be used in the first clause, in which case the relationship between the two clauses would be even more explicit. E.g. 你就是不愿意听，我也要说！

例句：　1) 你不爱听，我也要唱。
　　　　2) 你不爱喝茶，我也要你喝。

造句：

填充, incorporate this pattern into the completed sentences:

　　　1) 你功课再好，＿＿＿＿＿ (认真复习)。

　　　2) 你再累，＿＿＿＿＿ (完成工作)。

　　　3) 现在你不喜欢画画儿，＿＿＿＿ (画完)。

　　　4) 我不喜欢物理，可是为了考试，＿＿＿＿ (复习)。

13) 不是…吗？　　　　　　　她不是你的小学同学吗？ (p. 15)

This is a rhetorical question meaning "isn't it...?" and implying that it is indeed the case, but at the same time urging the other person to confirm or recognize the fact. This pattern can also be used to "enclose" two phrases, as in 你不是总批评我，说我对她不好吗？ (Cf. Part I, p. 79.)

例句：　1) 你不是比我大一岁吗？
　　　　2) 那对夫妻不是不吵嘴了吗？

造句：

填充：　1) 他有个 (tutoring) 老师，怎么还是沒考好？

　　　　2) 你已经 (review) 过了 (ancient literature), 对不对？

　　　　3) 那个 (wood-carved) (panda), 扔了 (rather) 可惜的。

改寫 - Reword the following sentence and the completed sentences in the preceding exercise, using this pattern: 爺爺昨晚生病了。 今天怎麼那麼早就起來了？

14)   Subject/topic, predicate/comment   韋老師的心，實在摸不透！ (p. 14)

A comma separating the subject or topic of a sentence from the predicate or "comment" provides a pause which lends greater focus or weight to the subject or topic. This focus can be further reinforced by adding 啊 (or any of the variants 呀, 哪, 哇), 呢, 嘛 or 吧 at the end of the subject or topic, as in 就上回打架吧， ⋯ (Cf. Part I, p. 114.)

例句：   1) 這篇古文，的確太難。
         2) 期末的評三好哇，挺讓學生害怕的。

填充：   1) 那個安然真不懂 (etiquette).
         2) 我完全看不懂這篇 (ancient literature).
         3) 沒去過農村的知識分子 (truly) 不 (understand) (peasants).
         4) 這個會 (contemplate) 的少女給我留下了很深的印象。

改寫 - Reword the completed sentences in the preceding exercise, using this pattern.

INCLUSIVE 翻譯 EXERCISE FOR SEGMENT I. The translation exercises are designed to provide practice in using the sentence patterns introduced in each segment. Therefore, each sentence in this section should contain at least one of the sentence patterns introduced in the segment.

1) In that case, why are you afraid?

2) What a cute panda!

3) When the two of them get to arguing; it's really something!

4) She did it that way solely (completely) for the sake of her daughters.

5) When did you become friends with that peasant? (make friends: 作朋友)

6) Even if you don't like to review, you've got to review.

7) Those eyes of hers, they are truly beautiful.

8 - 14) See bottom of facing page.

改写 - Reword the following sentence and the completed sentences in the preceding exercise, using this pattern: 爷爷昨晚生病了。今天怎么那么早就起来了？

14) Subject/topic, predicate/comment   韦老师的心，实在摸不透！ (p. 15)

A comma separating the subject or topic of a sentence from the predicate or "comment" provides a pause which lends greater focus or weight to the subject or topic. This focus can be further reinforced by adding 啊 (or any of the variants 呀, 哪, 哇), 呢, 嘛 or 吧 at the end of the subject or topic, as in 就上回打架吧，… (Cf. Part I, p. 115.)

例句： 1) 这篇古文，的确太难。
       2) 期末的评三好哇，挺让学生害怕的。

填充： 1) 那个安然真不懂 (etiquette).
       2) 我完全看不懂这篇 (ancient literature).
       3) 没去过农村的知识分子 (truly) 不 (understand) (peasants).
       4) 这个会 (contemplate) 的少女给我留下了很深的印象。

改写 - Reword the completed sentences in the preceding exercise, using this pattern.

INCLUSIVE 翻译 EXERCISE FOR SEGMENT I. The translation exercises are designed to provide practice in using the sentence patterns introduced in each segment. Therefore, each sentence in this section should contain at least one of the sentence patterns introduced in the segment.

1 - 7) See bottom of facing page.
   8) In getting married, there must be love. (emphatic statement)
   9) The vehicle is running faster and faster, yet you're still chasing (it)?
  10) That couple (pair of husband and wife) is indeed interesting.
  11) Our records are quite clear.
  12) That matter must not be forgotten.
  13) I just don't like history class.
  14) Didn't that panda starve to death?

SEGMENT II

1) Subject 來 VP   下面我來講講這句⋯ (p. 16)

來, used before a verb phrase, indicates that the subject intends to or is about to do something. This usage is similar to the usage of "go" in the English expression "I am going to...."

例句：   1) 誰能來編輯這本書呢？
            2) 你姐姐的英文不是挺好的？可以讓她來輔導你嘛。

填充, incorporate this pattern into the completed sentences:
            1) 誰能給我 (explain) 這個 (physics) 題目？我 _____ 。
            2) 誰願意 (wait upon, serve) 他？我今天沒事，_____ 。
            3) 誰有工夫 (look after) 這個病了的孩子？奶奶說：_____ 。
            4) 安靜對安然說：我 (married) 以後，你就得自己 __ (wash hair) 了。

2) (先)⋯再 VP   先按我的讀，下課，查查字典再說！ (p. 16)

The adverbs 先 and 再 used in two coordinate clauses indicate that the two events do, should, or are intended to occur in the sequence given. The adverb 先 in the first clause may be understood and omitted. This pattern is to be distinguished from the pattern 先⋯，⋯才⋯, which, in addition to indicating the same temporal sequence, also implies that the second event is later than expected or desired.

例句：   1) 從前在中國人們不是先有了愛情再結婚的。
            2) 在美國大學生是先進了大學再決定專業的。

造句：

填充：   1) 我打算 (review) 完 (physics) 以後就 (review ancient literature)。
            2) 大夫會給你 (examine) 了以後才告訴你得吃什麼藥。
            3) 你不必立刻去買 (stamps)，可以把信寫好了，然後去買。
            4) 每年都是 (end of semester) 考試完了就進行評"三好生"。

改寫 - Reword the completed sentences in the preceding exercise, using this pattern.

SEGMENT II

1) Subject 来 VP   下面我来讲讲这句… (p. 17)

来, used before a verb phrase, indicates that the subject intends to or is about to do something.
This usage is similar to the usage of "go" in the English expression "I am going to...."

例句：   1) 谁能来编辑这本书呢？
            2) 你姐姐的英文不是挺好的？可以让她来辅导你嘛。

填充, incorporate this pattern into the completed sentences:
            1) 谁能给我 (explain) 这个 (physics) 题目？我 _____。
            2) 谁愿意 (wait upon, serve) 他？我今天没事，_____。
            3) 谁有工夫 (look after) 这个病了的孩子？奶奶说：_____。
            4) 安静对安然说：我 (married) 以后，你就得自己 __ (wash hair) 了。

2) (先)…再 VP   先按我的读，下课，查查字典再说！ (p. 17)

The adverbs 先 and 再 used in two coordinate clauses indicate that the two events do, should, or are
intended to occur in the sequence given. The adverb 先 in the first clause may be understood and
omitted. This pattern is to be distinguished from the pattern 先…，…才…, which, in addition to
indicating the same temporal sequence, also implies that the second event is later than expected or
desired.

例句：   1) 从前在中国人们不是先有了爱情再结婚的。
            2) 在美国大学生是先进了大学再决定专业的。

造句：

填充：   1) 我打算 (review) 完 (physics) 以后就 (review ancient literature)。
            2) 大夫会给你 (examine) 了以后才告诉你得吃什么药。
            3) 你不必立刻去买 (stamps)，可以把信写好了，然后去买。
            4) 每年都是 (end of semester) 考试完了就进行评"三好生"。

改写 - Reword the completed sentences in the preceding exercise, using this pattern.

3)   在 V   我剛才看見你拿着在翻。 (p. 16)

在 is normally used to introduce a location or time element. But it can be used before a verb to indicate that the subject is in the midst of doing something. In English translation, this usage of 在 usually comes out as the progressive tense.

例句：   1) 他在檢查你的行李，你最好對他禮貌點兒。
         2) 上次叫你別抽煙，你怎麼又在抽煙了？

造句：

填充：   1) 安靜在幹什麼？ (Washing hair for An Ran).
         2) 米曉玲在做什麼？ (Doing her physics homework).
         3) 安然 (is tutoring) 劉冬虎 (in English).
         4) 韋老師在課上做什麼？ (Earnestly explaining ancient literature).

4)   在…上   大家在學習上，要更加踏實。 (p. 18)

This pattern means "speaking from the standpoint of...," and is a "situational" or "conditional" phrase that precedes the main verb phrase of the sentence.

例句：   1) 安靜在工作上非常認真。
         2) 安然在學習上是相當努力的。

造句：

填充：   1) 學生們的學習 (attitude) 應該 (set straight) 一點兒。
         2) 王洪衛的 (ancient literature) 不怎麼好，可是他的 (professional specialty) (quite) 不錯的。
         3) 在過去十年中，(peasant) 的生活比從前好多了，可是在 (education) 這方面，水平還很低。
         4) 安然雖然愛玩兒，可是她 (contemplate) 問題的時候挺像個大人的。

改寫 - Reword the completed sentences in the preceding exercise, using this pattern.

5)   Pronoun subject repeated at end of sentence [colloquial]   你欺負我，你。 (p. 20)

In colloquial speech, a pronoun-subject which occurs at the beginning of a sentence can be repeated at the end of the sentence for emphasis, as if to rub in or remind the listener who the subject is. 你 occurs most frequently as the subject in this pattern. This pattern can also be used in commands, in which

3)   在 V   我刚才看见你拿着在翻。 (p. 17)

在 is normally used to introduce a location or time element. But it can be used before a verb to indicate that the subject is in the midst of doing something. In English translation, this usage of 在 usually comes out as the progressive tense.

例句：   1) 他在检查你的行李，你最好对他礼貌点儿。
         2) 上次叫你别抽烟，你怎么又在抽烟了？

造句：

填充：   1) 安静在干什么？ (Washing hair for An Ran).
         2) 米晓玲在做什么？ (Doing her physics homework).
         3) 安然 (is tutoring) 刘冬虎 (in English).
         4) 韦老师在课上做什么？ (Earnestly explaining ancient literature).

4)   在···上   大家在学习上，要更加踏实。 (p. 19)

This pattern means "speaking from the standpoint of...," and is a "situational" or "conditional" phrase that precedes the main verb phrase of the sentence.

例句：   1) 安静在工作上非常认真。
         2) 安然在学习上是相当努力的。

造句：

填充：   1) 学生们的学习 (attitude) 应该 (set straight) 一点儿。
         2) 王洪卫的 (ancient literature) 不怎么好，可是他的 (professional specialty) (quite) 不错的。
         3) 在过去十年中，(peasant) 的生活比从前好多了，可是在 (education) 这方面，水平还很低。
         4) 安然虽然爱玩儿，可是她 (contemplate) 问题的时候挺象个大人的。

改写 - Reword the completed sentences in the preceding exercise, using this pattern.

5)   Pronoun subject repeated at end of sentence [colloquial]   你欺负我，你。 (p. 21)

In colloquial speech, a pronoun-subject which occurs at the beginning of a sentence can be repeated at the end of the sentence for emphasis, as if to rub in or remind the listener who the subject is. 你 occurs most frequently as the subject in this pattern. This pattern can also be used in commands, in which case the subject 你 may be omitted at the beginning of the sentence but retained at the end, e.g. 快走吧，你。 A similar usage in commands occurs in colloquial English, e.g., "You'd better listen, you!"

例句：　1) 你騙我，你。
　　　　2) 你怎麼了，你。

填充, incorporate this pattern into the completed sentences:
　　　1) 妻子打了丈夫，丈夫説：＿＿＿＿＿＿＿。
　　　2) 安然和安靜 (quarrel), 安靜説：你別 ＿＿＿＿＿＿＿。
　　　3) 爸爸 (smoke) 抽得很利害，媽媽説：＿＿＿＿＿＿＿。
　　　4) 媽媽怕安然考不好，不能 (graduate), 所以説："你專心做 (homework) 吧，你。"

6)　Object as topic of sentence　　　　　　　丟掉專業的滋味兒，你們知道。 (p. 20)

The logical object of a sentence may be shifted to topic position in front of the sentence in order to focus on it. The same nuance is conveyed in English not by a different word order, but by the use of stress and intonation.

例句：　1) 這玩意兒，你最好別多吃。
　　　　2) 剛下鄉的青年，農民要特別照顧。

造句：

填充：　1) 我實在不 (understand) 那句 (ancient literature).
　　　　2) 李老師非常 (earnest), 每星期都 (inspect/examine) 學生的作業。
　　　　3) 我並不賞識那套 (commemorative stamps).
　　　　4) 這學生雖然聰明，可是 (must) 端正他的學習 (attitude).

改寫 - Reword the completed sentences in the preceding exercise, using this pattern.

7)　Understood subjects　　　　　　　　　就會畫那些不被賞識的畫。 (p. 20)

The subject of a sentence, when understood, is often omitted. In the above example, 你 is the omitted subject.

例句：　1) 就知道玩兒。
　　　　2) 不知道他什麼時候學會了抽煙。

填充：　1) 挺喜歡在 (educational sector) 工作的。

case the subject 你 may be omitted at the beginning of the sentence but retained at the end, e.g. 快走吧，你。 A similar usage in commands occurs in colloquial English, e.g., "You'd better listen, you!"

例句：　1) 你骗我，你。
　　　　2) 你怎么了，你。

填充, incorporate this pattern into the completed sentences:
　　　　1) 妻子打了丈夫，丈夫说：＿＿＿＿＿＿＿。
　　　　2) 安然和安静 (quarrel), 安静说：你别 ＿＿＿＿＿＿＿。
　　　　3) 爸爸 (smoke) 抽得很利害，妈妈说：＿＿＿＿＿＿＿。
　　　　4) 妈妈怕安然考不好，不能 (graduate), 所以说："你专心做 (homework) 吧，你。"

6)　Object as topic of sentence　　　　　　　　丢掉专业的滋味儿，你们知道。 (p. 21)

The logical object of a sentence may be shifted to topic position in front of the sentence in order to focus on it. The same nuance is conveyed in English not by a different word order, but by the use of stress and intonation.

例句：　1) 这玩意儿，你最好别多吃。
　　　　2) 刚下乡的青年，农民要特别照顾。

造句：

填充：　1) 我实在不 (understand) 那句 (ancient literature).
　　　　2) 李老师非常 (earnest), 每星期都 (inspect/examine) 学生的作业。
　　　　3) 我并不赏识那套 (commemorative stamps).
　　　　4) 这学生虽然聪明，可是 (must) 端正他的学习 (attitude).

改写 - Reword the completed sentences in the preceding exercise, using this pattern.

7)　Understood subjects　　　　　　　　　　就会画那些不被赏识的画。 (p. 21)

The subject of a sentence, when understood, is often omitted. In the above example, 你 is the omitted subject.

例句：　1) 就知道玩儿。
　　　　2) 不知道他什么时候学会了抽烟。

填充：　1) 挺喜欢在 (educational sector) 工作的。

2) 老跟同學借 (physics homework), 這怎麼行呢？

3) 聰明是聰明，可是對老師的 (attitude) 實在不夠 (modest).

4) 姐姐 (marry) 了，以後就得自己 (wash hair) 了。

改寫, add a subject in each of the completed sentences in the preceding exercise.

8) 才   才不呢，… (p. 22)

One usage of 才, as exemplified in the above sentence, is to convey contradiction or defiance of an assumption, suggestion, or view which has just been expressed by the other person in the conversation or is prevalent. This usage of 才 occurs more frequently with a negative verb than with a positive one.

例句：   1) 安靜：安然的精力太過盛了！
            爸爸：這樣才好呢！
        2) A： 他們夫妻關係挺好吧？
            B： 才不呢，他們一天到晚吵嘴呢！

造句：

填充：   1) 安然：姐，你喜歡替我 (wash hair) 吧？
            安靜：才 _____，你從明天起就得自己洗了。
        2) 一位 (lady) 對她的丈夫說：你別以為女人都喜歡做家事。我有我的 (professional specialty), __ 不願意在家 (wait upon) 你呢。
        3) A： 像安然這麼一個又 (smart) 又 (earnest) 的學生，老師們一定都喜歡她。
            B： 才 ____! 老師們不 (understand) 她，以為她沒有 (etiquette).
        4) 因為安然喜歡在課上提問題，韋老師覺得她的 (attitude) 不好。其實，我覺得這 __ 是她的 (strong point).

9) V-O V 的 [colloquial]   你給我吃核桃吃的。 (p. 22)

This is a special form of the 是…的 pattern in which the verb is repeated just before the final 的 to indicate that a certain circumstance or state came about as a result of the verb.

例句：   1) 他那麼胖，是吃冰淇淋吃的。
        2) 他感冒了，是昨天出去玩兒吹風吹的。

填充, incorporate this pattern into the completed sentences:
        1) 他的牙齒發黃了，_____ (抽煙).
        2) 米曉玲的 (eyes) 紅了，是昨晚 _____ (流淚).

2) 老跟同学借 (physics homework)，这怎么行呢？

3) 聪明是聪明，可是对老师的 (attitude) 实在不够 (modest)．

4) 姐姐 (marry) 了，以后就得自己 (wash hair) 了。

改写, add a subject in each of the completed sentences in the preceding exercise.

8) 才　　　　　　　　　　　　　　　才不呢，… (p. 23)

One usage of 才, as exemplified in the above sentence, is to convey contradiction or defiance of an assumption, suggestion, or view which has just been expressed by the other person in the conversation or is prevalent. This usage of 才 occurs more frequently with a negative verb than with a positive one.

例句：　1) 安静：安然的精力太过盛了！
　　　　　　爸爸：这样才好呢！
　　　　2) A：他们夫妻关系挺好吧？
　　　　　　B：才不呢，他们一天到晚吵嘴呢！

造句：

填充：　1) 安然：姐，你喜欢替我 (wash hair) 吧？
　　　　　　安静：才 ＿＿＿＿，你从明天起就得自己洗了。
　　　　2) 一位 (lady) 对她的丈夫说：你别以为女人都喜欢做家事。我有我的 (professional specialty)，＿＿ 不愿意在家 (wait upon) 你呢。
　　　　3) A：象安然这么一个又 (smart) 又 (earnest) 的学生，老师们一定都喜欢她。
　　　　　　B：才 ＿＿＿＿！老师们不 (understand) 她，以为她没有 (etiquette)．
　　　　4) 因为安然喜欢在课上提问题，韦老师觉得她的 (attitude) 不好。其实，我觉得这 ＿＿
　　　　　　是她的 (strong point)．

9) V-O V 的 [colloquial]　　　　　　　　　你给我吃核桃吃的。 (p. 23)

This is a special form of the 是…的 pattern in which the verb is repeated just before the final 的 to indicate that a certain circumstance or state came about as a result of the verb.

例句：　1) 他那么胖，是吃冰淇淋吃的。
　　　　2) 他感冒了，是昨天出去玩儿吹风吹的。

填充, incorporate this pattern into the completed sentences:
　　　　1) 他的牙齿发黄了，＿＿＿＿＿＿＿＿ (抽烟)．
　　　　2) 米晓玲的 (eyes) 红了，是昨晚 ＿＿＿＿＿＿＿ (流泪)．

　　　3) 我右手那麼累是 ＿＿＿＿＿＿＿＿ (寫作業)。

　　　4) 安靜的文章寫得那麼好是年青的時候 ＿＿＿＿＿＿＿＿ (讀小說)。

10)　PN 這個/那個 N　　　　　　　　　你這個人哪，就一條優點，倔。 (p. 22)

When "這個/那個 so-and-so" comes immediately after a pronoun or a personal name, attention is being called to that person's disposition, habit, or personality, and usually to some negative aspect of it.

例句：　1) 你這個人哪，就是愛吵嘴。

　　　　2) 他這個老頭子，一天到晚要別人伺候他。

填充：　1) 那個學生學習 (attitude) 就是不夠 (modest).

　　　　2) 那個小孩子沒有人 (tutor) 的話就念不好書。

　　　　3) 你怎麼老是喜歡 (bully) 少女呢？

　　　　4) 他是個 (greatly capable person)，不必 (review) 也能考得很好。

改寫 - Reword the completed sentences in the preceding exercise, using this pattern.

11)　就 NP [colloquial]　　　　　　　　就一條優點，… (p. 22)

Since 就 is an adverb, it may seem odd that it is followed by a noun phrase and not by a verb. In colloquial speech, the verb 有 and 是 (unlike other verbs) can be omitted when the meaning of the sentence is clear without the 有 or 是. In the above example, the omitted verb is 有, so the phrase is actually derived from 就有一條優點。 (Cf. Grammatical Note V.4. for additional examples of the omission of 有 and 是.)

例句：　1) 安然就一個姐姐。

　　　　2) 沒什麼可說的，就這麼回事。

填充：　1) 上 (physics) 課的就有她一個女生。

　　　　2) 你覺得一對 (husband and wife) 就有一個孩子怎麼樣？

改寫 - Reword the completed sentences in the preceding exercise, using this pattern.

12)　又　　　　　　　　　　　　　我又怎麼了？ (p. 24)

Aside from its basic meaning of "again," 又 sometimes has the function of stressing a certain aspect of the expression. This second function can be conveyed in English not by translation but by stressing the relevant words. Context usually makes clear which of the two above meanings is intended. In the above

3) 我右手那么累是 ＿＿＿＿＿＿＿＿ (写作业)。

4) 安静的文章写得那么好是年青的时候 ＿＿＿＿＿＿＿＿ (读小说)。

10) PN 这/那个 N   你这个人哪，就一条优点，偃。 (p. 23)

When "这个/那个 so-and-so" comes immediately after a pronoun or a personal name, attention is being called to that person's disposition, habit, or personality, and usually to some negative aspect of it.

例句： 1) 你这个人哪，就是爱吵嘴。

2) 他这个老头子，一天到晚要别人伺候他。

填充： 1) 那个学生学习 (attitude) 就是不够 (modest).

2) 那个小孩子沒有人 (tutor) 的话就念不好书。

3) 你怎么老是喜欢 (bully) 少女呢？

4) 他是个 (greatly capable person)，不必 (review) 也能考得很好。

改写 - Reword the completed sentences in the preceding exercise, using this pattern.

11) 就 NP [colloquial]   就一条优点，… (p. 23)

Since 就 is an adverb, it may seem odd that it is followed by a noun phrase and not by a verb. In colloquial speech, the verb 有 and 是 (unlike other verbs) can be omitted when the meaning of the sentence is clear without the 有 or 是. In the above example, the omitted verb is 有, so the phrase is actually derived from 就有一条优点。 (Cf. Grammatical Note V.4. for additional examples of the omission of 有 and 是.)

例句： 1) 安然就一个姐姐。

2) 沒什么可说的，就这么回事。

填充： 1) 上 (physics) 课的就有她一个女生。

2) 你觉得一对 (husband and wife) 就有一个孩子怎么样？

改写 - Reword the completed sentences in the preceding exercise, using this pattern.

12) 又   我又怎么了？ (p. 25)

Aside from its basic meaning of "again," 又 sometimes has the function of stressing a certain aspect of the expression. This second function can be conveyed in English not by translation but by stressing the relevant words. Context usually makes clear which of the two above meanings is intended. In the above example, 又 probably carries both functions: the sense of "again" implies that the mother is again complaining about the father, and 我 is being emphasized.

例句：　1) 評不上三好生又怎麼樣？

　　　　2) 我下鄉的那時候又沒打算把我的專業丟掉。

填充：　1) (History) 不是他的 (professional specialty), 你怎麼能請他來給你 (tutor in history) 呢？

　　　　2) 你不是個小孩子，為什麼還要我來給你 (wash hair) 呢？

　　　　3) 他幹事 (truly) 不行，大學 (graduate) 怎麼樣？

　　　　4) 參考一下安然的 (physics homework) 不是什麼壞事。

改寫, insert a 又 into each of the completed sentences in the preceding exercise.

INCLUSIVE 翻譯 EXERCISE FOR SEGMENT II:

1) No one wants to take care of this lovable child? I'll take care of him.

2) With regard to his specialty, he is very earnest.

3) (You're) really too rude to the teacher of classical Chinese!

4) His illness comes from drinking.

5) So what if I want to wear a red blouse?!

6) First listen to the teacher explain (the lesson), then raise questions.

7) Enough! Don't talk anymore, you!

8) Short hair is good-looking. (contrary to the popular view that long hair is good-looking).

9) He, being such a greatly capable person, can do anything!

10) She's in the midst of washing her hair, so she can't come to the phone.

11) Physics tests are something that students all dread (are afraid of).

12) Nowadays each couple has only one child.

example, 又 probably carries both functions: the sense of "again" implies that the mother is again complaining about the father, and 我 is being emphasized.

例句： 1) 评不上三好生又怎么样？

2) 我下乡的那时候又沒打算把我的专业丢掉。

填充： 1) (History) 不是他的 (professional specialty)，你怎么能请他来给你 (tutor in history) 呢？

2) 你不是个小孩子，为什么还要我来给你 (wash hair) 呢？

3) 他干事 (truly) 不行，大学 (graduate) 怎么样？

4) 参考一下安然的 (physics homework) 不是什么坏事。

改写, insert a 又 into each of the completed sentences in the preceding exercise.

INCLUSIVE 翻译 EXERCISE FOR SEGMENT II:

1) No one wants to take care of this lovable child? I'll take care of him.

2) With regard to his specialty, he is very earnest.

3) (You're) really too rude to the teacher of classical Chinese!

4) His illness comes from drinking.

5) So what if I want to wear a red blouse?!

6) First listen to the teacher explain (the lesson), then raise questions.

7) Enough! Don't talk anymore, you!

8) Short hair is good-looking. (contrary to the popular view that long hair is good-looking).

9) He, being such a greatly capable person, can do anything!

10) She's in the midst of washing her hair, so she can't come to the phone.

11) Physics tests are something that students all dread (are afraid of).

12) Nowadays each couple has only one child.

SEGMENT III

1) 就是 　　　　　　　　　就是…就是有點兒羣眾關係不大好。 (p. 28)

就是 has many usages. Here, 就是, translatable as "it's just that...," is used to indicate that an otherwise fine thing, person, or situation is marred by a flaw. This pattern usually contains two clauses, the first one indicating that something is generally good, followed by the 就是 clause stating the flaw. The first clause, however, may be understood and omitted, as in the above example.

例句： 1) 其實教育部門的工作挺好的，就是工資太低了。
　　　 2) 安然挺聰明的，學習也很認真，就是對老師的態度不夠謙虛。

造句：

填充： 1) 她 ([academic] achievements) 很好，羣眾關係也不錯，只是不夠 (political qualifications).
　　　 2) 她 (end of semester) 考試都考得不錯，只是 (physics) 差一點兒。
　　　 3) 編輯對這 (M) (manuscript) 相當滿意，但是覺得它太長了一點兒。
　　　 4) 她的 ([fellow] alumni) 在專業上都很有發展，只有她一個到現在還當個 (office worker).

改寫 - Reword the completed sentences from the preceding exercise, using this pattern.

2) VP$_1$ 來/去 VP$_2$ 　　　　　用形容成人的話來説… (p. 28)

來 or 去, when used to link two verb phrases, indicates that the action of the first verb phrase serves to achieve the purpose stated in the second verb phrase. It can be translated as "in order to" or simply "to." The choice between 來 and 去 is determined by whether or not the action is close at hand.

例句： 1) 我打電話去聯繫這件事。
　　　 2) 他打算開一次校友會來見見一些多年沒見面的同學。

造句：

填充： 1) 為了讓更多的中國人也能看這本 (children's stories), 他要 (translate) 它。
　　　 2) 為了 (urge) 他別 (smoke), 我已經想了不少的法子，可是都沒用。
　　　 3) 為了 (commemorate) 一些外國同志，中國出了一套 (stamps).
　　　 4) 為了 (describe) 安然心裡的 (feelings), 小説的 (author) 用了樹上的 "(eyes)."

S E G M E N T   III

1)   就是   就是…就是有点儿群众关系不大好。(p. 29)

就是 has many usages. Here, 就是, translatable as "it's just that...," is used to indicate that an otherwise fine thing, person, or situation is marred by a flaw. This pattern usually contains two clauses, the first one indicating that something is generally good, followed by the 就是 clause stating the flaw. The first clause, however, may be understood and omitted, as in the above example.

例句：   1) 其实教育部门的工作挺好的，就是工资太低了。
        2) 安然挺聪明的，学习也很认真，就是对老师的态度不够谦虚。

造句：

填充：   1) 她 ([academic] achievements) 很好，群众关系也不错，只是不够 (political qualifications).
        2) 她 (end of semester) 考试都考得不错，只是 (physics) 差一点儿。
        3) 编辑对这 (M) (manuscript) 相当满意，但是觉得它太长了一点儿。
        4) 她的 ([fellow] alumni) 在专业上都很有发展，只有她一个到现在还当个 (office worker).

改写 - Reword the completed sentences from the preceding exercise, using this pattern.

2)   VP$_1$ 来/去 VP$_2$ 用形容成人的话来说… (p. 29)

来 or 去, when used to link two verb phrases, indicates that the action of the first verb phrase serves to achieve the purpose stated in the second verb phrase. It can be translated as "in order to" or simply "to." The choice between 来 and 去 is determined by whether or not the action is close at hand.

例句：   1) 我打电话去联系这件事。
        2) 他打算开一次校友会来见见一些多年没见面的同学。

造句：

填充：   1) 为了让更多的中国人也能看这本 (children's stories), 他要 (translate) 它。
        2) 为了 (urge) 他别 (smoke), 我已经想了不少的法子，可是都没用。
        3) 为了 (commemorate) 一些外国同志，中国出了一套 (stamps).
        4) 为了 (describe) 安然心里的 (feelings), 小说的 (author) 用了树上的 "(eyes)."

改寫 - Reword the completed sentences from the preceding exercise, using this pattern.

3) ···QW···, ···(就)···(QW)···   有啥說啥。 (p. 28)

The QW (啥 in this example) in this double VP pattern is to be interpreted in the all-inclusive sense. The first VP states a condition ("whatever..., however..., whoever..., however much..., etc.") and the second VP states the resultant action or conclusion. The QW stated in the first VP is usually, but not necessarily, repeated in the second VP to reinforce the sense of all-inclusiveness. The 就 is usually, but not necessarily, included in the second VP to reinforce the condition-result relationship between the two VPs. Sometimes, the VPs may be expanded into rather elaborate clauses, e.g. 你什麼時候有空，我就什麼時候來看你。 "I'll come visit you whenever you have time."

例句: 1) 哪天有空哪天去。
         2) 有什麼我就吃什麼，我一點兒也不在乎。

造句:

填充: 1) 爸爸喜歡 (smoke). 外國煙，中國煙都可以。
         2) 別急，(homework) 做不完沒關係。你能做多少就 _____ 吧。

改寫 - Reword the following sentences and the first sentence from the preceding exercise, using this pattern: 1) 他什麼英文書都翻譯。
         2) 今天我請客。你就吃你最喜歡的菜吧!

4) 什麼 N   和她唱過一首什麼歌，··· (p. 28)

Here, 什麼 is used in the indefinite sense, and can be translated as "some sort of..." Other question words may also be used in this way.

例句: 1) 安然昨天借了一本什麼童話給那個小姑娘。
         2) 去年你不是寫了一本什麼小說?

填充: 1) 她告訴別人他是個作家，(actually) 他只是個 (office worker).
         2) 我記不清楚他在哪兒工作了，就知道是在一個 (education department).
         3) 韋老師寫了一首 (poem), 那 (M) (manuscript) 我還看過呢。
         4) 自從她朋友 (discover) 她從前有過 (political) 問題，對她的 (attitude) 就不一樣了。

改寫, insert 什麼 into each of the completed sentences from the preceding exercise.

改写 - Reword the completed sentences from the preceding exercise, using this pattern.

3)   ···QW··· , ···(就)···(QW)···   有啥说啥。 (p. 29)

The QW (啥 in this example) in this double VP pattern is to be interpreted in the all-inclusive sense. The first VP states a condition ("whatever..., however..., whoever..., however much..., etc.") and the second VP states the resultant action or conclusion. The QW stated in the first VP is usually, but not necessarily, repeated in the second VP to reinforce the sense of all-inclusiveness. The 就 is usually, but not necessarily, included in the second VP to reinforce the condition-result relationship between the two VPs. Sometimes, the VPs may be expanded into rather elaborate clauses, e.g. 你什么时候有空，我就什么时候来看你。 "I'll come visit you whenever you have time."

例句： 1) 哪天有空哪天去。
        2) 有什么我就吃什么，我一点儿也不在乎。

造句：

填充： 1) 爸爸喜欢 (smoke). 外国烟，中国烟都可以。
        2) 别急，(homework) 做不完沒关系。你能做多少就 _____ 吧。

改写 - Reword the following sentences and the first sentence from the preceding exercise, using this pattern: 1) 他什么英文书都翻译。
        2) 今天我请客。你就吃你最喜欢的菜吧！

4)   什么 N   和她唱过一首什么歌，··· (p. 29)

Here, 什么 is used in the indefinite sense, and can be translated as "some sort of..." Other question words may also be used in this way.

例句： 1) 安然昨天借了一本什么童话给那个小姑娘。
        2) 去年你不是写了一本什么小说？

填充： 1) 她告诉别人他是个作家，(actually) 他只是个 (office worker).
        2) 我记不清楚他在哪儿工作了，就知道是在一个 (education department).
        3) 韦老师写了一首 (poem), 那 (M) (manuscript) 我还看过呢。
        4) 自从她朋友 (discover) 她从前有过 (political) 问题，对她的 (attitude) 就不一样了。

改写, insert 什么 into each of the completed sentences from the preceding exercise.

5)   N 這兒/那兒   去一個業餘作者那兒了。 (p. 30)

Certain verbs such as 在, 到, 來, and 去 require place-word objects. Certain nouns such as 中國 and 學校 can serve as place words, but personal nouns and pronouns, and most other nouns cannot. In order to use these non-place-word pronouns and nouns as objects of such verbs, they must be turned into place words by the addition of 這兒 (這裡) or 那兒 (那裡). The choice between 這兒 and 那兒 is determined by whether or not the location is close by in reference to the speaker.

例句: 1) 參考書都在我這兒。
          2) 你的物理作業怎麼會在米曉玲那兒呢？

造句:

填充, incorporate this pattern into the completed sentences:
          1) 媽媽拿了安靜的朋友給她寫的信。安靜的信 _____。
          2) (Married) 以後，他把錢都給了他的愛人。他的錢 _____。
          3) 編輯拿了他的 (manuscript). 他的 (manuscript) _____。
          4) 那件紅 (blouse) 在椅子上。紅 (blouse) _____。

6)   也 VP   精力也太過盛啦！ (p. 32)

Here, 也 does not mean "also," but conveys a sense of emphasis. In English translation, the sense can be conveyed by the word "after all," or by appropriate intonation.

例句: 1) 我寫稿子也寫得夠累的了。
          2) 這兒出了好幾件事，他也夠倒霉的了。

填充: 1) 哎呀，我對韋老師夠 (courteous) 了，怎麼她還說我對她的 (attitude) 不好呢？
          2) 安然太喜歡 (have contact with) 男同學了。
          3) 祝文娟讀書太 (earnest) 了，連星期天都不 (rest a bit).
          4) 你呀，太愛 (dress up) 了，最好樸素一點兒。

改寫, insert a 也 into each of the completed sentences from the preceding exercise.

7)   V 成   真長成大姑娘了，啊？ (p. 32)

When 成 follows a verb, it can be interpreted in two different ways: a) As a resultative verb, 成 means "to succeed in V-ing, to satisfactorily complete the V-ing." In this usage, V 成 may or may not be followed by an object. E.g. 那本書寫成了。 我今年才寫成了那本書。 b) 成 can also be a postverb, in which case V 成 means "to V into..., to V as...," and is always followed by an object. E.g. 寫成小說。 造成房子。 The second usage is exemplified by the sentence above.

5)   N 这儿/那儿   去一个业余作者那儿了。 (p. 31)

Certain verbs such as 在, 到, 来, and 去 require place-word objects. Certain nouns such as 中国 and 学校 can serve as place words, but personal nouns and pronouns, and most other nouns cannot. In order to use these non-place-word pronouns and nouns as objects of such verbs, they must be turned into place words by the addition of 这儿 (这里) or 那儿 (那里). The choice between 这儿 and 那儿 is determined by whether or not the location is close by in reference to the speaker.

例句：   1) 参考书都在我这儿。
         2) 你的物理作业怎么会在米晓玲那儿呢？

造句：

填充, incorporate this pattern into the completed sentences:
         1) 妈妈拿了安静的朋友给她写的信。安静的信 _____。
         2) (Married) 以后，他把钱都给了他的爱人。他的钱 _____。
         3) 编辑拿了他的 (manuscript). 他的 (manuscript) _____。
         4) 那件红 (blouse) 在椅子上。红 (blouse) _____。

6)   也 VP   精力也太过盛啦！ (p. 33)

Here, 也 does not mean "also," but conveys a sense of emphasis. In English translation, the sense can be conveyed by the word "after all," or by appropriate intonation.

例句：   1) 我写稿子也写得够累的了。
         2) 这儿出了好几件事，他也够倒霉的了。

填充：   1) 哎呀，我对韦老师够 (courteous) 了，怎么她还说我对她的 (attitude) 不好呢？
         2) 安然太喜欢 (have contact with) 男同学了。
         3) 祝文娟读书太 (earnest) 了，连星期天都不 (rest a bit).
         4) 你呀，太爱 (dress up) 了，最好朴素一点儿。

改写, insert a 也 into each of the completed sentences from the preceding exercise.

7)   V 成   真长成大姑娘了，啊？ (p. 33)

When 成 follows a verb, it can be interpreted in two different ways: a) As a resultative verb, 成 means "to succeed in V-ing, to satisfactorily complete the V-ing." In this usage, V 成 may or may not be followed by an object. E.g. 那本书写成了。 我今年才写成了那本书。 b) 成 can also be a postverb, in which case V 成 means "to V into..., to V as...," and is always followed by an object. E.g. 写成小说。 造成房子。 The second usage is exemplified by the sentence above.

例句：　　1) 他二十年後才寫成了一本童話。
　　　　　2) 妹妹吃成一個小胖子了。

造句：

填充：　　1) 韋老師認為米曉玲是一個不 (earnest) 的學生。
　　　　　2) 他用這塊木頭做了一個 (splendid) 的 (wood sculpture).
　　　　　3) 他就在這個學校讀過一年書，沒畢業，但是同學們還是認為他是個 (alumnus).
　　　　　4) 那天她看見 (peasant) 時有了特別的感覺，回家後就寫了一首詩。

改寫 - Reword the completed sentences from the preceding exercise, using the pattern 把⋯V 成.
(Hint: used 看成 in sentences 1 and 3)

8)　　把 A 當 B (來) V　　　　　　　　你老把我當男孩子看待,⋯ (p. 32)

The meaning of this pattern is "to take A and do V to it as though it were B," implying that A is being treated or used in a way different from its normal role.

例句：　　1) 我要把這個學生當自己的孩子來教育。
　　　　　2) 他把毛筆當筷子用。

造句：

填充：　　1) 他很會 (contemplate), 所以很多人都覺得他是個 (adult) 了。
　　　　　2) 媽媽不小心，以為 (manuscript) 是廢紙，就把它 (throw away) 了。
　　　　　3) 他現在是個 (director [of films]) 了，你怎麼能還以為他是個 (office worker) 呢？

改寫 - Reword the following sentence and the completed sentences from the preceding exercise, using this pattern: 這孩子老是吃糖，吃飽了就吃不下飯了。

INCLUSIVE 翻譯 EXERCISE FOR SEGMENT III:

1) Actually, his English is rather good. It's just that his pronunciation is sometimes inaccurate.

2) He treats his spare time work as his profession.

3) She gave up (cast away) her (professional) specialty in order to create "political conditions" for her children.

4) That young girl has become (changed into) a very thoughtful (contemplative) person.

5 - 8) See bottom of facing page.

例句：　1) 他二十年后才写成了一本童话。
　　　　2) 妹妹吃成一个小胖子了。

造句：

填充：　1) 韦老师认为米晓玲是一个不 (earnest) 的学生。
　　　　2) 他用这块木头做了一个 (splendid) 的 (wood sculpture).
　　　　3) 他就在这个学校读过一年书，沒毕业，但是同学们还是认为他是个 (alumnus).
　　　　4) 那天她看见 (peasant) 时有了特别的感觉，回家后就写了一首诗。

改写 - Reword the completed sentences from the preceding exercise, using the pattern 把…V 成.
(Hint: used 看成 in sentences 1 and 3)

8)　把 A 当 B (来) V　　　　　　　你老把我当男孩子看待,… (p. 33)
The meaning of this pattern is "to take A and do V to it as though it were B," implying that A is being treated or used in a way different from its normal role.

例句：　1) 我要把这个学生当自己的孩子来教育。
　　　　2) 他把毛笔当筷子用。

造句：

填充：　1) 他很会 (contemplate), 所以很多人都觉得他是个 (adult) 了。
　　　　2) 妈妈不小心，以为 (manuscript) 是废纸，就把它 (throw away) 了。
　　　　3) 他现在是个 (director [of films]) 了，你怎么能还以为他是个 (office worker) 呢？

改写 - Reword the following sentence and the completed sentences from the preceding exercise, using this pattern: 这孩子老是吃糖，吃饱了就吃不下饭了。

INCLUSIVE 翻译 EXERCISE FOR SEGMENT III:

1 - 4) See bottom of facing page.
　5) I'll wear whichever shirt is clean.
　6) She's certainly pitiful enough, the teacher should give her some special consideration.
　7) I heard that they are planning to have some sort of alumni party.
　8) That manuscript is still at the editor's.

SEGMENT IV

1) V 個 O [colloquial]   看個電視那麼認真啊？ (p. 40)

This is a special colloquial usage of 個, in which 個 is not preceded by a specifier or number and is not strictly speaking a measure. It can be seen as a small "irregularity" to call attention to the verb or to the entire statement. Another example of this usage is "有草梅醬我買個十瓶" (Part I, p. 90). Even greater attention can be called by adding 他 in front of 個, e.g. 買他個十瓶。 This usage of 個 can also be applied to sentences involving an action verb followed by a stative verb, producing a similar effect. E.g. 玩兒個痛快。玩兒他個痛快。

例句：   1) 學個外語有什麼難呢？
            2) 今天是星期天，咱們去逛個街吧。

填充：   1) 他愛人可利害呢。他在家 (smoke) 都不行。
            2) 穿穿紅 (blouse) 算什麼？韋老師怎麼能說這就是不 (simple and plain) 的表現呢？

改寫, insert 個 into the following sentences and the completed sentences in the preceding exercise:
            1) 講課不必穿得那麼漂亮。
            2) 你那麼聰明，考大學還不容易？

2) ⋯怕什麼？   議論我褲子怕什麼？ (p. 40)

Unlike the verb "afraid" in English, which is linked to an object by the preposition "of" or by the relative pronoun "that," the Chinese verb 怕 can be followed immediately by an object (including the QW-objects 什麼 and 誰). This phenomenon applies to the verbs 笑 "laugh," 哭 "cry," and 氣 "angry" as well. Secondly, what we have here is a loosely constructed colloquial pattern with the clause 議論我褲子 as the topic (in front of the sentence) and the logical subject (我, 我們, or 你) understood and omitted. Lastly, "⋯怕什麼？" (literally "What's there to be afraid of?") is a rhetorical question, implying that there is nothing to be afraid of.

例句：   1) 背幾篇古文怕什麼？
            2) 向韋老師提個問題怕什麼？

造句：

填充：   1) 不必怕別人在 (behind someone's back) (discuss).
            2) 不必怕 (political qualifications) 不好。
            3) 不必怕韋老師不 (understand) 你。

SEGMENT IV

1)   V 个 O [colloquial]   看个电视那么认真啊？ (p. 41)

This is a special colloquial usage of 个, in which 个 is not preceded by a specifier or number and is not strictly speaking a measure. It can be seen as a small "irregularity" to call attention to the verb or to the entire statement. Another example of this usage is "有草梅酱我买个十瓶" (Part I, p. 91). Even greater attention can be called by adding 他 in front of 个, e.g. 买他个十瓶。 This usage of 个 can also be applied to sentences involving an action verb followed by a stative verb, producing a similar effect. E.g. 玩儿个痛快。玩儿他个痛快。

例句：   1) 学个外语有什么难呢？
           2) 今天是星期天，咱们去逛个街吧。

填充：   1) 他爱人可利害呢。他在家 (smoke) 都不行。
           2) 穿穿红 (blouse) 算什么？韦老师怎么能说这就是不 (simple and plain) 的表现呢？

改写, insert 个 into the following sentences and the completed sentences in the preceding exercise:
          1) 讲课不必穿得那么漂亮。
          2) 你那么聪明，考大学还不容易？

2)   …怕什么？   议论我裤子怕什么？ (p. 41)

Unlike the verb "afraid" in English, which is linked to an object by the preposition "of" or by the relative pronoun "that," the Chinese verb 怕 can be followed immediately by an object (including the QW-objects 什么 and 谁). This phenomenon applies to the verbs 笑 "laugh," 哭 "cry," and 气 "angry" as well. Secondly, what we have here is a loosely constructed colloquial pattern with the clause 议论我裤子 as the topic (in front of the sentence) and the logical subject (我, 我们, or 你) understood and omitted. Lastly, "…怕什么？" (literally "What's there to be afraid of?") is a rhetorical question, implying that there is nothing to be afraid of.

例句：   1) 背几篇古文怕什么？
           2) 向韦老师提个问题怕什么？

造句：

填充：   1) 不必怕别人在 (behind someone's back) (discuss).
          2) 不必怕 (political qualifications) 不好。
          3) 不必怕韦老师不 (understand) 你。

4) 不必怕 (pronunciation) 不準，你姐姐可以來 (tutor) 你。

改寫 - Reword the completed sentences in the preceding exercise, using this pattern.

3)   V 一下   叫你…輔導一下外語都不幹。 (p. 42)

V 一下 means "to V a bit." 一下 is grammatically a measure of the intensity or duration of the action, and it indicates that the action is carried out briefly and lightly. If the verb takes an object, the object comes after 一下; and if the completion aspect is indicated for the verb, the 了 comes after the verb and before the 一下. E.g. 昨天晚上我看了一下書。

例句： 1) 他喜歡睡覺前看一下小說。
        2) 飯前最好洗一下手。

造句：

填充： 1) 我只是 (bring up) 我的意見，我們不必 (quarrel).
        2) 這次的 (physics homework) 我能不能 (ask you for advice)?
        3) 去參加晚會以前，最好 (wash hair), (dress up).
        4) "Cow" 這個音我還是發不準，你能不能形容 (tongue) 應該怎麼樣?

改寫, insert 一下 into each of the completed sentences in the preceding exercise.

4)   …都…   叫你幫我請個你老同學幫我輔導一下外語都不幹。 (p. 42)

This is the 連…都/也… pattern in disguise. In colloquial speech, the 連 is often omitted, leaving just 都 or 也 to convey the meaning "even (in the adverbial sense)." The pitfall is that students, when speaking Chinese, often equate "even" with 連 and overlook the indispensable 都/也 part.

例句： 1) 他很髒，褲子穿了一個月都不洗。
        2) 他的舌頭太硬了，"cow" 這個簡單的音都發不準。

造句：

填充, incorporate this pattern into the completed sentences:
        1) 他太沒良心了，_____。
        2) 你怎麼那麼傻，_____。
        3) 安然很樂意協助同學們，_____。
        4) 這位老師很耐心，_____。

4) 不必怕 (pronunciation) 不准，你姐姐可以来 (tutor) 你。

改写 - Reword the completed sentences in the preceding exercise, using this pattern.

3)   V 一下   叫你…辅导一下外语都不干。 (p. 43)

V 一下 means "to V a bit." 一下 is grammatically a measure of the intensity or duration of the action, and it indicates that the action is carried out briefly and lightly. If the verb takes an object, the object comes after 一下; and if the completion aspect is indicated for the verb, the 了 comes after the verb and before the 一下. E.g. 昨天晚上我看了一下书。

例句：   1) 他喜欢睡觉前看一下小说。
         2) 饭前最好洗一下手。

造句：

填充：   1) 我只是 (bring up) 我的意见，我们不必 (quarrel).
         2) 这次的 (physics homework) 我能不能 (ask you for advice)?
         3) 去参加晚会以前，最好 (wash hair), (dress up).
         4) "Cow" 这个音我还是发不准，你能不能形容 (tongue) 应该怎么样？

改写, insert 一下 into each of the completed sentences in the preceding exercise.

4)   …都…   叫你帮我请个你老同学帮我辅导一下外语都不干。 (p. 43)

This is the 连…都/也… pattern in disguise. In colloquial speech, the 连 is often omitted, leaving just 都 or 也 to convey the meaning "even (in the adverbial sense)." The pitfall is that students, when speaking Chinese, often equate "even" with 连 and overlook the indispensable 都/也 part.

例句：   1) 他很脏，裤子穿了一个月都不洗。
         2) 他的舌头太硬了，"cow" 这个简单的音都发不准。

造句：

填充, incorporate this pattern into the completed sentences:
         1) 他太沒良心了，＿＿＿＿＿＿＿。
         2) 你怎么那么傻，＿＿＿＿＿＿＿。
         3) 安然很乐意协助同学们，＿＿＿＿＿＿＿。
         4) 这位老师很耐心，＿＿＿＿＿＿＿。

5) 還不是⋯   還不是因為這個家! (p. 42)

This is a rhetorical expression in which the speaker conveys his/her strong conviction in a rueful or contemptuous tone.

例句: 1) 還不是為了給你們創造好的政治條件!
        2) 還不是因為你太愛背後議論別人了。

造句:

填充, incorporate this pattern into the completed sentences:
        1) 中學生那麼認真讀書, ＿＿＿＿＿＿＿＿＿。
        2) 老師要學生端正學習態度, ＿＿＿＿＿＿＿＿＿。
        3) 其實她沒有什麼優點, 能當上班長, ＿＿＿＿＿＿＿＿＿。
        4) 她那麼積極地幫助韋老師, ＿＿＿＿＿＿＿＿＿。

6) 都 [colloquial]   都十六歲了。 (p. 44)

Instead of its usual totalizing function, 都 means "already" in this context.

例句: 1) 還不夠高啊? 都六尺二了!
        2) 還笑! 人家都煩惱死了。

造句:

填充, incorporate this pattern into the completed sentences:
        1) 你現在才起床? ＿＿＿＿＿＿＿＿＿。
        2) 他現在才把第二課的作業做好, ＿＿＿＿＿＿＿＿＿。
        3) 你還寫信給他? ＿＿＿＿＿＿＿＿＿。
        4) ＿＿＿＿＿＿＿＿＿, 你還把我當孩子看待。

7) 要 SV/VP [colloquial]   反正大人的煩惱, 總比小孩兒要多。 (p. 44)

要 preceding an SV or a VP can have the following two functions: a) It can be an AV meaning "want to be SV" or "want to VP (do something)." E.g. 我要高一點兒。他要請我輔導他。 b) It can be an adverb meaning "certainly," conveying the speaker's estimation. This function of 要 is often used in comparisons, as in the example from the script above. The given context usually clarifies which of the two functions is intended.

5)   还不是…   还不是因为这个家！   (p. 43)

This is a rhetorical expression in which the speaker conveys his/her strong conviction in a rueful or contemptuous tone.

例句：   1) 还不是为了给你们创造好的政治条件！
        2) 还不是因为你太爱背后议论别人了。

造句：

填充, incorporate this pattern into the completed sentences:
        1) 中学生那么认真读书，_____。
        2) 老师要学生端正学习态度，_____。
        3) 其实她没有什么优点，能当上班长，_____。
        4) 她那么积极地帮助韦老师，_____。

6)   都 [colloquial]   都十六岁了。 (p. 45)

Instead of its usual totalizing function, 都 means "already" in this context.

例句：   1) 还不够高啊？都六尺二了!
        2) 还笑! 人家都烦恼死了。

造句：

填充, incorporate this pattern into the completed sentences:
        1) 你现在才起床？_____。
        2) 他现在才把第二课的作业做好，_____。
        3) 你还写信给他？_____。
        4) _____，你还把我当孩子看待。

7)   要 SV/VP [colloquial]   反正大人的烦恼，总比小孩儿要多。 (p. 45)

要 preceding an SV or a VP can have the following two functions: a) It can be an AV meaning "want to be SV" or "want to VP (do something)." E.g. 我要高一点儿。他要请我辅导他。 b) It can be an adverb meaning "certainly," conveying the speaker's estimation. This function of 要 is often used in comparisons, as in the example from the script above. The given context usually clarifies which of the two functions is intended.

例句：　1) 就是很好的夫妻，有時候還是要吵嘴的。

　　　　2) 他留過學，所以他的外語一定比我們的要好。

填充：　1) 你別看我那麼有 (energy)，有時候也一定會累的。

　　　　2) (Professional artist) 的作品一定會比 (spare-time, amateur) 的好一些。

　　　　3) 你現在上 (second year high school) 了，還有兩年就要考大學了，必得 (earnest) 一點兒了。

改寫 - Reword the following sentence and the completed sentences in the preceding exercise, using this pattern: 女人一生了孩子總是會比從前胖一點兒的。

8) SV着呢 [colloquial]　　　　　　　　　　你不知道的事情還多着呢。 (p. 46)

The 着呢 following an SV is a much more colloquial way of conveying the meaning 很 or 極了.

例句：　1) 他的麻煩多着呢。

　　　　2) 湯剛拿出來，還熱着呢。

填充：　1) 你的 (useless prattle) 可真多。

　　　　2) 社會上有很多年輕人 (maltreat) 老人。

　　　　3) 要看的 (manuscripts) 太多了。雖然是星期天，安靜還很忙。

　　　　4) 宿舍裡 (all day long) 都很吵，我怎麼能 (review) 功課呢？

改寫 - Reword the completed sentences in the preceding exercise, using this pattern.

9) QW 也/都 (不)…　　　　　　　　　　我誰也不像，… (p. 46)

When a question word (什麼, 誰, 多少, etc.) is followed by the adverb 也 or 都, it is used in the all-inclusive sense ("whoever, whatever, etc.") and not in the interrogative sense. This all-inclusive sense is best conveyed in English translation by the use of "every" or "any."

例句：　1) 他什麼事情都來請教我。

　　　　2) 我剛來這個學校，誰也不認識。

造句：

填充：　1) 他做事老是不 (patient).

　　　　2) 人人感覺到他很有 (conscience).

例句：　1) 就是很好的夫妻，有时候还是要吵嘴的。

　　　　2) 他留过学，所以他的外语一定比我们的要好。

填充：　1) 你别看我那么有 (energy)，有时候也一定会累的。

　　　　2) (Professional artist) 的作品一定会比 (spare-time, amateur) 的好一些。

　　　　3) 你现在上 (second year high school) 了，还有两年就要考大学了，必得 (earnest) 一点儿了。

改写 - Reword the following sentence and the completed sentences in the preceding exercise, using this pattern: 女人一生了孩子总是会比从前胖一点儿的。

8)　SV着呢 [colloquial]　　　　　　　　　　　　你不知道的事情还多着呢。 (p. 47)

The 着呢 following an SV is a much more colloquial way of conveying the meaning 很 or 极了.

例句：　1) 他的麻烦多着呢。

　　　　2) 汤刚拿出来，还热着呢。

填充：　1) 你的 (useless prattle) 可真多。

　　　　2) 社会上有很多年轻人 (maltreat) 老人。

　　　　3) 要看的 (manuscripts) 太多了。虽然是星期天，安静还很忙。

　　　　4) 宿舍里 (all day long) 都很吵，我怎么能 (review) 功课呢？

改写 - Reword the completed sentences in the preceding exercise, using this pattern.

9)　QW 也/都 (不)…　　　　　　　　　　　　我谁也不象，… (p. 47)

When a question word (什么, 谁, 多少, etc.) is followed by the adverb 也 or 都, it is used in the all-inclusive sense ("whoever, whatever, etc.") and not in the interrogative sense. This all-inclusive sense is best conveyed in English translation by the use of "every" or "any."

例句：　1) 他什么事情都来请教我。

　　　　2) 我刚来这个学校，谁也不认识。

造句：

填充：　1) 他做事老是不 (patient).

　　　　2) 人人感觉到他很有 (conscience).

3) (World) 上所有的 (nation) 都有他們的 (strong points).

4) 你要來借 (children's stories) 書嗎？我今天都不出門，你可以隨時來。

改寫 - Reword the completed sentences in the preceding exercise, using this pattern.

INCLUSIVE 翻譯 EXERCISE FOR SEGMENT IV:

1) There are plenty of couples who don't get along (their relationships are bad).

2) Final exams are already almost here. You're still not reviewing?

3) Even her math grades (achievements) are poor, how can she study physics?

4) It's no big deal to raise a question in class. (⋯也沒什麼。)

5) Your dad's a high-level cadre, (so) why be afraid of not measuring up academically (academic achievements are poor)?

6) When he graduated he didn't know how to do anything.

7) Young girls always (must) love to make themselves up more so than adults.

8) Isn't it just because the teacher likes her that she got to be a "three good student?"

9) What I just said is very important, so let me repeat it (a bit).

3) (World) 上所有的 (nation) 都有他们的 (strong points).

4) 你要来借 (children's stories) 书吗？我今天都不出门，你可以随时来。

改写 - Reword the completed sentences in the preceding exercise, using this pattern.

INCLUSIVE 翻译 EXERCISE FOR SEGMENT IV:

1) There are plenty of couples who don't get along (their relationships are bad).

2) Final exams are already almost here. You're still not reviewing?

3) Even her math grades (achievements) are poor, how can she study physics?

4) It's no big deal to raise a question in class. (···也沒什么。)

5) Your dad's a high-level cadre, (so) why be afraid of not measuring up academically (academic achievements are poor)?

6) When he graduated he didn't know how to do anything.

7) Young girls always (must) love to make themselves up more so than adults.

8) Isn't it just because the teacher likes her that she got to be a "three good student?"

9) What I just said is very important, so let me repeat it (a bit).

SEGMENT V

1) “…”地 [colloquial]   一個人老“可是可是”地過日子，… (p. 54)

Often a stative verb may be used adverbially by adding 地 (pronounced -de) to it; and in this adverbializing process, it may also be reduplicated (e.g.: 高興, 高興地, 高高興興地). This kind of "adverbializing" can extend to just about any other type of words by quotation-marking and adding 地 after it. Thus, the above example may be translated as "If one keeps living from day to day in a 'but ...but...' way, ..." This is an example of how the Chinese language can be made colorful by the creative applications of standard grammatical patterns.

例句：   1) 不要總是“如果如果”地說話。
          2) 他老是“明天明天”地答應人。
填充：   1) 打球的時候，他老叫“(Aiya)！”
          2) 安然小時候常常喜歡問“(How come)…”
          3) 媽，我已經是 (adult) 了，你不必老 (urge) 我說“小心”了。

改寫 - Reword the following sentence and the completed sentences in the preceding exercise, using this pattern: 我最不喜歡他那樣老說“說不定”。

2) 因…而… (formal)   …，但小狗不因大狗的存在而惶惑。 (p. 54)

This is a more formal way of expressing the 因為…所以… relationship. When used in tandem, the adverbs 因 and 而 indicate that the state/circumstance/action stated after 因 is the direct cause or motivation for the state/circumstance/action stated after 而. In English translation, the two phrases are usually reversed from their order in Chinese. Thus, the above example can be translated as "The little dog would not be alarmed by the big dog's existence."

例句：   1) 大家不因他政治條件不好而看不起他。
          2) 我因不舒服而沒去講課。

造句：

填充：   1) 因為她 (husband) (maltreats) 她，她決定離婚了。
          2) 這位 (artist) 的作品得不到好的 (evaluation)，是因為 (elucidativeness) 不夠 (strong)。
          3) 我認為不應該只因為 (relationship with people) 好就選上“三好生”。
          4) 他那本小說 (political) 意識太強是因為 (the times) 的 (influence)。

改寫 - Reword the completed sentences in the preceding exercise, using this pattern.

SEGMENT V

1)   "…" 地 [colloquial]   一个人老 "可是可是" 地过日子，… (p. 55)

Often a stative verb may be used adverbially by adding 地 (pronounced _-de_) to it; and in this adverbializing process, it may also be reduplicated (e.g.: 高兴, 高兴地, 高高兴兴地). This kind of "adverbializing" can extend to just about any other type of words by quotation-marking and adding 地 after it. Thus, the above example may be translated as "If one keeps living from day to day in a 'but …but…' way, …" This is an example of how the Chinese language can be made colorful by the creative applications of standard grammatical patterns.

例句：   1) 不要总是 "如果如果" 地说话。
          2) 他老是 "明天明天" 地答应人。

填充：   1) 打球的时候，他老叫 "(Aiya)！"
          2) 安然小时候常常喜欢问 "(How come)…"
          3) 妈，我已经是 (adult) 了，你不必老 (urge) 我说 "小心" 了。

改写 - Reword the following sentence and the completed sentences in the preceding exercise, using this pattern: 我最不喜欢他那样老说 "说不定"。

2)   因…而… (formal)   …，但小狗不因大狗的存在而惶惑。 (p. 55)

This is a more formal way of expressing the 因为…所以… relationship. When used in tandem, the adverbs 因 and 而 indicate that the state/circumstance/action stated after 因 is the direct cause or motivation for the state/circumstance/action stated after 而. In English translation, the two phrases are usually reversed from their order in Chinese. Thus, the above example can be translated as "The little dog would not be alarmed by the big dog's existence."

例句：   1) 大家不因他政治条件不好而看不起他。
          2) 我因不舒服而没去讲课。

造句：

填充：   1) 因为她 (husband) (maltreats) 她，她决定离婚了。
          2) 这位 (artist) 的作品得不到好的 (evaluation), 是因为 (elucidativeness) 不够 (strong)。
          3) 我认为不应该只因为 (relationship with people) 好就选上 "三好生"。
          4) 他那本小说 (political) 意识太强是因为 (the times) 的 (influence)。

改写 - Reword the completed sentences in the preceding exercise, using this pattern.

3) 像…一樣/一個樣   正像人在說謊的時候，偏要加大嗓門兒一個樣。 (p. 56)

This pattern means "(the subject) is just like..." The ellipsis may be filled by a simple noun, a noun phrase, an elaborate clause, or even a two-phrase clause separated by a comma, as in the above example. 像…一個樣 is not used nearly as commonly as 像…一樣.

例句：　1) 他們團結得像兄弟一樣。
　　　　2) 他的房間像剛來了個颱風，弄得亂七八糟一樣。

造句：

填充：　1) 安靜像媽媽年輕的時候一個樣，沒有什麼 (worries)。
　　　　2) 考上了大學，就不像在 (high school third year) 的時候 (all day long) 都得讀書
　　　　　　一樣了。
　　　　3) 他吃得像三天沒吃飯，快要 (die from hunger) 了一樣。
　　　　4) 他 (fight) 的時候，像一個 (hoodlum)，一點道理都不講一樣。

4) …(有/是)…   咱們學校好幾個這樣的人。 (p. 56)

In Chinese colloquial speech, the verbs 有 and 是 (unlike other verbs) can be understood and omitted when the meaning of the sentence is clear without them. In the above example, the omitted verb is 有.

例句：　1) 安然今年十六歲了嗎？
　　　　2) 我們班上好些聰明的學生。

填充：　1) 她常常 (marry) 又離婚，已經有好幾個 (husbands) 了。
　　　　2) 這部 (film) 有兩個女 (protagonist)，沒有男 (protagonist)。
　　　　3) 她 (academic achievements) 又好，(relationship with people) 又好，年年都是三好生。
　　　　4) 這個班高中三年就有一個 (class monitor)，每年都是祝文娟。

改寫- Reword the completed sentences in the preceding exercise, deleting the understood verb 有 or 是.

5) 連 VP 都 不/沒 VP   連看都不看她一眼。 (p. 58)

The coverb 連 "even" is most often followed by a nominal object. But it may also take a verbal object, as in this pattern. This pattern reinforces the negative aspect that something hadn't been done or isn't being done. It can best be translated as "doesn't/didn't even VP."

例句：　1) 他那天連說都沒說一聲就走了。
　　　　2) 今天他病得厲害，連吃一口飯都沒吃。

3)　　象…一样/一个样　　　　　　　　　正象人在说谎的时候，偏要加大嗓门儿一个样。 (p. 57)

This pattern means "(the subject) is just like..." The ellipsis may be filled by a simple noun, a noun phrase, an elaborate clause, or even a two-phrase clause separated by a comma, as in the above example. 象…一个样 is not used nearly as commonly as 象…一样.

例句：　1) 他们团结得象兄弟一样。
　　　　2) 他的房间象刚来了个台风，弄得乱七八糟一样。

造句：

填充：　1) 安静象妈妈年轻的时候一个样，没有什么 (worries)。
　　　　2) 考上了大学，就不象在 (high school third year) 的时候 (all day long) 都得读书
　　　　　 一样了。
　　　　3) 他吃得象三天没吃饭，快要 (die from hunger) 了一样。
　　　　4) 他 (fight) 的时候，象一个 (hoodlum)，一点道理都不讲一样。

4)　　…(有/是)…　　　　　　　　　　　咱们学校好几个这样的人。 (p. 57)

In Chinese colloquial speech, the verbs 有 and 是 (unlike other verbs) can be understood and omitted when the meaning of the sentence is clear without them. In the above example, the omitted verb is 有.

例句：　1) 安然今年十六岁了吗？
　　　　2) 我们班上好些聪明的学生。

填充：　1) 她常常 (marry) 又离婚，已经有好几个 (husbands) 了。
　　　　2) 这部 (film) 有两个女 (protagonist)，没有男 (protagonist)。
　　　　3) 她 (academic achievements) 又好，(relationship with people) 又好，年年都是三好生。
　　　　4) 这个班高中三年就有一个 (class monitor)，每年都是祝文娟。

改写- Reword the completed sentences in the preceding exercise, deleting the understood verb 有 or 是.

5)　　连 VP 都 不/没 VP　　　　　　　连看都不看她一眼。 (p. 59)

The coverb 连 "even" is most often followed by a nominal object. But it may also take a verbal object, as in this pattern. This pattern reinforces the negative aspect that something hadn't been done or isn't being done. It can best be translated as "doesn't/didn't even VP."

例句：　1) 他那天连说都没说一声就走了。
　　　　2) 今天他病得厉害，连吃一口饭都没吃。

造句:

填充:　1) 他怎麼能當 (writer)? 連 (essay) 都作不好。
　　　　2) 那對 (husband and wife) (relationship) 很好，從來沒吵過嘴。
　　　　3) 學生很怕韋老師，有問題的時候都不敢 (ask advice from) 她。
　　　　4) 這次 (physics) 考試你沒 (review), 怎麼能考好呢？

改寫 - Reword the completed sentences in the preceding exercise, using this pattern.

6)　非…不可　　　　　　　　　　她幹嘛非影響我不可？ (p. 58)

非…不可 is a double-negative pattern, literally meaning "(if) not..., then it is not permissible." It is a very forceful statement (or resolution if the subject is 我) that something absolutely must be done. There is no ideal English translation for this pattern, but the idea can be conveyed through the use of appropriate stress and intonation. When 非…不可 is embedded in a question (with either 嗎 at the end or 為什麼/幹嘛 before the verb phrase), the question becomes rhetorical, implying disagreement with the notion that something must be a certain way.

例句:　1) 我們為什麼非學外語不可？
　　　　2) 安然幹嘛非要評上三好生不可？

造句:

填充:　1) 學生為什麼一定要 (respect) 老師呢？
　　　　2) 爸爸老了，(eyes) 越來越不行了，現在就一定要戴 (glasses) 了。
　　　　3) 女人幹嘛必得 (wait upon) 男人呢？
　　　　4) 這句 (famous saying) 有意思，我一定要記住。

改寫 - Reword the completed sentences in the preceding exercise, using this pattern.

7)　Subject V-O VP　　　　　　　她辦事說到能做到，… (p. 58)

On the surface, this sentence pattern consists of a subject, a V-O, and a predicate. In reality, the V-O is actually a part of the sentence topic, upon which the predicate 說到能做到 is a comment.

例句:　1) 她學科學是因為受了她丈夫的影響。
　　　　2) 媽媽丟掉專業未必就能給安靜、安然創造政治條件。

造句:

造句：

填充：　1) 他怎么能当 (writer)? 连 (essay) 都作不好。

2) 那对 (husband and wife) (relationship) 很好，从来沒吵过嘴。

3) 学生很怕韦老师，有问题的时候都不敢 (ask advice from) 她。

4) 这次 (physics) 考试你没 (review), 怎么能考好呢？

改写 - Reword the completed sentences in the preceding exercise, using this pattern.

6)　非…不可　　　　　　　　她干嘛非影响我不可？ (p. 59)

非…不可 is a double-negative pattern, literally meaning "(if) not..., then it is not permissible." It is a very forceful statement (or resolution if the subject is 我) that something absolutely must be done. There is no ideal English translation for this pattern, but the idea can be conveyed through the use of appropriate stress and intonation. When 非…不可 is embedded in a question (with either 吗 at the end or 为什么/干嘛 before the verb phrase), the question becomes rhetorical, implying disagreement with the notion that something must be a certain way.

例句：　1) 我们为什么非学外语不可？

2) 安然干嘛非要评上三好生不可？

造句：

填充：　1) 学生为什么一定要 (respect) 老师呢？

2) 爸爸老了，(eyes) 越来越不行了，现在就一定要戴 (glasses) 了。

3) 女人干嘛必得 (wait upon) 男人呢？

4) 这句 (famous saying) 有意思，我一定要记住。

改写 - Reword the completed sentences in the preceding exercise, using this pattern.

7)　Subject V-O VP　　　　　　她办事说到能做到，… (p. 59)

On the surface, this sentence pattern consists of a subject, a V-O, and a predicate. In reality, the V-O is actually a part of the sentence topic, upon which the predicate 说到能做到 is a comment.

例句：　1) 她学科学是因为受了她丈夫的影响。

2) 妈妈丢掉专业未必就能给安静、安然创造政治条件。

造句：

填充：　1) 她 (play role of) (female protagonist) 非常合適。

2) 我們追求 (truth) 要追求 (whole life)。

3) 他 (teach, lecture) (truly) 是經過一番的準備。

4) 我 (write essay) 要寫一些自個兒 (contemplate) 出來的東西。

8) 少/多 (了) O　　　　　　　　　少了一個聽眾，… (p. 60)

多 and 少 are primarily stative verbs, but can also function as transitive verbs, as in the above example.

例句：　1) 那本手冊多了一條說明。

2) 這篇作文少了一些廢話就好了。

造句：

填充, incorporate this pattern into the completed sentences:

1) 安靜給了我一套新 (stamps), 現在我的本子裡又 _____。

2) 安靜結了婚，家裡就 _____。

3) 這兒的工作太多了，如果能 ___ 幾個 (office workers) 就好了。

4) 我們 (must) 想辦法讓社會 ___ 一些 (hoodlum)。

9) (如果)…，… (omission of "linking adverbs")　　　　餓了，櫃子裡有點心。 (p. 60)

The relationship between two adjoining clauses is usually made clear by the use of an adverb in one or both of the clauses. However, when the relationship is clear from the context, these adverbs may be omitted. In the above example, the omitted adverb is 要是 or 如果 in the first clause. Incidentally, the subject 你 in the first clause is also understood and omitted.

例句：　1) 吃虧了，下次就領教了。

2) 一個人力量不夠，多請些朋友來幫忙是可以的。

填充：　1) 要是你想看 (novel), 可以來我這兒借。

2) 如果紅 (blouse) (dirty) 了，床上有乾淨的襯衫。

3) 如果看 (ancient literature) 時遇到不認識的字，可以查一查 (《Cihai》 [a dictionary])。

4) 如果想 (elect) 上三好生，就得把 (relationship with people) 弄好。

改寫 - Reword the completed sentences in the preceding exercise, omitting the linking adverbs.

填充： 1) 她 (play role of) (female protagonist) 非常合适。

2) 我们追求 (truth) 要追求 (whole life).

3) 他 (teach, lecture) (truly) 是经过一番的准备。

4) 我 (write essay) 要写一些自个儿 (contemplate) 出来的东西。

8) 少/多 (了) O   少了一个群众，…（p. 61)

多 and 少 are primarily stative verbs, but can also function as transitive verbs, as in the above example.

例句： 1) 那本手册多了一条说明。

2) 这篇作文少了一些废话就好了。

造句：

填充, incorporate this pattern into the completed sentences:

1) 安静给了我一套新 (stamps), 现在我的本子里又 _____。

2) 安静结了婚，家里就 _____。

3) 这儿的工作太多了，如果能 ___ 几个 (office workers) 就好了。

4) 我们 (must) 想办法让社会 ___ 一些 (hoodlum).

9) (如果)…，… (omission of "linking adverbs")   饿了，柜子里有点心。 (p. 61)

The relationship between two adjoining clauses is usually made clear by the use of an adverb in one or both of the clauses. However, when the relationship is clear from the context, these adverbs may be omitted. In the above example, the omitted adverb is 要是 or 如果 in the first clause. Incidentally, the subject 你 in the first clause is also understood and omitted.

例句： 1) 吃亏了，下次就领教了。

2) 一个人力量不够，多请些朋友来帮忙是可以的。

填充： 1) 要是你想看 (novel), 可以来我这儿借。

2) 如果红 (blouse) (dirty) 了，床上有干净的衬衫。

3) 如果看 (ancient literature) 时遇到不认识的字，可以查一查 (《Cihai》
[a dictionary])。

4) 如果想 (elect) 上三好生，就得把 (relationship with people) 弄好。

改写 - Reword the completed sentences in the preceding exercise, omitting the linking adverbs.

10) 拿 X (來) V⋯   就拿我們的班長祝文娟同學講，⋯ (p. 62)

This pattern means "to take X as the focus, the representative example, or the point of departure in V-ing," or "to V from the point of view of X." A paraphrase of this pattern is often less awkward than a literal translation. For example, the above sentence can be paraphrased as "take our class monitor Zhu Wenjuan for example, ..."

例句：　1) 這傢伙一點兒也不尊敬老師，就拿他對韋老師的態度來講，⋯
　　　　2) 他很滑稽，就拿他跳水的樣子來講吧，他跳得像一隻狗。

填充：　1) (The times) 對美術有很大的 (influence)，比方說，八十年代的小說⋯
　　　　2) 女人一結了婚就沒有從前那麼 (go after) 她們的 (professional specialty) 了。安然的媽媽就是個例子，她⋯
　　　　3) 米曉玲的 (homework) 老做不好。她的作文就是個例子，總是 (a mess) 的。
　　　　4) 安然常常會替別人打抱不平，比方說，那次劉冬虎和 (hoodlum) (fight)，⋯

改寫 - Reword the completed sentences in the preceding exercise, using this pattern.

11) 從(來) 不/沒⋯   從不和人吵架；⋯ (p. 62)

The adverb 從(來) is always used with a negative - 不 or 沒. 從來沒 implies that something has never happened in the past, but makes no assumptions about the present or future (i.e., that something may or may not happen in the future). 從(來)不 implies that something has never happened in the past and would not in the present or future. 從 is short for 從來, and is used only in colloquial speech.

例句：　1) 安然非常誠實，從不說謊。
　　　　2) 她從來沒當過班長。

造句：

填充：　1) 我有個 (understand) 我的姐姐，所以沒有 (vexation).
　　　　2) 她 (all day long) 在外頭忙，老是不在家。
　　　　3) 他有一個 (virtue, strong point), 沒有 (behind people's back) (discuss) 過別人。
　　　　4) 安然從小就有個姐姐 (wait upon) 她，所以到現在還沒自己洗過頭呢。

改寫 - Reword the completed sentences in the preceding exercise, using this pattern.

10) 拿 X (来) V…   就拿我们的班长祝文娟同学讲，… (p. 63)

This pattern means "to take X as the focus, the representative example, or the point of departure in V-ing," or "to V from the point of view of X." A paraphrase of this pattern is often less awkward than a literal translation. For example, the above sentence can be paraphrased as "take our class monitor Zhu Wenjuan for example, ..."

例句：   1) 这家伙一点儿也不尊敬老师，就拿他对韦老师的态度来讲，…
         2) 他很滑稽，就拿他跳水的样子来讲吧，他跳得象一只狗。

填充：   1) (The times) 对美术有很大的 (influence)，比方说，八十年代的小说…
         2) 女人一结了婚就没有从前那么 (go after) 她们的 (professional specialty) 了。安然的
            妈妈就是个例子，她…
         3) 米晓玲的 (homework) 老做不好。她的作文就是个例子，总是 (a mess) 的。
         4) 安然常常会替别人打抱不平，比方说，那次刘冬虎和 (hoodlum) (fight)，…

改写 - Reword the completed sentences in the preceding exercise, using this pattern.

11) 从(来) 不/没…   从不和人吵架；… (p. 63)

The adverb 从(来) is always used with a negative - 不 or 没. 从来没 implies that something has never happened in the past, but makes no assumptions about the present or future (i.e., that something may or may not happen in the future). 从(来)不 implies that something has never happened in the past and would not in the present or future. 从 is short for 从来, and is used only in colloquial speech.

例句：   1) 安然非常诚实，从不说谎。
         2) 她从来没当过班长。

造句：

填充：   1) 我有个 (understand) 我的姐姐，所以没有 (vexation)。
         2) 她 (all day long) 在外头忙，老是不在家。
         3) 他有一个 (virtue, strong point)，没有 (behind people's back) (discuss) 过别人。
         4) 安然从小就有个姐姐 (wait upon) 她，所以到现在还没自己洗过头呢。

改写 - Reword the completed sentences in the preceding exercise, using this pattern.

INCLUSIVE 翻译 EXERCISE FOR SEGMENT V: See next page.

INCLUSIVE 翻譯 EXERCISE FOR SEGMENT V:

1) Young people, due to the influence of the times, all wanted to study science.

2) There are two tickets on your desk, for you and your husband.

3) The motherland has many problems at present, all the nationalities (ethnic groups) must unite together.

4) Since you joined in our work, we have gained a great deal of strength.

5) Looking from the point of view of her essays, her thoughts are rather comprehensive.

6) Comrades must work in a "mutually assisting" way.

7) Having learned a foreign language, one must use it often. Otherwise, it's like not ever having learned it.

8) He isn't even selective (doesn't even select) when he buys fruit, so he often ends up with bad ones.

9) We must pursue (go after) truth our whole lives. (In pursuing truth, we must ...)

10) This artist is never influenced by others' evaluation.

11) If you don't like writing essays, then write a poem.

7) …的   講起三國演義來一套一套的…… (p. 10)

In colloquial Chinese, one way to describe something (a person, a matter, a phenomenon, etc.) is to use a descriptive predicate made by adding 的 to a phrase or a stock expression. Thus 一套一套的 means "in a well-organized, set by set, manner."

例句： 1) 他吃飯一大碗一大碗的。
        2) 他愛唱歌，一首接一首的。

填充, incorporate this pattern into the completed sentences:
        1) 他愛講故事，_____ (一個又一個)。
        2) 他寫的毛筆字 _____ (漂亮)。
        3) 祝文娟複習起功課來 _____ (認真)。
        4) 這對夫妻吵起嘴來 _____ (打，罵)。

8) 為 O (V)   那就為你自己？ (p. 10)

為 can be the main verb of a sentence meaning "for, for the sake of" as in the above example, or it can be a coverb in the context of 為 O V "to V for the sake of...." Note that when 為 is used in this sense, it is pronounced in the fourth tone and not the second tone as in 以為.

例句： 1) 我不能老為你洗衣服啊！
        2) 你就知道為你自己。

造句 - Create sentences, incorporating the vocabulary items given and this pattern.
        1) 洗頭髮
        2) 做飯
        3) 輔導古文
        4) 做物理作業

9) O 不能/可/應該…   話不能這麼說。 (p. 10)·

This is an injunction against doing something. But to tone down the harshness of it, the sentence is cast in the "notional passive" form in the following way: the logical subject 你 is omitted from the standard pattern "你不能/可/應該 VP," and the object is shifted to the topic position in front of the sentence in order to focus on it. The same effect is achieved in English by using passive voice. E.g., "You shouldn't tell others about that matter." vs. "That matter shouldn't be told to others."

例句： 1) 事情不應該這麼做。
        2) 這種酒不能多喝。

1) "…" 什麼 (呀/嘛)？　　[colloquial]　　　　　　　　　　"噢" 什麼呀？ (p. 66)

This is a very colloquial pattern through which the speaker expresses skepticism, disapproval, disagreement, or irritation with the previous speaker. The word preceding 什麼 in this pattern is repeated from the immediately preceding utterance of the other speaker, and is the crux of the skepticism, disapproval, disagreement, or irritation. In the above example, "噢" is the crux of the irritation, that is, An Ran is irritated with her father for his minimal and noncommittal comment on her essay.

例句：　1)　A：我這個短篇夠精確了吧？
　　　　　　B：嗯…
　　　　　　A："嗯"什麼呀？
　　　　2)　A：唉？你怎麼能穿這條褲子去講課？
　　　　　　B："唉"什麼嘛？學生們是來聽課，不是來看我的褲子。

填充, incorporate this pattern into the completed sentences:
　　　　1)　媽：你看這次安然該 (elect) 上 (class monitor) 了吧？
　　　　　　爸：＿＿。
　　　　　　媽：＿＿＿＿＿＿＿＿＿＿！
　　　　2)　媽：唉，你別給孩子 (instill) 你那套思想了！
　　　　　　爸：＿＿＿＿＿，我這套才是 (truth) 呢。
　　　　3)　安然：這篇作文把祝文娟 (summarize) 得夠 (comprehensive) 了吧？
　　　　　　安靜：＿＿。
　　　　　　安然：＿＿＿＿＿＿＿＿？！
　　　　4)　媽：咳，你看安然這孩子老喜歡 (have contact with) 男生！
　　　　　　爸：＿＿＿＿＿＿，(have contact with) 男生又怎麼樣？我覺得挺好的。

2) V 起 O　　　　　　　　　　　　你怎麼寫起班長啦？ (p. 66)

The 起 in this pattern functions as the complement attached to the preceding verb, and it carries the meaning "to begin to..., to up and..." A common variation of this pattern, without any change in the meaning, is V 起 O 來. In this latter pattern, the 來 follows the object and is not "suffixed" to 起, i.e., "V 起來 O" is incorrect. (Cf. Grammatical Note I.6.)

例句：　1) 爸爸又抽起煙了！
　　　　2) 她不到十二歲就戴起眼鏡來了。

SEGMENT VI

1) "…" 什么 (呀/嘛)?   [colloquial]   "噢" 什么呀? (p. 67)

This is a very colloquial pattern through which the speaker expresses skepticism, disapproval, disagreement, or irritation with the previous speaker. The word preceding 什么 in this pattern is repeated from the immediately preceding utterance of the other speaker, and is the crux of the skepticism, disapproval, disagreement, or irritation. In the above example, "噢" is the crux of the irritation, that is, An Ran is irritated with her father for his minimal and noncommittal comment on her essay.

例句：   1)   A：我这个短篇够精确了吧?
        B：嗯…
        A："嗯" 什么呀?

        2)   A：唉? 你怎么能穿这条裤子去讲课?
        B："唉" 什么嘛? 学生们是来听课, 不是来看我的裤子。

填充, incorporate this pattern into the completed sentences:

   1)   妈：你看这次安然该 (elect) 上 (class monitor) 了吧?
        爸：___。
        妈：_____!

   2)   妈：唉, 你别给孩子 (instill) 你那套思想了!
        爸：_____, 我这套才是 (truth) 呢。

   3)   安然：这篇作文把祝文娟 (summarize) 得够 (comprehensive) 了吧?
        安静：___。
        安然：_____? !

   4)   妈：咳, 你看安然这孩子老喜欢 (have contact with) 男生!
        爸：_____, (have contact with) 男生又怎么样? 我觉得挺好的。

2) V 起 O   你怎么写起班长啦? (p. 67)

The 起 in this pattern functions as the complement attached to the preceding verb, and it carries the meaning "to begin to..., to up and..." A common variation of this pattern, without any change in the meaning, is V 起 O 来. In this latter pattern, the 来 follows the object and is not "suffixed" to 起, i.e., "V 起来 O" is incorrect. (Cf. Grammatical Note I.6.)

例句：   1) 爸爸又抽起烟了!
        2) 她不到十二岁就戴起眼镜来了。

造句：

填充：　　1) 那個 (peasant) 做買賣了。
　　　　　2) 這個詩人什麼時候寫 (short stories) 了？
　　　　　3) 經過一個時期的 (review), 媽媽最近又作她原來的 (professional specialty) 了。
　　　　　4) 米曉玲是挺 (well-behaved) 的，怎麼會 (engage in) 這些 (muddled) 的事呢？

改寫, insert 起 into each of the completed sentences in the preceding exercise.

3)　沒什麼 VP/SV　　　　　　　　　班長沒什麼不能寫，⋯ (p. 66)
沒什麼 preceding a verb phrase (stative verb or action verb) indicates that there isn't anything sufficient for, or worthy of, the action or circumstance stated in the verb phrase. The positive form of this pattern occurs only in questions, but usually in the rhetorical sense (with the same negative implication as the negative form). E.g. 班長有什麼不能寫？ "What's there about the class monitor that cannot be written about?" implying that there is nothing that cannot be written about.

例句：　　1) 這兒風景沒什麼好看。
　　　　　2) 他作的那首詩有什麼特別？

造句：

填充：　　1) 這些 (procedures are not particularly difficult to deal with)。
　　　　　2) 這個夢 (isn't anything mysterious)。
　　　　　3) 安然對韋老師 (isn't particularly disrespectful)。
　　　　　4) (Dean's office) 怎麼能說米曉玲 (withdraw from school) (isn't particularly important) 呢？

4)　倒　　　　　　　　　　　　　　這倒怪了。 (p. 66)
As a verb, 倒 means "to reverse." As an adverb, it indicates that the speaker's opinion or the reality expressed by the statement is contrary to (reverse of) what's expected or assumed.

例句：　　1) 這次倒好，她終於贏了。
　　　　　2) 你倒舒服，不工作也不學習。

造句：

填充：　　1) 這問題不大，請她 (husband) 來幫個忙就行了。
　　　　　2) 他們家孩子多，可是 (economic) 情況不錯。

造句:

填充:　1) 那个 (peasant) 做买卖了。

2) 这个诗人什么时候写 (short stories) 了?

3) 经过一个时期的 (review), 妈妈最近又作她原来的 (professional specialty) 了。

4) 米晓玲是挺 (well-behaved) 的, 怎么会 (engage in) 这些 (muddled) 的事呢?

改写, insert 起 into each of the completed sentences in the preceding exercise.

3)　没什么 VP/SV　　　　　　　　班长没什么不能写, … (p. 67)

没什么 preceding a verb phrase (stative verb or action verb) indicates that there isn't anything sufficient for, or worthy of, the action or circumstance stated in the verb phrase. The positive form of this pattern occurs only in questions, but usually in the rhetorical sense (with the same negative implication as the negative form). E.g. 班长有什么不能写? "What's there about the class monitor that cannot be written about?" implying that there is nothing that cannot be written about.

例句:　1) 这儿风景没什么好看。

2) 他作的那首诗有什么特别?

造句:

填充:　1) 这些 (procedures are not particularly difficult to deal with).

2) 这个梦 (isn't anything mysterious).

3) 安然对韦老师 (isn't particularly disrespectful).

4) (Dean's office) 怎么能说米晓玲 (withdraw from school) (isn't particularly important) 呢?

4)　倒　　　　　　　　　　　这倒怪了。 (p. 67)

As a verb, 倒 means "to reverse." As an adverb, it indicates that the speaker's opinion or the reality expressed by the statement is contrary to (reverse of) what's expected or assumed.

例句:　1) 这次倒好, 她终于赢了。

2) 你倒舒服, 不工作也不学习。

造句:

填充:　1) 这问题不大, 请她 (husband) 来帮个忙就行了。

2) 他们家孩子多, 可是 (economic) 情况不错。

3) 找個 (someone to take over a job) 不算難，但是要找個 (honest one) 不容易。

4)   A： 聽說他 (drop out of school) 了。

B： 這不錯，班上少了個 (hoodlum) 了。

改寫, insert 倒 into each of the completed sentences in the preceding exercise.

5) 這麼/那麼一 V, …   你這麼一說，我非連穿它三天不可。 (p. 66)

這麼一 V, "as soon as (Subj.) V in this way," is the first clause in a two-clause sentence. It indicates that the action or circumstance stated in the second clause is the direct and immediate consequence of the action or circumstance stated in the first clause. Just as in the pattern "…一…，…就…," the adverb 就 often, but not necessarily, occurs in the second clause. 那麼 can replace 這麼 in this pattern; 這麼 indicates that the action happened close at hand, whereas 那麼 indicates that there is some distance between the action and the speaker.

例句：   1) 她這麼一解釋，大家馬上就明白了。
        2) 媽媽那麼一說安然，安然真的生氣了。

填充, incorporate this pattern into the completed sentences:

1) 你那麼一 (yield to) 她，她以後就更 (unbridled) 了。

2) 韋老師 _____，祝文娟就把她的 (《Cihai》) 收起來了。

3) 多年沒見面，我們那麼 __ (chat)，就想起很多 (young girl) (era) 的事了。

4) 我 _____ 想，真覺得 (life's journey) 上有 (countless) 的機會。

6) 別…就…   你別覺得自己考得不錯就放肆，… (p. 68)

The pattern "別…就…" is used in admonishing someone against doing something just because of a certain situation. Logically, there should be a 因為 after 別, but this 因為 is often understood and omitted. Notice that in English translation, the order of the two phrases in this Chinese pattern is reversed. Thus, the above example can be translated as "Don't be so cocky just because you feel you've done pretty well on the exams."

例句：   1) 你別看他表面謙虛就相信他。
        2) 你別以為自己有錢就看不起沒錢的人。

造句：

填充, incorporate this pattern into the completed sentences:

1) 你別看她才十五歲就認為她一定不懂得 (human nature and ways of the world).

3) 找个 (someone to take over a job) 不算难，但是要找个 (honest one) 不容易。

4)　A：听说他 (drop out of school) 了。

　　B：这不错，班上少了个 (hoodlum) 了。

改写, insert 倒 into each of the completed sentences in the preceding exercise.

5)　这么/那么一 V, …　　　　　　　　你这么一说，我非连穿它三天不可。 (p. 67)

这么一 V, "as soon as (Subj.) V in this way," is the first clause in a two-clause sentence. It indicates that the action or circumstance stated in the second clause is the direct and immediate consequence of the action or circumstance stated in the first clause. Just as in the pattern "…一…，…就…," the adverb 就 often, but not necessarily, occurs in the second clause. 那么 can replace 这么 in this pattern; 这么 indicates that the action happened close at hand, whereas 那么 indicates that there is some distance between the action and the speaker.

例句：　1) 她这么一解释，大家马上就明白了。

　　　　2) 妈妈那么一说安然，安然真的生气了。

填充, incorporate this pattern into the completed sentences:

　　　　1) 你那么一 (yield to) 她，她以后就更 (unbridled) 了。

　　　　2) 韦老师 _____，祝文娟就把她的 (《Cihai》) 收起来了。

　　　　3) 多年没见面，我们那么 __ (chat)，就想起很多 (young girl) (era) 的事了。

　　　　4) 我 _____ 想，真觉得 (life's journey) 上有 (countless) 的机会。

6)　别…就…　　　　　　　　　　你别觉得自己考得不错就放肆，… (p. 69)

The pattern "别…就…" is used in admonishing someone against doing something just because of a certain situation. Logically, there should be a 因为 after 别, but this 因为 is often understood and omitted. Notice that in English translation, the order of the two phrases in this Chinese pattern is reversed. Thus, the above example can be translated as "Don't be so cocky just because you feel you've done pretty well on the exams."

例句：　1) 你别看他表面谦虚就相信他。

　　　　2) 你别以为自己有钱就看不起没钱的人。

造句：

填充, incorporate this pattern into the completed sentences:

　　　　1) 你别看她才十五岁就认为她一定不懂得 (human nature and ways of the world)。

   2) 別以為 (academic achievement) 好就 _____ ，考大學可比平常的考試難得多。

   3) 你別看他英語 (pronunciation) 發得不準就 _____ ，他作 (translation) 還是挺不錯的。

   4) 你別覺得別人會有 (report [on you]) 就 _____ ，做一個 (artist) 必須用自己的 (eyes) 看。

7)   SV 什麼?   好什麼? (p. 68)

SV 什麼? can be translated as "What's so SV about it?" Its function is similar to that of the pattern "…" 什麼? (Cf. Grammatical Note VI.1.).

例句: 1)   A：我看安然挺耐心的。
               B：耐心什麼? 她輔導劉冬虎英語的時候就一點兒也不耐心。
         2)   A：那個少女真美啊!
               B：美什麼? 瘦成那個樣子!

造句:

填充, incorporate this pattern into the completed sentences:
         1)   某同學：我看祝文娟挺 (honest) 的
               安然：_____ , _____ 。
         2)   A：韋老師那首 (poem) 很好嘛。
               B：_____ ? _____ 。
         3)   A：安然的家好像挺 (perfectly satisfactory) 的。
               B：_____ ? 他們常常 (quarrel).
         4)   A：當個高中生夠苦的了。
               B：_____ ? 什麼 (worries) 都沒有，只要好好兒地學習。

8)   SV 而 V [literary]   忽忽而過。 (p. 74)

This pattern, which occurs frequently in poetry and songs, has a literary flavor to it. The SV describes the manner in which the action of the V occurs. In keeping with the literary/poetic nature of this pattern, the SV is often reduplicated. In mundane vernacular speech, the same idea is expressed by SV-地 V.

例句: 1) 那天我們吵了嘴以後是不歡而散的。
         2) 春風慢慢而吹來。

2) 别以为 (academic achievement) 好就 _____ ，考大学可比平常的考试难得多。

3) 你别看他英语 (pronunciation) 发得不准就 _____ ，他作 (translation) 还是挺不错的。

4) 你别觉得别人会有 (report [on you]) 就 _____ ，做一个 (artist) 必须用自己的 (eyes) 看。

7) SV 什么？   好什么？ (p. 69)

SV 什么？ can be translated as "What's so SV about it?" Its function is similar to that of the pattern "…" 什么？ (Cf. Grammatical Note VI.1.).

例句： 1) A：我看安然挺耐心的。
            B：耐心什么？她辅导刘冬虎英语的时候就一点儿也不耐心。
        2) A：那个少女真美啊！
            B：美什么？瘦成那个样子！

造句：

填充, incorporate this pattern into the completed sentences:
        1) 某同学：我看祝文娟挺 (honest) 的
            安然：_____，_____。
        2) A：韦老师那首 (poem) 很好嘛。
            B：_____？_____。
        3) A：安然的家好象挺 (perfectly satisfactory) 的。
            B：_____？他们常常 (quarrel).
        4) A：当个高中生够苦的了。
            B：_____？什么 (worries) 都没有，只要好好儿地学习。

8) SV 而 V [literary]   匆匆而过。 (p. 75)

This pattern, which occurs frequently in poetry and songs, has a literary flavor to it. The SV describes the manner in which the action of the V occurs. In keeping with the literary/poetic nature of this pattern, the SV is often reduplicated. In mundane vernacular speech, the same idea is expressed by SV-地 V.

例句： 1) 那天我们吵了嘴以后是不欢而散的。
        2) 春风慢慢而吹来。

填充：　1) 安然和安靜看了那 <u>(M)</u> <u>(poem)</u> 就不約而同地説：「這還算是 <u>(poetry)</u> ?!」
　　　　2) 今天評三好生，安然上學是 <u>(worrying)</u> 而去的。
　　　　3) 他 <u>(journey)</u> 上遇到一些不愉快的事，所以他不滿而歸了。
　　　　4) 她和那個外國人 <u>(marry)</u> 之後，就遠遠而去，再也不回來了。

翻譯 - Translate the completed sentences in the preceding exercise into English.

9)　Ｖ了又Ｖ　　　　　　　　　　　把繁星數了又數。 (p. 74)

This pattern indicates that the action of the verb has occurred again and again, not necessarily just twice (as in a literal interpretation), but possibly numerous times.

例句：　1) 他把那本童話看了又看，還是覺得有意思。
　　　　2) 我跟他説了又説，可他還是沒聽懂。

造句：

填充：　1) 我們都常常勸爸爸，可是他還是 <u>(smoke)</u>。
　　　　2) 那幅畫我看了好幾次，還是看不出來它的 <u>(strong points)</u>。
　　　　3) 安然不停地唱 <u>(that song)</u>，我們都不願意聽了。
　　　　4) 你那條 <u>(slacks)</u>，我洗了好幾次，還是洗不乾淨。

改寫 - Reword the completed sentences in the preceding exercise, using this pattern.

INCLUSIVE 翻譯 EXERCISE FOR SEGMENT VI:

1) A: This poem is excellent!

    B: What's so good about it? It doesn't have the least bit of fervor to it.

2) I washed that pair of slacks repeatedly, but they're still filthy.

3) I began dreaming soon after I fell asleep.

4) That day I passed by hurriedly, so I didn't see it clearly.

5) Rest assured, your husband's illness is not in any way dangerous.

6) A: H'm...

    B: What's this "H'm...?" How come you don't have the least bit of reaction?

7) She has all along lived by herself, and yet she doesn't feel lonely.

8) Don't think (erroneously) that she doesn't understand human nature and ways of the world just because she is a young girl.

9) As soon as she examined (it) (in that way), (she) knew that it wasn't real.

填充： 1) 安然和安靜看了那 (M) (poem) 就不约而同地说："这还算是 (poetry) ?!"
2) 今天评三好生，安然上学是 (worrying) 而去的。
3) 他 (journey) 上遇到一些不愉快的事，所以他不满而归了。
4) 她和那个外国人 (marry) 之后，就远远而去，再也不回来了。

翻译 - Translate the completed sentences in the preceding exercise into English.

9) V 了又 V   把繁星数了又数。 (p. 75)

This pattern indicates that the action of the verb has occurred again and again, not necessarily just twice (as in a literal interpretation), but possibly numerous times.

例句： 1) 他把那本童话看了又看，还是觉得有意思。
2) 我跟他说了又说，可他还是沒听懂。

造句：

填充： 1) 我们都常常劝爸爸，可是他还是 (smoke).
2) 那幅画我看了好几次，还是看不出来它的 (strong points).
3) 安然不停地唱 (that song)，我们都不愿意听了。
4) 你那条 (slacks)，我洗了好几次，还是洗不干净。

改写 - Reword the completed sentences in the preceding exercise, using this pattern.

INCLUSIVE 翻译 EXERCISE FOR SEGMENT VI:

1) A: This poem is excellent!

   B: What's so good about it? It doesn't have the least bit of fervor to it.

2) I washed that pair of slacks repeatedly, but they're still filthy.

3) I began dreaming soon after I fell asleep.

4) That day I passed by hurriedly, so I didn't see it clearly.

5) Rest assured, your husband's illness is not in any way dangerous.

6) A: H'm...

   B: What's this "H'm...?" How come you don't have the least bit of reaction?

7) She has all along lived by herself, and yet she doesn't feel lonely.

8) Don't think (erroneously) that she doesn't understand human nature and ways of the world just because she is a young girl.

9) As soon as she examined (it) (in that way), (she) knew that it wasn't real.

SEGMENT VII

1) …以上   十五歲以上就是青年。 (p. 78)

以上 following a number-measure or just a number means "above (that certain quantity)." Similarly,
以下 in this pattern means "below (that certain quantity)."

例句: 1) 成績要在九十分以上才能考上大學。
           2) 一萬字以上就算是中篇小說。

造句:

填充: 1) 他的 (academic achievements) 每門課都是九十多分。
           2) 這地方的 (peasant) (economic) 情況不錯，差不多每家房子的 (surface area) 都不只
              八十平方米。
           3) 過了十二歲，坐 (airplane), 看 (movies) 等等都得買全票。
           4) 在過去十年中，物理專業的 (graduates [graduating students]) 每年 (on the average)
              五十多名。

改寫 - Reword the completed sentences in the preceding exercise, using this pattern.

2) 要…了   米曉玲要工作了，… (p.80)

This pattern conveys the sense that an event or action is imminent (i.e., it will occur soon). The
same idea can be conveyed by using 快, 快要, or 就要 instead of 要. But in all these cases, the 了 at
the end is indispensable.

例句: 1) 天不早了，我要走了。
           2) 你最好今天去找他，他明天要旅遊去了。

造句:

填充: 1) 他在研究院已經五年了，明年就得到 (Ph. D.) 學位了。
           2) 我們快 (graduate) 了，很快就 (separate) 了，但是我一定忘不了我們的
              (friendship).
           3) 你寫了一年多的小說快 (completed) 了，你的 (frame of mind) 一定很愉快!
           4) 米曉玲快畢業了，怎麼這個時候 (withdraw from school) 呢? 真 (a pity)!

改寫, incorporate 要…了 into each of the completed sentences in the preceding exercise.

68

SEGMENT VII

1) …以上   十五岁以上就是青年。 (p. 79)

以上 following a number-measure or just a number means "above (that certain quantity)." Similarly, 以下 in this pattern means "below (that certain quantity)."

例句：　1) 成绩要在九十分以上才能考上大学。
　　　　2) 一万字以上就算是中篇小说。

造句：

填充：　1) 他的 (academic achievements) 每门课都是九十多分。
　　　　2) 这地方的 (peasant) (economic) 情况不错，差不多每家房子的 (surface area) 都不只八十平方米。
　　　　3) 过了十二岁，坐 (airplane), 看 (movies) 等等都得买全票。
　　　　4) 在过去十年中，物理专业的 (graduates [graduating students]) 每年 (on the average) 五十多名。

改写 - Reword the completed sentences in the preceding exercise, using this pattern.

2) 要…了   米晓玲要工作了，… (p.81)

This pattern conveys the sense that an event or action is imminent (i.e., it will occur soon). The same idea can be conveyed by using 快, 快要, or 就要 instead of 要. But in all these cases, the 了 at the end is indispensable.

例句：　1) 天不早了，我要走了。
　　　　2) 你最好今天去找他，他明天要旅游去了。

造句：

填充：　1) 他在研究院已经五年了，明年就得到 (Ph. D.) 学位了。
　　　　2) 我们快 (graduate) 了，很快就 (separate) 了，但是我一定忘不了我们的 (friendship)。
　　　　3) 你写了一年多的小说快 (completed) 了，你的 (frame of mind) 一定很愉快！
　　　　4) 米晓玲快毕业了，怎么这个时候 (withdraw from school) 呢？真 (a pity)!

改写, incorporate 要…了 into each of the completed sentences in the preceding exercise.

3) 什麼…(啊)   什麼朋友啊，友誼啊，都是瞎扯。 (p. 80)

什麼 followed by a noun phrase is an expression of contempt for a hypocritical claim or a false pretense. The expression often, but not necessarily, ends in an exclamatory particle 啊/呀/哇/哪. This expression defies direct translation and can only be paraphrased into something like "What do you mean, ...!" "..., indeed!" or "..., my foot!"

例句： 1) 什麼耐心啊，她教了劉冬虎不到三分鐘就開始笑他了。
        2) 什麼西瓜啊、蘋果啊，都不好吃。

填充： 1) 什麼 (friendship) 啊，一、兩天不見面就忘了。
        2) 什麼 (unity) 啊，還不是 (all day long) 吵嘴！
        3) 什麼 (honesty) 啊，＿＿＿＿＿＿＿＿！
        4) 什麼 (love) 啊，結了婚不到一年就＿＿＿＿＿＿＿＿。

4) Nu 來 M   你媽都活到五十來歲了，… (p. 80)

來 following a round number means "around, approximately (that certain number)." This usage of 來 can be better understood and remembered if one associates it with the concept of "approaching" rather than "coming."

例句： 1) 他去了四十來天了。
        2) 今年我們家的菜園收獲了二十來斤青菜。

造句：

填充： 1) 我們在中國 (travel) 了差不多三十天。
        2) (Humankind) 搞 (outer-space travel) 已經有三十多年的歷史了。
        3) 他在 (science) 研究院已經幹了差不多十年了。
        4) 你別 (believe lightly) 他。他哪兒是二十八歲？我看他已經有差不多四十歲了。

改寫 - Reword the completed sentences in the preceding exercise, using this pattern.

5) 來 NP   再來一個。 (p. 82)

In this idiomatic pattern, 來 means "make come (someone, something)," and is used in a command, suggestion, or plea. The expression can be paraphrased variously depending on the context:

來人哪！   Help! Somebody! or: Will someone please come?!
來一杯水。   Bring a cup of water.

3) 什么…(啊)   什么朋友啊，友谊啊，都是瞎扯。 (p. 81)

什么 followed by a noun phrase is an expression of contempt for a hypocritical claim or a false pretense. The expression often, but not necessarily, ends in an exclamatory particle 啊/呀/哇/哪. This expression defies direct translation and can only be paraphrased into something like "What do you mean, ...!" "..., indeed!" or "..., my foot!"

例句：   1) 什么耐心啊，她教了刘冬虎不到三分钟就开始笑他了。
        2) 什么西瓜啊、苹果啊，都不好吃。

填充：   1) 什么 (friendship) 啊，一、两天不见面就忘了。
        2) 什么 (unity) 啊，还不是 (all day long) 吵嘴！
        3) 什么 (honesty) 啊，_____！
        4) 什么 (love) 啊，结了婚不到一年就 _____。

4)   Nu 来 M   你妈都活到五十来岁了，… (p. 81)

来 following a round number means "around, approximately (that certain number)." This usage of 来 can be better understood and remembered if one associates it with the concept of "approaching" rather than "coming."

例句：   1) 他去了四十来天了。
        2) 今年我们家的菜园收获了二十来斤青菜。

造句：

填充：   1) 我们在中国 (travel) 了差不多三十天。
        2) (Humankind) 搞 (outer-space travel) 已经有三十多年的历史了。
        3) 他在 (science) 研究院已经干了差不多十年了。
        4) 你别 (believe lightly) 他。他哪儿是二十八岁？我看他已经有差不多四十岁了。

改写 - Reword the completed sentences in the preceding exercise, using this pattern.

5)   来 NP   再来一个。 (p. 83)

In this idiomatic pattern, 来 means "make come (someone, something)," and is used in a command, suggestion, or plea. The expression can be paraphrased variously depending on the context:

来人哪!   Help! Somebody!   or: Will someone please come?!
来一杯水。   Bring a cup of water.

Used idiomatically, 來 does not necessarily mean "come," but can take the place of another verb, e.g.:

再來一杯!   Have (drink) another cup!
再來一次!   Do it again!

例句: 1) 上個星期天我們在海邊玩得很痛快,下星期想再來一次。
      2) 兩個孩子已經太多了,不能再來一個了!

造句:

填充: 1) 我們每年都開一次 (alumni) 會。
      2) 她兩次 (marry) 都不 (perfectly satisfactory),所以不想再 (marry) 了。
      3) (Dean's office) 昨天對他說:"你常常在學校打架,如果再打一次,就要 (withdraw from school) 了。"
      4) 這 (watermelon) 真甜,我們再買一個,怎麼樣?

改寫 - Reword the completed sentences in the preceding exercise, using this pattern.

6) 只有…才…   只有結種子,才算完成了植物生長的全過程。 (p. 84)

In this two-clause sentence, the first clause indicates a necessary (but not necessarily sufficient) condition for the circumstance stated in the second clause. The same meaning can be conveyed by using only 才, without using 只有 (in fact, this is the more common pattern), but 只有 lends greater emphasis on the necessity of the circumstance stated in the first clause.

例句: 1) 只有關心別人,別人才會關心你。
      2) 只有真理才是有價值的。

造句:

填充, incorporate this pattern into the completed sentences:
      1) 只有把 (economy) 搞好,(only then can the nation become strong)。
      2) 只有用自個兒的眼睛看,(only then can [one] be a true artist)。
      3) 只有 (open-mindedly) 請教老師,_____。
      4) _____,屋子才不會亂七八糟。

Used idiomatically, 来 does not necessarily mean "come," but can take the place of another verb, e.g.:

再来一杯！   Have (drink) another cup!

再来一次！   Do it again!

例句：   1) 上个星期天我们在海边玩得很痛快，下星期想再来一次。

2) 两个孩子已经太多了，不能再来一个了！

造句：

填充：   1) 我们每年都开一次 (alumni) 会。

2) 她两次 (marry) 都不 (perfectly satisfactory)，所以不想再 (marry) 了。

3) (Dean's office) 昨天对他说："你常常在学校打架，如果再打一次，就要 (withdraw from school) 了。"

4) 这 (watermelon) 真甜，我们再买一个，怎么样？

改写 - Reword the completed sentences in the preceding exercise, using this pattern.

6)   只有…才…   只有结种子，才算完成了植物生长的全过程。 (p. 85)

In this two-clause sentence, the first clause indicates a necessary (but not necessarily sufficient) condition for the circumstance stated in the second clause. The same meaning can be conveyed by using only 才, without using 只有 (in fact, this is the more common pattern), but 只有 lends greater emphasis on the necessity of the circumstance stated in the first clause.

例句：   1) 只有关心别人，别人才会关心你。

2) 只有真理才是有价值的。

造句：

填充, incorporate this pattern into the completed sentences:

1) 只有把 (economy) 搞好，(only then can the nation become strong)。

2) 只有用自个儿的眼睛看，(only then can [one] be a true artist)。

3) 只有 (open-mindedly) 请教老师，_____。

4) _____，屋子才不会乱七八糟。

INCLUSIVE 翻译 EXERCISE FOR SEGMENT VII: See next page.

INCLUSIVE 翻譯 EXERCISE FOR SEGMENT VII:

1) The process is about to be completed. Please, everyone, bear with it (work hard) just a bit more.

2) This university graduates approximately eighty Ph.D.'s a year.

3) The natural conditions here are poor; only by expending a great deal of human labor can a good harvest be obtained.

4) On An Ran's report card, every course is above ninety (points).

5) Concern, indeed! He's only concerned about himself!

6) Don't feel bad about not passing the college entrance exam. You can try again next year.

SEGMENT VIII

1)   PW V   [request/invitation]   裡邊兒坐，… (p. 88)

The normal pattern involving verbs such as 坐, 站, 躺 and location is V (在) PW, but when the expression is a request or invitation for someone to do something at a certain place, an alternative pattern is PW V. Note that the "normal" pattern is used in 坐那邊兒 in the next line in the script.

例句： 1) 外邊兒玩兒去，我要在這兒看稿子。
           2) 後邊兒去，那兒有座位。

填充, incorporate this pattern into the completed sentences:
      1) (Sit upstairs), 那兒安靜些。
      2) (Let's sit in the kitchen), 那兒暖和些。
      3) 幹嘛 (stand outside the door)? 快進來吧。

2)   V 作…   我把它叫作… (p. 90)

This pattern means "to take A and V it as/by/into B." The exact preposition used in the English translation is determined by the verb. The subject of the sentence is the agent who takes something (A) and processes it (by the action of V), so that it emerges as something else (B).

例句： 1) 他把木刻熊貓看作真熊貓了。
           2) 劉冬虎老把 "cow" 讀作 "cough"。

造句：

填充, incorporate this pattern into the completed sentences:
      1) 他把 "福" 字 _____ (寫)。
      2) 很多美國人把廚房 _____ (當)。
      3) 她把貓的叫聲 _____ (聽)。
      4) 除了安然以外，大家都把祝文娟 _____ (看)。

3)   看…   [colloquial]   看你多好，… (p. 92)

看, followed by a clause, means "look how...." In using this pattern, the speaker asks the listener to look at a fact, calls the listener's attention to something, or expresses an opinion to the listener.

例句： 1) 你看他多笨，腦子裡是空空的。
           2) 看她多難看，只知道趕時髦。

SEGMENT VIII

1)   PW V   [request/invitation]   里边儿坐，… (p. 89)

The normal pattern involving verbs such as 坐, 站, 躺 and location is V (在) PW, but when the expression is a request or invitation for someone to do something at a certain place, an alternative pattern is PW V. Note that the "normal" pattern is used in 坐那边儿 in the next line in the script.

    例句：   1) 外边儿玩儿去，我要在这儿看稿子。

             2) 后边儿去，那儿有座位。

    填充, incorporate this pattern into the completed sentences:

          1) (Sit upstairs), 那儿安静些。

          2) (Let's sit in the kitchen), 那儿暖和些。

          3) 干嘛 (stand outside the door)? 快进来吧。

2)   V 作…   我把它叫作… (p. 91)

This pattern means "to take A and V it as/by/into B." The exact preposition used in the English translation is determined by the verb. The subject of the sentence is the agent who takes something (A) and processes it (by the action of V), so that it emerges as something else (B).

    例句：   1) 他把木刻熊猫看作真熊猫了。

             2) 刘冬虎老把 "cow" 读作 "cough"。

    造句：

    填充, incorporate this pattern into the completed sentences:

          1) 他把 "福" 字 ＿＿＿＿＿＿(写)。

          2) 很多美国人把厨房 ＿＿＿＿＿＿(当)。

          3) 她把猫的叫声 ＿＿＿＿＿＿(听)。

          4) 除了安然以外，大家都把祝文娟 ＿＿＿＿＿＿(看)。

3)   看…   [colloquial]   看你多好，… (p. 93)

看, followed by a clause, means "look how...." In using this pattern, the speaker asks the listener to look at a fact, calls the listener's attention to something, or expresses an opinion to the listener.

    例句：   1) 你看他多笨，脑子里是空空的。

             2) 看她多难看，只知道赶时髦。

填充： 1) 你多不要臉，＿＿＿＿＿＿＿＿＿＿。
        2) 看她多有 (energy)，＿＿＿＿＿＿＿＿＿＿。
        3) 你們的生活多 (abundant, rich)，＿＿＿＿＿＿＿＿＿。
        4) 你看祝文娟多 (cocky)，＿＿＿＿＿＿＿＿＿。

改寫, insert 看 into sentences 1) and 3) in the preceding exercise.

4) 並 不/沒 VP   我並不想上班，… (p. 92)

並 "actually (not)" is used only with a negative (不 or 沒). It conveys the sense that reality differs from an assumption or a commonly held view.

例句： 1) 他並沒把這件事處理好。
        2) 韋老師並不喜歡安然。

造句：

填充： 1) (Housewives) 不一定喜歡做 (housework).
        2) 你看他被 (criticized) 以後也不 (regret)，還是跟從前一樣 (unbridled).
        3) 你 (declared [your] position) 是 ＿＿＿＿ 了，但是不 (clear).
        4) 她是個 (hard to come by) 的好老師，可是沒把自己的孩子 (nurture) 好。你說奇怪不奇怪。

改寫, include the word 並 in each of the completed sentences in the preceding exercise.

5) 一MM   看見一個個背着書包，… (p. 92)

一MM is a contraction of 一M一M (with the second 一 understood and omitted). It carries two possible meanings: a) It indicates that the manner in which the action or circumstance of the verb phrase occurs is that of orderly succession, in which case it can be translated as "one by one." b) It conveys the sense that the things in question are numerous and that the sentence applies to each and every one of them. The 一M一M pattern can be generalized to Nu-M Nu-M, with 一 being replaced with another number. But when the Nu is anything other than 一, then the second occurrence of the Nu cannot be omitted; e.g., one can say 兩個兩個 "two by two," but not 兩個個.

例句： 1) 劉冬虎看見了一個個大西瓜。
        2) 小朋友們數着夜空上的一顆顆星星。

造句：

填充：　1) 你多不要脸，＿＿＿＿＿＿＿＿＿＿＿＿。
　　　　2) 看她多有 (energy), ＿＿＿＿＿＿＿＿＿＿＿＿。
　　　　3) 你们的生活多 (abundant, rich), ＿＿＿＿＿＿＿＿＿＿。
　　　　4) 你看祝文娟多 (cocky), ＿＿＿＿＿＿＿＿＿＿＿。

改写, insert 看 into sentences 1) and 3) in the preceding exercise.

4)　并 不/沒 VP　　　　　　　　　　　　我并不想上班，⋯ (p. 93)

并 "actually (not)" is used only with a negative (不 or 沒). It conveys the sense that reality differs from an assumption or a commonly held view.

例句：　1) 他并沒把这件事处理好。
　　　　2) 韦老师并不喜欢安然。

造句：

填充：　1) (Housewives) 不一定喜欢做 (housework).
　　　　2) 你看他被 (criticized) 以后也不 (regret), 还是跟从前一样 (unbridled).
　　　　3) 你 (declared [your] position) 是 ＿＿＿＿＿ 了，但是不 (clear).
　　　　4) 她是个 (hard to come by) 的好老师，可是沒把自己的孩子 (nurture) 好。你说奇怪
　　　　　 不奇怪。

改写, include the word 并 in each of the completed sentences in the preceding exercise.

5)　一MM　　　　　　　　　　　　　　看见一个个背着书包,⋯ (p. 93)

一MM is a contraction of 一M一M (with the second 一 understood and omitted). It carries two possible meanings: a) It indicates that the manner in which the action or circumstance of the verb phrase occurs is that of orderly succession, in which case it can be translated as "one by one." b) It conveys the sense that the things in question are numerous and that the sentence applies to each and every one of them. The 一M一M pattern can be generalized to Nu-M Nu-M, with 一 being replaced with another number. But when the Nu is anything other than 一, then the second occurrence of the Nu cannot be omitted; e.g., one can say 两个两个 "two by two," but not 两个个.

例句：　1) 刘冬虎看见了一个个大西瓜。
　　　　2) 小朋友们数着夜空上的一颗颗星星。

造句：

填充：　1) 安然在樹皮上 (discover) 了很多隻 "(eye)".

　　　　2) 這個畫家連在夢裡也看見每一 (M) 畫兒。

　　　　3) 這班學生不錯，每一個都有 (progress).

　　　　4) 媽在菜場看見很多 (M) (fresh) 的魚，可惜買不起。

改寫 - Reword the completed sentences in the preceding exercise, using this pattern.

6)　　…如何？　　[literary/formal]　　　　　　　　今天進展如何？ (p. 94)

如何 is a synonym of 怎麼樣, but it carries a literary or formal flavor. Both 如何 and 怎麼樣 can come before a verb phrase (to ask how something is done), or at the end of a sentence (to ask for an opinion, or for a report on a situation or an event).

例句：　1) 那個餐館做的豆腐湯如何？

　　　　2) 讓你丈夫來幹家務活兒如何？

造句：

填充：　1) 那幅名為 "(kiss)" 的畫怎麼樣？

　　　　2) 你上次買的 (sold at reduced price) (canned goods) 好不好？

　　　　3) 咱們把這個家 (decorate) 一下，好不好？

　　　　4) 爸、媽 (married) 二十五 (anniversary)，咱們預備個 (gift) 給他們，怎麼樣？

改寫 - Reword the completed sentences in the preceding exercise, using this pattern.

7)　　一 V 就是…　　　　　　　　　　　　　　一當就是十年，… (p. 96)

This pattern indicates that the duration of the action of the verb, or the state resulting from the action, is much longer than expected or desired at the outset. There is no direct translation of this expression in English, and its meaning is best conveyed by paraphrasing.

例句：　1) 他們一談就是三個小時。

　　　　2) 米曉玲一上班就是十個小時。

造句：

填充, incorporate this pattern into the completed sentences:

　　　　1) 他好像三天沒吃飯了，一吃就是 _____。

　　　　2) 媽一進 (kitchen) 就是 _____。

填充： 1) 安然在树皮上 (discover) 了很多只 "(eye)".

2) 这个画家连在梦里也看见每一 (M) 画儿。

3) 这班学生不错，每一个都有 (progress).

4) 妈在菜场看见很多 (M) (fresh) 的鱼，可惜买不起。

改写 - Reword the completed sentences in the preceding exercise, using this pattern.

6) …如何？　[literary/formal]　　　　　　　　今天进展如何？ (p. 95)

如何 is a synonym of 怎么样, but it carries a literary or formal flavor. Both 如何 and 怎么样 can come before a verb phrase (to ask how something is done), or at the end of a sentence (to ask for an opinion, or for a report on a situation or an event).

例句： 1) 那个餐馆做的豆腐汤如何？

2) 让你丈夫来干家务活儿如何？

造句：

填充： 1) 那幅名为 "(kiss)" 的画怎么样？

2) 你上次买的 (sold at reduced price) (canned goods) 好不好？

3) 咱们把这个家 (decorate) 一下，好不好？

4) 爸、妈 (married) 二十五 (anniversary)，咱们预备个 (gift) 给他们，怎么样？

改写 - Reword the completed sentences in the preceding exercise, using this pattern.

7) 一 V 就是…　　　　　　　　　　　一当就是十年，… (p. 97)

This pattern indicates that the duration of the action of the verb, or the state resulting from the action, is much longer than expected or desired at the outset. There is no direct translation of this expression in English, and its meaning is best conveyed by paraphrasing.

例句： 1) 他们一谈就是三个小时。

2) 米晓玲一上班就是十个小时。

造句：

填充, incorporate this pattern into the completed sentences:

1) 他好象三天没吃饭了，一吃就是 _____。

2) 妈一进 (kitchen) 就是 _____。

3) _____ 就是三個月。

4) 爸一 (start smoking) 就是 _____。

8)　滿 N… [somewhat uncommon]　　　　　　　滿腦子油鹽醬醋。 (p. 96)

Notice that there is no verb in this pattern. Logically, 都是 should be inserted after 滿 N. But since 都是 is understood, it can be omitted. There is no direct translation of this expression in English, but it can be paraphrased as "the entire N is filled with...."

例句：　1) 教室裡滿地(都是)廢紙。

　　　　2) 星期天下午滿街(都是)行人汽車。

填充：　1) 我 (do accounts) 算了一整天，滿腦子都是 _____。

　　　　2) 安靜的辦公室裡，滿桌子 _____。

　　　　3) 那個小姑娘愛看 (children's stories)，她房間裡滿書架上 _____。

　　　　4) 秋天到了，樹林裡滿地 _____。

9)　有 O VP　　　　　　　　　　　　　　我還有話跟你談，… (p. 96)

This pattern means "there is N to VP." The VP may be a simple verb (e.g. 我有錢用。 "I have money to spend.") or a verb phrase that includes a CV-O, as in the above example. So the above example can be translated as "I've got something to say to you."

例句：　1) 媽媽有事要跟安然說。

　　　　2) 安然有問題要請教老師。

造句：

填充：　1) 今天還要做很多 (housework)，沒法子 (interview) 那位 (editor) 了。

　　　　2) (Research institute) 裡還 (must deal with) 不少問題。

　　　　3) 米曉玲要送一些 (sold at reduced price) (canned goods) 給安然。

改寫 - Reword the following sentence and the completed sentences in the preceding exercise, using this pattern: 安然要和安靜談一些心事。

3) _____ 就是三个月。

4) 爸一 (start smoking) 就是 _____。

8) 满 N··· [somewhat uncommon]   满脑子油盐酱醋。 (p. 97)

Notice that there is no verb in this pattern. Logically, 都是 should be inserted after 满 N. But since 都是 is understood, it can be omitted. There is no direct translation of this expression in English, but it can be paraphrased as "the entire N is filled with...."

例句：   1) 教室里满地(都是)废纸。

2) 星期天下午满街(都是)行人汽车。

填充：   1) 我 (do accounts) 算了一整天，满脑子都是 _____。

2) 安静的办公室里，满桌子 _____。

3) 那个小姑娘爱看 (children's stories), 她房间里满书架上 _____。

4) 秋天到了，树林里满地 _____。

9) 有 O VP   我还有话跟你谈，··· (p. 97)

This pattern means "there is N to VP." The VP may be a simple verb (e.g. 我有钱用。"I have money to spend.") or a verb phrase that includes a CV-O, as in the above example. So the above example can be translated as "I've got something to say to you."

例句：   1) 妈妈有事要跟安然说。

2) 安然有问题要请教老师。

造句：

填充：   1) 今天还要做很多 (housework), 没法子 (interview) 那位 (editor) 了。

2) (Research institute) 里还 (must deal with) 不少问题。

3) 米晓玲要送一些 (sold at reduced price) (canned goods) 给安然。

改写 - Reword the following sentence and the completed sentences in the preceding exercise, using this pattern: 安然要和安静谈一些心事。

INCLUSIVE 翻译 EXERCISE FOR SEGMENT VIII: See next page.

INCLUSIVE 翻譯 EXERCISE FOR SEGMENT VIII:

1) The kitchen is full of dirty dishes.

2) We don't care whether or not he's a Ph.D. We only want to know how his work is.

3) The research institute <u>didn't</u> make any headway (contrary to expectations).

4) She's a writer. How can you take her to be a housewife?

5) Please come in, (and) sit in the living room.

6) Look at how regretful she is about having given up her career!

7) In the beginning I was very worried. But later on the problems got resolved one by one.

8) Today I've got something that I have to deal with, so I'll be home a little late.

9) I thought I could finish writing that book in a year. But once I started writing it, it went on for ten years!

SEGMENT IX

1) 既然　　　　　　　　　　　　　你既然什麼都知道，幹嘛還拿人一把？　(p. 98)

The movable adverb 既然, meaning "given the fact that, since," marks the first clause in a two- or multiple-clause sentence in which the 既然 clause states the given situation (which cannot be altered or challenged) and the final clause states the conclusion or result. The final clause may be either a statement or a question (usually rhetorical).

例句：　1) 他既然不虛心學習，你幹嘛還要輔導他？
　　　　2) 你既然反對他的主張，開會的時候就應該提出你的意見。

造句：

填充, incorporate this pattern into the completed sentences:
　　1) 他既然對你那麼沒有 (conscience) _____。
　　2) _____ ，你怎麼 (in the beginning) (choose) 了這個 (professional specialty) 呢？
　　3) 你既然把你的心 (present to) 了 (motherland)，_____。
　　4) _____ ，你就不應該再 (believe lightly) 他了。

2) V 什麼 (O)　　　　　　　　　　去逛什麼白洋淀？！　(p. 98)

This is a rhetorical question which expresses the speaker's disapproval of something that someone has done or is about to do. The expression defies translation, and can only be paraphrased as something like "what's this...?!" or "what is this...all about?!"

例句：　1) 你這樣的人寫什麼詩？一點激情都沒有。
　　　　2) 她這個人學什麼數學？一天到晚只知道打扮。

造句：　1) 做什麼翻譯
　　　　2) 追求什麼真理
　　　　3) 喊什麼口號
　　　　4) 聽什麼現代音樂

3) 何必…?　　　　　　　　　　　何必那麼偷偷摸摸的？　(p. 98)

"Why must...?" This is a rhetorical question implying that there is no need to do that certain thing.

例句：　1) 他又不是你的好朋友，何必生氣呢？
　　　　2) 你又不會游泳，何必跳水？

86

SEGMENT IX

1) 既然   你既然什么都知道，干嘛还拿人一把？ (p. 99)

The movable adverb 既然, meaning "given the fact that, since," marks the first clause in a two- or multiple-clause sentence in which the 既然 clause states the given situation (which cannot be altered or challenged) and the final clause states the conclusion or result. The final clause may be either a statement or a question (usually rhetorical).

例句： 1) 他既然不虚心学习，你干嘛还要辅导他？
        2) 你既然反对他的主张，开会的时候就应该提出你的意见。

造句：

填充, incorporate this pattern into the completed sentences:

    1) 他既然对你那么没有 (conscience), _____。
    2) _____, 你怎么 (in the beginning) (choose) 了这个 (professional specialty) 呢？
    3) 你既然把你的心 (present to) 了 (motherland), _____。
    4) _____, 你就不应该再 (believe lightly) 他了。

2) V 什么 (O)   去逛什么白洋淀？！ (p. 99)

This is a rhetorical question which expresses the speaker's disapproval of something that someone has done or is about to do. The expression defies translation, and can only be paraphrased as something like "what's this...?!" or "what is this...all about?!"

例句： 1) 你这样的人写什么诗？一点激情都没有。
        2) 她这个人学什么数学？一天到晚只知道打扮。

造句： 1) 做什么翻译
        2) 追求什么真理
        3) 喊什么口号
        4) 听什么现代音乐

3) 何必…？   何必那么偷偷摸摸的？ (p. 99)

"Why must...?" This is a rhetorical question implying that there is no need to do that certain thing.

例句： 1) 他又不是你的好朋友，何必生气呢？
        2) 你又不会游泳，何必跳水？

造句：

填充, incorporate this pattern into the completed sentences:

    1) 你又不是自己 (ability) 不夠，_____？

    2) _____，何必把事情搞得那麼 (complicated) 呢？

    3) 他那麼 (selfish)，我們何必 _____？

    4) _____，你何必 (interrogate) 她呢？

4)   什麼…?   什麼專找?   (p. 100)

The effect of this expression is similar to that in Grammatical Note IX.2. Both convey the speaker's disapproval or disagreement with the other person. The difference between the two patterns is this: the pattern here is used in a two-way argument; the word following 什麼 in this pattern has been spoken in a prior utterance by the other person, and it is the crux of the speaker's disapproval or disagreement.

例句：   1) 什麼自私？我最關心別人的了。

           2) 什麼精力過盛？她上課時沒精打彩的。

造句：

填充：   1) 什麼 (upright)？他老是 (furtively) 的！

          2) 什麼 (frame of mind) 不好？_____。

          3) 什麼 (innocent)？_____。

          4) 什麼 (knowledgeable [have knowledge])？他連一個 (century) 是多少年都不知道。

5)   V 起 (O) 來   打起精神來。 (p. 102)

The V 起 (O) 來 pattern has already appeared in Grammatical Notes I.6. and VI.2. Aside from the usages introduced earlier, 起…來 can also indicate an "uplifting." Moreover, a few phrases with this usage have become idiomatic expressions, with the force of urging someone on. E.g.

               打起精神來!   Come on, get your spirits up!

               鼓起勇氣來!   Come on, get your courage up!

例句：   1) 不必害怕，鼓起勇氣來!

           2) 最近她寫起詩來了。

填充：   1) 她為什麼開始 (vexed) 了？

          2) 這孩子真的成熟了，你看，他開始講 (principles) 了。

造句：

填充, incorporate this pattern into the completed sentences:

1) 你又不是自己 (ability) 不够，_____？
2) _____，何必把事情搞得那么 (complicated) 呢？
3) 他那么 (selfish)，我们何必 _____？
4) _____，你何必 (interrogate) 她呢？

4)　什么…？　　　　　　　　　　　　　　什么专找？　(p. 101)

The effect of this expression is similar to that in Grammatical Note IX.2. Both convey the speaker's disapproval or disagreement with the other person. The difference between the two patterns is this: the pattern here is used in a two-way argument; the word following 什么 in this pattern has been spoken in a prior utterance by the other person, and it is the crux of the speaker's disapproval or disagreement.

例句：　1) 什么自私？我最关心别人的了。
　　　　2) 什么精力过盛？她上课时沒精打采的。

造句：

填充：　1) 什么 (upright)？他老是 (furtively) 的！
　　　　2) 什么 (frame of mind) 不好？_____。
　　　　3) 什么 (innocent)？_____。
　　　　4) 什么 (knowledgeable [have knowledge])？他连一个 (century) 是多少年都不知道。

5)　V 起 (O) 来　　　　　　　　　　　　打起精神来。　(p. 103)

The V 起 (O) 来 pattern has already appeared in Grammatical Notes I.6. and VI.2. Aside from the usages introduced earlier, 起…来 can also indicate an "uplifting." Moreover, a few phrases with this usage have become idiomatic expressions, with the force of urging someone on. E.g.

打起精神来！　　　Come on, get your spirits up!
鼓起勇气来！　　　Come on, get your courage up!

例句：　1) 不必害怕，鼓起勇气来！
　　　　2) 最近她写起诗来了。

填充：　1) 她为什么开始 (vexed) 了？
　　　　2) 这孩子真的成熟了，你看，他开始讲 (principles) 了。

改寫 - Reword the following sentences and the completed sentences in the preceding exercise, using this
pattern: 1) 你怎麼批評班長了？

2) 你怎麼不複習功課而看電影了？

6)   …的地方   你有過…不尊重老師的地方…？   (p. 104)

地方 doesn't always refer to a concrete place. It can refer to something abstract, as in this example.

地方 in the abstract sense can be translated as "aspect" or "respect."

例句：   1) 對這道題，你有沒有不明白的地方？

2) 你的家庭有不幸福的地方嗎？

造句：

填充：   1) 我的 (pronunciation) 如果什麼地方不 (accurate), 請你多多 (correct).

2) 編輯說這個短篇小說還不夠 (comprehensive), 發表以前 (must) 改一改。

3) 祝文娟 (advocate) 的做法，同學們一點兒都不 (object, oppose).

4) (Actually), 安然是個又 (innocent) 又 (honest) 的少女，一點兒都不 "(complicated)".

改寫 - Reword the completed sentences in the preceding exercise, using this pattern.

7)   … 什麼的   專愛表現自己什麼的。 (p. 104)

什麼的 following a listing of items means "so on and so forth, etc."

例句：   1) 爸爸喜歡安然這樣會思考、有精力什麼的。

2) 有人說你幹事偷偷摸摸什麼的。

造句：

填充：   1) 章老師 (criticize) 安然 (attitude) 不夠 (modest), 愛 (put on make-up) 等等。

2) 你 (since) 覺得他太 (selfish), 沒 (proper upbringing) 等等，何必還跟他作朋友呢？

3) 她要 (wait upon her husband), (nurture) 孩子等等，怎麼能把自己的 (professional
specialty) 搞好呢？

改寫 - Reword the following sentence and the completed sentences in the preceding exercise, using this
pattern: 你怎麼不自己多複習，偏要給劉冬虎輔導英語、借作業給米曉玲等等？

改写 - Reword the following sentences and the completed sentences in the preceding exercise, using this pattern:　1) 你怎么批评班长了？

2) 你怎么不复习功课而看电影了？

6)　…的地方　　　　　　　　　　　　你有过…不尊重老师的地方…?　　(p. 105)

地方 doesn't always refer to a concrete place. It can refer to something abstract, as in this example. 地方 in the abstract sense can be translated as "aspect" or "respect."

例句:　1) 对这道题，你有沒有不明白的地方？

2) 你的家庭有不幸福的地方吗？

造句:

填充:　1) 我的 (pronunciation) 如果什么地方不 (accurate), 请你多多 (correct).

2) 编辑说这个短篇小说还不够 (comprehensive), 发表以前 (must) 改一改。

3) 祝文娟 (advocate) 的做法，同学们一点儿都不 (object, oppose).

4) (Actually), 安然是个又 (innocent) 又 (honest) 的少女，一点儿都不 "(complicated)".

改写 - Reword the completed sentences in the preceding exercise, using this pattern.

7)　… 什么的　　　　　　　　　　　专爱表现自己什么的。　(p. 105)

什么的 following a listing of items means "so on and so forth, etc."

例句:　1) 爸爸喜欢安然这样会思考、有精力什么的。

2) 有人说你干事偷偷摸摸什么的。

造句:

填充:　1) 韦老师 (criticize) 安然 (attitude) 不够 (modest), 爱 (put on make-up) 等等。

2) 你 (since) 觉得他太 (selfish), 沒 (proper upbringing) 等等，何必还跟他作朋友呢？

3) 她要 (wait upon her husband), (nurture) 孩子等等，怎么能把自己的 (professional specialty) 搞好呢？

改写 - Reword the following sentence and the completed sentences in the preceding exercise, using this pattern:　你怎么不自己多复习，偏要给刘冬虎辅导英语、借作业给米晓玲等等？

8) 再也 不/沒…   她再也不找我了。 (p. 104)

This is an emphatic and colloquial way of saying "never VP again/anymore." A more prosaic way of saying the same thing is "不/沒 再 VP 了." In both these patterns, 不 implies that the act <u>was</u> never done again and/or <u>will</u> never again be done, and 沒 only implies that the act has never again been done since a certain time in the past (e.g. 以後，我們再也沒見到他了。), with no implications for the future.

例句：   1) 這次旅行他表現得那麼自私，我再也不願意跟他接觸了。
         2) 那個流氓再也沒做過壞事了。

造句：

填充：   1) 我以後一定不會 (believe lightly) 這種不 (honest) 的人了。
         2) 米曉玲 (go to work) 以後就沒 (study) 了。
         3) 那次被 (Dean's office) 叫去 (interrogate) 後，他就不敢 (fight) 了。
         4) 她生了個兒子以後，她父母就不 (oppose) 她跟那個 (peasant) (marry) 了。

改寫, insert 再也 into each of the completed sentences in the preceding exercise.

INCLUSIVE 翻譯 EXERCISE FOR SEGMENT IX:

1) What's this about studying Chinese? He can't even learn French.
2) Since you are against her dropping out of school, why didn't you urge her (not to drop out)?
3) Mother: I don't like that furtive way of yours.

    An Ran: "Furtive" my foot! I've never been furtive!
4) If you have no assurance that you can finish it, why must you guarantee that you can?
5) Does this manuscript have some spots that should be corrected?
6) Classmates said that she likes to follow fashion, loves to make (herself) up, and so on.
7) I'll never believe you again!
8) Don't be so listless. Come on, get your spirits up!

8)   再也 不/沒⋯   她再也不找我了。 (p. 105)

This is an emphatic and colloquial way of saying "never VP again/anymore." A more prosaic way of saying the same thing is "不/沒 再 VP 了." In both these patterns, 不 implies that the act was never done again and/or will never again be done, and 沒 only implies that the act has never again been done since a certain time in the past (e.g. 以后，我们再也沒见到他了。), with no implications for the future.

例句：   1) 这次旅行他表现得那么自私，我再也不愿意跟他接触了。
         2) 那个流氓再也沒做过坏事了。

造句：

填充：   1) 我以后一定不会 (believe lightly) 这种不 (honest) 的人了。
         2) 米晓玲 (go to work) 以后就沒 (study) 了。
         3) 那次被 (Dean's office) 叫去 (interrogate) 后，他就不敢 (fight) 了。
         4) 她生了个儿子以后，她父母就不 (oppose) 她跟那个 (peasant) (marry) 了。

改写, insert 再也 into each of the completed sentences in the preceding exercise.

INCLUSIVE 翻译 EXERCISE FOR SEGMENT IX:

1) What's this about studying Chinese? He can't even learn French.

2) Since you are against her dropping out of school, why didn't you urge her (not to drop out)?

3) Mother: I don't like that furtive way of yours.

    An Ran: "Furtive" my foot! I've never been furtive!

4) If you have no assurance that you can finish it, why must you guarantee that you can?

5) Does this manuscript have some spots that should be corrected?

6) Classmates said that she likes to follow fashion, loves to make (herself) up, and so on.

7) I'll never believe you again!

8) Don't be so listless. Come on, get your spirits up!

SEGMENT X

1) 難道…   難道你晚上來了，就能找着嗎？ (p. 110)

難道 cannot be taken for its literal meaning "difficult to say." It is a movable adverb conveying disbelief in the information given in the rest of the sentence, and can be translated as "You mean to say...?" or "Can it be that...?"

例句：   1) 難道一個結了婚、有了孩子的女人，就不能在事業上有毅力嗎？

          2) 難道科學家、數學家就沒有幻想嗎？

造句：

填充：   1) 這怎麼能 (prove) 他不是 (thief) 呢？

          2) 在課上 (point out) 老師或 (class monitor) 的錯是應該的，怎麼能算是 (arrogant) 的表現呢？

          3) 你和劉冬虎住一幢樓已經 (exceed) 十年了，怎麼能不 (understand) 他的 (family situation) 呢？

          4) (Cadres) 不一定就對 (peasant) 沒有 (warmheartedness).

改寫 - Reword the completed sentences in the preceding exercise, using this pattern.

2) 只好…   只好拿回家去校對。 (p. 112)

只好 is an adverb meaning "can only..., have no choice but..." Note that the meaning of 好 in this pattern is far removed from the primary meaning of this word; i.e., 好 does not mean "good" here, but rather, "possible."

例句：   1) 只好吃西瓜，沒別的水果可吃。

          2) 自己能力不夠，只好請別人來幫個忙。

造句：

填充：   1) 這個星期我 (too busy to manage everything)，你那件事下星期辦吧。

          2) 韋老師那麼一說，張曉英不得不 (raise hand) (vote) 了。

          3) 她 (housework) 重，又想給孩子創造一些 (political qualifications)，所以不得不把專業 (discard) 了.

          4) 我真不願意 (believe) 他作了 (thief)，但是有了這麼多 (evidence)，我也沒法子不 (believe) 了。

SEGMENT X

1) 难道…   难道你晚上来了，就能找着吗？ (p. 111)

难道 cannot be taken for its literal meaning "difficult to say." It is a movable adverb conveying disbelief in the information given in the rest of the sentence, and can be translated as "You mean to say...?" or "Can it be that...?"

例句：   1) 难道一个结了婚、有了孩子的女人，就不能在事业上有毅力吗？
          2) 难道科学家、数学家就没有幻想吗？

造句：

填充：   1) 这怎么能 (prove) 他不是 (thief) 呢？
          2) 在课上 (point out) 老师或 (class monitor) 的错是应该的，怎么能算是 (arrogant) 的
             表现呢？
          3) 你和刘冬虎住一幢楼已经 (exceed) 十年了，怎么能不 (understand) 他的 (family
             situation) 呢？
          4) (Cadres) 不一定就对 (peasant) 没有 (warmheartedness).

改写 - Reword the completed sentences in the preceding exercise, using this pattern.

2) 只好…   只好拿回家去校对。 (p. 113)

只好 is an adverb meaning "can only..., have no choice but..." Note that the meaning of 好 in this pattern is far removed from the primary meaning of this word; i.e., 好 does not mean "good" here, but rather, "possible."

例句：   1) 只好吃西瓜，没别的水果可吃。
          2) 自己能力不够，只好请别人来帮个忙。

造句：

填充：   1) 这个星期我 (too busy to manage everything), 你那件事下星期办吧。
          2) 韦老师那么一说，张晓英不得不 (raise hand) (vote) 了。
          3) 她 (housework) 重，又想给孩子创造一些 (political qualifications), 所以不得不把
             专业 (discard) 了.
          4) 我真不愿意 (believe) 他作了 (thief), 但是有了这么多 (evidence), 我也没法子不
             (believe) 了。

改寫 - Reword the completed sentences in the preceding exercise, using this pattern.

3)   是…，可(是)…   安然同學學習成績是不錯，可總感覺有點兒… (p. 114)

This is a two-clause sentence in which the first clause concedes a fact, and the second clause states a countering fact or opinion. The 是 in the first clause is best conveyed in English translation by putting stress on the verb (e.g. "An Ran's academic work <u>is</u> quite good, ..."). Sometimes the sense of this 是 can be conveyed by the word "alright" at the end of the first clause (e.g. 她忙是忙，可是… "She is busy alright, but...").

例句：   1) 你的毛筆字是很漂亮，可還是不夠有力。
          2) 他是十分聰明，可不夠認真。

造句：

填充：   1) 張曉英是舉了手，可 _____。
          2) 爸爸的畫兒是非常有特色，可 _____。
          3) 安然是被選上了"三好生"，可 _____。
          4) 安然考完試那天是和一羣男生到白洋淀玩兒去了，可 _____。

4)   就説…(吧)，…   就説上次上語文課，… (p. 114)

"就説…" is not to be taken literally in this context. It actually means "just take...as an example" or "even considering just...alone." In supporting one's argument, the "就説…" clause raises an example of one's point, and at the same time implies that there are even stronger, though unnamed, instances.

例句：   1) 就説你這次考試吧，如果你好好兒地複習就一定能比上次考得好。
          2) 就説你的發言吧，你應該實事求是地評價一個人。

填充：   1) 劉冬虎 <u>(adverb conveying surprise)</u> 會 <u>(bully)</u> 農民。就説那次他在路邊買水果吧，
          _____。
          2) 安然對他的同學們是很 <u>(warmhearted)</u> 的。就説米曉玲 <u>(withdraw from school)</u> 這件事吧，_____。
          3) 安靜很會 <u>(look after)</u> 她的妹妹。就説 <u>(wash hair)</u> 這件事吧，_____。
          4) 媽媽 <u>(fundamentally)</u> 不喜歡安然和米曉玲作朋友。就説那次安然要請米曉玲到家來吃飯吧，_____。

改写 - Reword the completed sentences in the preceding exercise, using this pattern.

3)   是···，可(是)···   安然同学学习成绩是不错，可总感觉有点儿··· (p. 115)

This is a two-clause sentence in which the first clause concedes a fact, and the second clause states a countering fact or opinion. The 是 in the first clause is best conveyed in English translation by putting stress on the verb (e.g. "An Ran's academic work <u>is</u> quite good, ..."). Sometimes the sense of this 是 can be conveyed by the word "alright" at the end of the first clause (e.g. 她忙是忙，可是··· "She is busy alright, but...").

例句：   1) 你的毛笔字是很漂亮，可还是不够有力。
          2) 他是十分聪明，可不够认真。

造句：

填充：   1) 张晓英是举了手，可 _____。
          2) 爸爸的画儿是非常有特色，可 _____。
          3) 安然是被选上了"三好生"，可 _____。
          4) 安然考完试那天是和一群男生到白洋淀玩儿去了，可 _____。

4)   就说···(吧)，···   就说上次上语文课，··· (p. 115)

"就说···" is not to be taken literally in this context. It actually means "just take...as an example" or "even considering just...alone." In supporting one's argument, the "就说···" clause raises an example of one's point, and at the same time implies that there are even stronger, though unnamed, instances.

例句：   1) 就说你这次考试吧，如果你好好儿地复习就一定能比上次考得好。
          2) 就说你的发言吧，你应该实事求是地评价一个人。

填充：   1) 刘冬虎 (adverb conveying surprise) 会 (bully) 农民。就说那次他在路边买水果吧，
              _____。

          2) 安然对他的同学们是很 (warmhearted) 的。就说米晓玲 (withdraw from school) 这件
             事吧，_____。

          3) 安静很会 (look after) 她的妹妹。就说 (wash hair) 这件事吧，_____。

          4) 妈妈 (fundamentally) 不喜欢安然和米晓玲作朋友。就说那次安然要请米晓玲到
             家来吃饭吧，_____。

5) 居然   她居然還指導老師。 (p. 114)

居然 has no equivalent in English. It is an adverb indicating that the event or situation comes as a surprise. Often it also implies surprise at someone's impudence.

例句： 1) 米曉玲居然哭了。
        2) 這個十五歲的少女居然挺有毅力的。

造句：

填充： 1) 沒想到韋老師的那首口號式的詩 (publish) 了。
        2) 沒想到會有同學站起來為安然說些 (fair, just) 的話。
        3) 沒想到在 (appraise and elect) "三好生" 的那天，安然還敢穿那件 (red blouse).
        4) 她那麼一個 (simple and plain) 的少女，沒想到最近 (put on make-up) 起來了。

改寫 - Reword the completed sentences in the preceding exercise, using this pattern.

6) …吧，… [colloquial]   就上回打架吧，… (p. 114)
    Cf. Grammatical Note I.14.

例句： 1) 學外語吧，他的發音不夠好；學數學吧，他又沒興趣。
        2) 老同學寄來的這首詩該怎麼處理呢？退回去吧，會讓她生氣；發表吧，又實在不合適。

填充： 1) 她是需要 (guidance) 的，可是 (correct) 她吧，_____。
        2) 十五歲的姑娘已經不是孩子了，可是說她是 (adult) 吧，_____。
        3) 祝文娟對誰都是和和氣氣的，可是說她 (warmhearted) 吧，_____。
        4) 同學們 (point out) 的這些事實吧，就能 (prove) 她是個相當 (selfish) 的人。

7) Subject 不知怎麼，VP [colloquial]   她不知怎麼，有個勁兒，… (p. 116)
    Here, the phrase 不知怎麼 has been interjected between the subject and predicate of the sentence. The understood (and unstated) subject of 不知怎麼 is not necessarily the subject of the sentence, but is often the speaker, as is the case in the above example.

例句： 1) 他不知怎麼，總覺得自己了不起。
        2) 他不知怎麼，做事總是偷偷摸摸的。

5) 居然   她居然还指导老师。(p. 115)

居然 has no equivalent in English. It is an adverb indicating that the event or situation comes as a surprise. Often it also implies surprise at someone's impudence.

例句：　1) 米晓玲居然哭了。
　　　　2) 这个十五岁的少女居然挺有毅力的。

造句：

填充：　1) 沒想到韦老师的那首口号式的诗 (publish) 了。
　　　　2) 沒想到会有同学站起来为安然说些 (fair, just) 的话。
　　　　3) 沒想到在 (appraise and elect) "三好生" 的那天，安然还敢穿那件 (red blouse).
　　　　4) 她那么一个 (simple and plain) 的少女，沒想到最近 (put on make-up) 起来了。

改写 - Reword the completed sentences in the preceding exercise, using this pattern.

6) …吧，… [colloquial]   就上回打架吧，… (p. 115)
    Cf. Grammatical Note I.14.

例句：　1) 学外语吧，他的发音不够好；学数学吧，他又沒兴趣。
　　　　2) 老同学寄来的这首诗该怎么处理呢？退回去吧，会让她生气；发表吧，又实在
　　　　　 不合适。

填充：　1) 她是需要 (guidance) 的，可是 (correct) 她吧，＿＿＿＿＿＿＿＿＿。
　　　　2) 十五岁的姑娘已经不是孩子了，可是说她是 (adult) 吧，＿＿＿＿＿＿＿＿＿。
　　　　3) 祝文娟对谁都是和和气气的，可是说她 (warmhearted) 吧，＿＿＿＿＿＿＿＿。
　　　　4) 同学们 (point out) 的这些事实吧，就能 (prove) 她是个相当 (selfish) 的人。

7) Subject 不知怎么, VP [colloquial]   她不知怎么，有个劲儿，… (p. 117)
    Here, the phrase 不知怎么 has been interjected between the subject and predicate of the sentence. The understood (and unstated) subject of 不知怎么 is not necessarily the subject of the sentence, but is often the speaker, as is the case in the above example.

例句：　1) 他不知怎么，总觉得自己了不起。
　　　　2) 他不知怎么，做事总是偷偷摸摸的。

填充：　1) 米曉玲説着説着就 <u>(start to cry)</u> 了。

　　　　2) 韋老師老愛 <u>(to discuss behind people's back)</u> 別人。

　　　　3) 她最近老是 <u>(frame of mind, mood)</u> 不好。

　　　　4) 劉冬虎在古文課上老是 <u>(listless)</u> 的。

改寫, insert 不知怎麼 into each of the completed sentences in the preceding exercise.

INCLUSIVE 翻譯 EXERCISE FOR SEGMENT X:

1) He has awakened alright, but he's not fully clear-headed yet.

2) Everything has gone up in cost. Just take watermelons for example, they are twice as expensive as last year.

3) We couldn't prove that he was the thief, so had no choice but to let him go.

4) She is <u>actually</u> better than her male classmates in math. (stating a surprising fact)

5) That essay she wrote, well, it really "seeks truth from reality."

6) (I) don't know why, but recently he hasn't been as warmhearted toward me as before.

7) You mean to say only cadres can speak up?

填充: 1) 米晓玲说着说着就 <u>(start to cry)</u> 了。

2) 韦老师老爱 <u>(to discuss behind people's back)</u> 别人。

3) 她最近老是 <u>(frame of mind, mood)</u> 不好。

4) 刘冬虎在古文课上老是 <u>(listless)</u> 的。

改写, insert 不知怎么 into each of the completed sentences in the preceding exercise.

INCLUSIVE 翻译 EXERCISE FOR SEGMENT X:

1) He has awakened alright, but he's not fully clear-headed yet.

2) Everything has gone up in cost. Just take watermelons for example, they are twice as expensive as last year.

3) We couldn't prove that he was the thief, so had no choice but to let him go.

4) She is <u>actually</u> better than her male classmates in math. (stating a surprising fact)

5) That essay she wrote, well, it really "seeks truth from reality."

6) (I) don't know why, but recently he hasn't been as warmhearted toward me as before.

7) You mean to say only cadres can speak up?

1)　　V 爲　　　　　　　　　　　　　　　　早日成長爲一名優秀的青年。 (p. 122)

This pattern is synonymous with V 成 O. Both consist of a verb followed by a postverb (成 or 爲)
meaning "to V into..." 成 is the more commonly used postverb in this construction, but 爲 is chosen for
the example above to avoid repeating the 成 in 成長.

　　例句：　1) 安然被評選爲一名"三好生"。
　　　　　　2) 他是今年才升爲幹部的。

填充, incorporate this pattern into the completed sentences:
　　　　　1) 法院把他 (adjudicate as hoodlum)。
　　　　　2) 不必把這件小事 ＿＿＿ 一個 (terrific, extraordinary) 的 (difficult problem)。
　　　　　3) 深圳這個城 (develop) 得很快，不到十年就 ＿＿＿ 一個工商業中心了。
　　　　　4) 你別把這種草 ＿＿＿ 一種不起眼的 (plant), 它是一種 (precious) 的藥呢！

2)　　…幹嘛？　　[colloquial]　　　　　　　您坐在這兒看我幹嘛？　(p. 122)

As noted in Vocabulary Annotation I.72 (Part I, p. 12), 幹嘛 is a very colloquial equivalent of 爲什麼
or 做什麼. It can be used as a movable adverb at the beginning of the sentence, or at the end of the
sentence (with no appreciable difference in meaning). The nuance of 幹嘛 at the end of the sentence is
that the speaker is annoyed or irritated. 做什麼, but not 爲什麼, can similarly be used at the end of
a sentence.

　　例句：　1) 媽，你嘮嘮叨叨幹嘛？
　　　　　　2) 韋老師既然不喜歡安然，幹嘛要表揚她呢？

造句：

填充：　1) 爸，你爲什麼老畫這種 (elucidativeness) 不 (strong) 的畫兒？
　　　　2) 祝文娟爲什麼不說些 (seek truth from facts) 的話呢？
　　　　3) 安靜爲什麼要 (request a leave of absence) 去秦皇島？
　　　　4) 你爲什麼老愛 (behind people's back) (criticize) 別的同學？

改寫 - Reword the completed sentences in the preceding exercise, using this pattern.

SEGMENT XI

1) V 为   早日成长为一名优秀的青年。(p. 123)

This pattern is synonymous with V 成 O. Both consist of a verb followed by a postverb (成 or 为) meaning "to V into..." 成 is the more commonly used postverb in this construction, but 为 is chosen for the example above to avoid repeating the 成 in 成长.

例句： 1) 安然被评选为一名"三好生"。
        2) 他是今年才升为干部的。

填充, incorporate this pattern into the completed sentences:

1) 法院把他 <u>(adjudicate as hoodlum)</u>.
2) 不必把这件小事 _____ 一个 <u>(terrific, extraordinary)</u> 的 <u>(difficult problem)</u>.
3) 深圳这个城 <u>(develop)</u> 得很快，不到十年就 _____ 一个工商业中心了。
4) 你别把这种草 _____ 一种不起眼的 <u>(plant)</u>, 它是一种 <u>(precious)</u> 的药呢！

2) …干嘛？ [colloquial]   您坐在这儿看我干嘛？ (p. 123)

As noted in Vocabulary Annotation I.72 (Part I, p. 12), 干嘛 is a very colloquial equivalent of 为什么 or 做什么. It can be used as a movable adverb at the beginning of the sentence, or at the end of the sentence (with no appreciable difference in meaning). The nuance of 干嘛 at the end of the sentence is that the speaker is annoyed or irritated. 做什么, but not 为什么, can similarly be used at the end of a sentence.

例句： 1) 妈，你唠唠叨叨干嘛？
        2) 韦老师既然不喜欢安然，干嘛要表扬她呢？

造句：

填充： 1) 爸，你为什么老画这种 <u>(elucidativeness)</u> 不 <u>(strong)</u> 的画儿？
        2) 祝文娟为什么不说些 <u>(seek truth from facts)</u> 的话呢？
        3) 安静为什么要 <u>(request a leave of absence)</u> 去秦皇岛？
        4) 你为什么老爱 <u>(behind people's back)</u> <u>(criticize)</u> 别的同学？

改写 - Reword the completed sentences in the preceding exercise, using this pattern.

3)   沒個⋯   [colloquial]   這個家呀，沒個安寧。 (p. 126)

沒個, meaning 沒有一點兒 or 一點兒也不, usually takes as its object an abstract quality (rather than a noun referring to a concrete object), and is used only in colloquial speech.

例句：   1) 你呀，沒個正經。
         2) 這孩子，他的媽一不在家就打他的弟弟，簡直沒個老實。

填充：   1) 看你，已經上高三了，還那麼不 (earnest)，怎麼能考上大學？
         2) 她的成績非常 (outstanding)，可是她的父母還是對她不 (satisfied).
         3) 劉冬虎的爸媽 (all day long) (quarrel)，對他一點兒也不 (concerned).
         4) 她呀，就知道忙她的 (professional specialty)，對 (housework) 一點兒都不 (gungho, enthusiastic).

改寫 - Reword the completed sentences in the preceding exercise, using this pattern.

4)   正要   我正要告訴你一件事兒。 (p. 126)

正要 (or just 要) is an adverb meaning "just about to, on the point of." Sometimes it is used in the first clause of a two-clause sentence to indicate that the two actions or events are linked by a coincidence, e.g. 我們正要出門，有客人來了。

例句：   1) 我正要發言，韋老師先說話了。
         2) 大家正要向她祝賀，她却哭了。

造句：

填充, incorporate this pattern into the completed sentences:
         1) 同學們正要 (criticize) 安然，韋老師倒 (commend) 她了。
         2) 你那 (M) (slacks) (dirty) 了，交給我吧。今晚我 ＿＿＿＿＿＿。
         3) 你先別走，我 ＿＿＿＿＿＿＿＿＿。
         4) 那年我大學剛 (graduate)，＿＿＿＿＿＿＿＿ 的時候，文化大革命開始了，我就 (go down to the countryside) 去了。

5)   等⋯再⋯   ⋯等我回來再說不行嗎？ (p. 128)

"Wait until...(and) then..." The meaning of 再 in this pattern is the same as in "先⋯，再⋯ (first..., then...)." Remember that 再 has nothing to do with "again" in this context.

3) 沒個⋯ [colloquial]   这个家呀，沒个安宁。 (p. 127)

沒个, meaning 沒有一点儿 or 一点儿也不, usually takes as its object an abstract quality (rather than a noun referring to a concrete object), and is used only in colloquial speech.

例句： 1) 你呀，沒个正经。
         2) 这孩子，他的妈一不在家就打他的弟弟，简直沒个老实。

填充： 1) 看你，已经上高三了，还那么不 (earnest)，怎么能考上大学？
         2) 她的成绩非常 (outstanding)，可是她的父母还是对她不 (satisfied)。
         3) 刘冬虎的爸妈 (all day long) (quarrel)，对他一点儿也不 (concerned)。
         4) 她呀，就知道忙她的 (professional specialty)，对 (housework) 一点儿都不 (gungho, enthusiastic)。

改写 - Reword the completed sentences in the preceding exercise, using this pattern.

4) 正要   我正要告诉你一件事儿。 (p. 127)

正要 (or just 要) is an adverb meaning "just about to, on the point of." Sometimes it is used in the first clause of a two-clause sentence to indicate that the two actions or events are linked by a coincidence, e.g. 我们正要出门，有客人来了。

例句： 1) 我正要发言，韦老师先说话了。
         2) 大家正要向她祝贺，她却哭了。

造句：

填充, incorporate this pattern into the completed sentences:
         1) 同学们正要 (criticize) 安然，韦老师倒 (commend) 她了。
         2) 你那 (M) (slacks) (dirty) 了，交给我吧。今晚我 ＿＿＿＿＿＿＿。
         3) 你先别走，我 ＿＿＿＿＿＿＿＿＿＿。
         4) 那年我大学刚 (graduate)，＿＿＿＿＿＿＿＿ 的时候，文化大革命开始了，我就 (go down to the countryside) 去了。

5) 等⋯再⋯   ⋯等我回来再说不行吗？ (p. 129)

"Wait until...(and) then..." The meaning of 再 in this pattern is the same as in "先⋯，再⋯ (first..., then...)." Remember that 再 has nothing to do with "again" in this context.

例句：　1) 等你到那兒再決定吧。

　　　　2) 等她看完了那本童話再借下一本給她吧。

造句：

填充, incorporate this pattern into the completed sentences:

1) 等我 (encounter difficulty) 時再 ＿＿＿＿＿＿＿＿＿ 。

2) 等 ＿＿＿＿＿＿＿＿＿ 再來 (congratulate) 我吧。

3) 等她 (frame of mind, mood) 好些 ＿＿＿＿＿＿＿＿＿ 。

4) 等 (cake) 做好了 ＿＿＿＿＿＿＿＿＿ 。

INCLUSIVE 翻譯 EXERCISE FOR SEGMENT XI:

1) I was just about to commend him, (but) he disappeared.

2) He's not the least bit careful in doing things, (and) often makes a big mess.

3) Don't transfer schools until the court has decided. (Wait until...and then...)

4) How come you trusted that hoodlum? (conveying irritation)

5) This little matter must be dealt with. Otherwise, it could become a difficult problem.

例句：　　1) 等你到那儿再决定吧。

　　　　　2) 等她看完了那本童话再借下一本给她吧。

造句：

填充, incorporate this pattern into the completed sentences:

1) 等我 (encounter difficulty) 时再 _____ 。

2) 等 _____ 再来 (congratulate) 我吧。

3) 等她 (frame of mind, mood) 好些 _____ 。

4) 等 (cake) 做好了 _____ 。

INCLUSIVE 翻译 EXERCISE FOR SEGMENT XI:

1) I was just about to commend him, (but) he disappeared.

2) He's not the least bit careful in doing things, (and) often makes a big mess.

3) Don't transfer schools until the court has decided. (Wait until...and then...)

4) How come you trusted that hoodlum? (conveying irritation)

5) This little matter must be dealt with. Otherwise, it could become a difficult problem.

SEGMENT XII

1) 好 VP   好早點兒回家。 (p. 134)

As an adverb, 好 can mean "easy to..." E.g. 人多好做事. In the above context, the adverbial 好 is used in another common meaning, which is "in order to..., so as to..."

例句：   1) 認真複習，好考個好成績。
          2) 説話誠實，好作個正直的青年。

造句:

填充：   1) 爸爸 (hope) 家裡能 (tranquil) 些，這樣就能在家畫畫兒了。
          2) 做老師的應當細心地 (observe) 每一個學生，這樣才能真正地 (understand) 他們。
          3) 這位女 (mathematician) 為了能 (go after) 她的專業，(move) 到 (research institute) 去了。這樣她就不必幹 (housework) 了。
          4) 我要在星期五晚上趕快把 (housework) 做完，這樣週末就 _____。

改寫 - Reword the four completed sentences in the preceding exercise, using this pattern.

2) VP time-span 了   已經死了好久了。 (p. 136)

A time-span expression within the pattern "VP time-span 了" indicates either the duration of an action up to the present time, or the amount of time lapse since an action or event has occurred. The choice between these two possibilities can usually be determined by the nature of the verb. If the verb refers to an on-going action, the time-span refers to the duration of the action up to the present (我念了三年中文了。). If the verb refers to an event like 死了 or a one-time action (not on-going) like 退學, then the time-span refers to the time lapse, up to the present, since the event or action occurred. This latter usage can be translated as "It has been...since..."

例句：   1) 他大學畢業三年了，現在才找到一個合適的工作。
          2) 我把這首詩寄去已經三個月了，今天才收到編輯的回信。

造句:

填充：   1) 米曉玲是三個月以前 (withdrew from school) 的。
          2) 媽是二十來年以前把她的 (professional specialty) (cast away) 的。
          3) 我是一個星期前聽到這個 (news) 的，所以已經不能算是 (news) 了。
          4) 我們倆是五年前就 (decide) (marry) 的，到現在才有房子能結婚了。

SEGMENT XII

1) 好 VP   好早点儿回家。 (p. 135)

As an adverb, 好 can mean "easy to..." E.g. 人多好做事. In the above context, the adverbial 好 is used in another common meaning, which is "in order to..., so as to..."

例句：   1) 认真复习，好考个好成绩。
         2) 说话诚实，好作个正直的青年。

造句:

填充：   1) 爸爸 (hope) 家里能 (tranquil) 些，这样就能在家画画儿了。
         2) 做老师的应当细心地 (observe) 每一个学生，这样才能真正地 (understand) 他们。
         3) 这位女 (mathematician) 为了能 (go after) 她的专业，(move) 到 (research institute)
            去了。这样她就不必干 (housework) 了。
         4) 我要在星期五晚上赶快把 (housework) 做完，这样周末就 _____ 。

改写 - Reword the four completed sentences in the preceding exercise, using this pattern.

2) VP time-span 了   已经死了好久了。 (p. 137)

A time-span expression within the pattern "VP time-span 了" indicates either the duration of an action up to the present time, or the amount of time lapse since an action or event has occurred. The choice between these two possibilities can usually be determined by the nature of the verb. If the verb refers to an on-going action, the time-span refers to the duration of the action up to the present (我念了三年中文了。). If the verb refers to an event like 死了 or a one-time action (not on-going) like 退学, then the time-span refers to the time lapse, up to the present, since the event or action occurred. This latter usage can be translated as "It has been...since..."

例句：   1) 他大学毕业三年了，现在才找到一个合适的工作。
         2) 我把这首诗寄去已经三个月了，今天才收到编辑的回信。

造句：

填充：   1) 米晓玲是三个月以前 (withdrew from school) 的。
         2) 妈是二十来年以前把她的 (professional specialty) (cast away) 的。
         3) 我是一个星期前听到这个 (news) 的，所以已经不能算是 (news) 了。
         4) 我们俩是五年前就 (decide) (marry) 的，到现在才有房子能结婚了。

改寫 - Reword the four completed sentences from the preceding exercise, using this pattern.

INCLUSIVE 翻譯 EXERCISE FOR SEGMENT XII:

1) I want to go up the mountain by myself, in order to think about my future cool-headedly.

2) It's been two weeks since my article was published. How come you still haven't read it?

改写 - Reword the four completed sentences from the preceding exercise, using this pattern.

INCLUSIVE 翻译 EXERCISE FOR SEGMENT XII:

1) I want to go up the mountain by myself, in order to think about my future cool-headedly.

2) It's been two weeks since my article was published. How come you still haven't read it?